BELIEVER

BELIEVER

Conversations with Mike Moore

Peter Parussini

upstart press

A catalogue record for this book is available from the National Library of New Zealand

ISBN 978-1-990003-04-2

An Upstart Press Book
Published in 2020 by Upstart Press Ltd
Level 6, BDO Tower, 19–21 Como St, Takapuna
Auckland 0622, New Zealand

Designed by CVD Limted (www.cvdgraphics.nz)
Printed by Everbest Printing Co., China
Cover photo: NZPA/NZME

Contents

Introduction 7

1. Tuna Town 13
2. 'A nice boy' 33
3. 'New Zealanders look to great things from you' 50
4. Second in command of a one-man dredge 74
5. A medical diagnosis or an opinion? 102
6. The Madman Fraser file 129
7. 'And he's the man who fights the bull' 155
8. Young horses 186
9. Chardonnay socialists or dry reds 218
10. The Democratic Coalition 232
11. Justice now: finish the round 254
12. Mr Raymond Poynter 285
13. A work in progress 305

Epilogue 323
Acknowledgements 331
Rt Hon Mike Moore, ONZ, AO 334
About the Author 336

Introduction

March 2017.

The solid mahogany family dining table is fully extended, and he's sitting at its head nearly touching the wall behind, like his old Bowen House desk in Wellington. In front of him are nine chairs — beautifully padded — at attention, waiting for a meeting.

The ashtray, the smell of old cigarettes and the mountains of memos, speeches, press releases and newspaper clippings in two giant piles either side are gone and replaced with flowers from the garden, ornaments from world travels, the stinging sun and the smell of sea air coming through the veranda doors.

The books — biographies and the latest economic and business thoughts from academics and leaders from around the globe — are still strewn everywhere. But now there's also a neat pile of them — *Go Fish*, *From Different Villages*, *Muslim Heritage in our World* and *The Penguin History of New Zealand* — lying on each other directly in front of him with a computer laptop, wirelessly connected, on top.

A pint glass of iced water is just in front of his left hand. His black contact pocket-book, with bits of paper still sticking out and dog-eared pages, is near his resting right hand.

The scene isn't much different to his old office which had those veneer desks common across Wellington's public service in the 1970s and 1980s — fake light walnut in colour and big; more than a human wingspan.

He also used to have it jammed up almost to the window, but with just enough space to squeeze in a comfortable high-backed chair and a pole with the New Zealand flag draped from it. A framed photo of the bespectacled Michael Joseph Savage hung on the wall and looked down across the room.

Laid out in front of the desk — all connected — were a series of tables in the same public service cardigan dullness, not quite matching the desk, butted up against each other to form a long table that could be surrounded by 10 chairs.

With cupboards and bookcases on one side of the room and windows on the other overlooking the prize — the Beehive — across Bowen Street there was little choice but to sit and meet with him when you walked through the door to his office.

With the familiar, the greeting is still the same. The dimple on his left cheek engages a pursed-lip teethless smile, his eyebrows lift, his blue eyes gaze up and there's a soft 'Gidday mate, how are ya?'. It's more a statement than a question and the sentence peters away, like he's thinking of something else.

He pushes his mouse awkwardly with his left hand and clicks it.

These days he doesn't politely stand when you walk in the room and his handshake doesn't feel like your dad's; more like your granddad's — wanting to be firm but with a couple of stiff fingers and not able to engage all the muscles.

Yvonne hasn't changed: there's still the optimistic smile, the greeting-kiss on the cheek with a hug, and offers of coffee and water. The savouries, sandwiches and cakes come back minutes later, out of their little white paper bags, cut up and returned on plates with napkins.

'How do you think they're going?' he starts the conversation. But it's a different query. The 42-year-old version of him would have followed up his question with a quick precis about how he thought 'they' — the New Zealand Labour Party — were going.

There's a pause. Did he actually want an answer? I've accidentally slipped into my old ways of more than 25 years earlier, creating a gap for him to answer his own question.

I hurriedly tell him what everyone else is saying, knowing it's hardly an observant answer for someone who always craves insight: 'Little's a nice and capable enough chap but he isn't the person to lead Labour out of the wilderness; but who knows who is.'

There's another pause and he states matter-of-factly: 'They've got to change that constitution to create a process that brings forward a leader that has broad electoral appeal, that doesn't have to pander to a handful of people who have privileged positions in the party.

'We need someone who appeals to the next generation and unashamedly dreams big for New Zealand because that's what great Labour leaders do.'

In the past he would have said that with an angry and exasperated voice. Talk about 'his' party and its processes would often result in his eyes bulging forward and a deep staccato-like voice.

Now his tone is calm. He's not bland. It's just softer and a conversational reflection that invites other opinions.

He is thirsty, though, keen for a chat about all matters politics: what's happening around Parliament and what others are saying about Labour and its key players.

Having given him some savouries, I slowly offer him something else: 'Mike. If you're up to it, I'm keen to talk about the early days — your mum and dad, growing up in Kawakawa, about being packed off to Dilworth School in Auckland.'

He relaxes his face, his dimple goes up, his eyebrows rise and his eyes look forward fixed on something beyond the end of the room . . .

****

There was hardly anyone there this midweek afternoon. No advance had been done to check out the location and drum up a crowd.

But Prime Minister Mike Moore went seeking the public like some missile homing in on targets. He cold-called many bewildered shoppers, stuck a hand out and introduced himself with a bevy of journalists and cameras in tow. Many politicians find the process of meeting members of the public awkward; not Moore, who seemed to enjoy their company more than the familiar faces of the media pack.

Few really wanted to chat. Many turned their eyes down and politely walked away after shaking his hand which, in itself, was an achievement given the hatred the country had towards Labour in 1990.

There was hardly anything exciting to report upon other than the depressing reception the prime minister was receiving at the Coastlands Shopping Mall in the marginal Labour seat of Kapiti, just north of Wellington. But that was a story that had already been written weeks earlier about Labour's re-election chances. No chance but we'll cut him a break and see what he can do, the Press Gallery seemed to think unconsciously.

As we wandered aimlessly through the mall, the photographer accompanying me spotted a giant panda sign at a nearby coffee shop,

Panda's Café. He said I should convince the thirty-fourth prime minister of New Zealand to pose in front of it. Instead of telling him how undignified that would be for a prime minister, in my youthful naivety I asked Moore if he'd oblige.

I hadn't calculated ahead that by asking him for this favour that might be my one and only following him around on the campaign trail. The older and wiser ones in the Press Gallery would probably have held back, saving up their one 'ask' for something more important — the inside word on an announcement or an exclusive story.

I also hadn't thought through the consequences of Moore barking back at me for being so stupid and how that would have put me even further down the pecking order of respect among my colleagues.

Fortunately, he agreed despite the background protests of his media minder. It seemed a fitting photo of Moore's campaign and, perhaps, his career: dark-ringed, tired and sad eyes attached to an optimistic and otherwise likeable and entertaining man prepared to try anything for the cause.

Moore never held that photo against me. I would have. In fact, a few months after losing the general election he offered me a job in his office.

Many of my colleagues thought I was mad going to work for him. He was too volatile, too erratic, too unfocused, too this, too that. I don't know why I did but I couldn't resist, much in the same way many New Zealanders were naturally attracted to his personality.

What followed were three intoxicating, exhilarating, hard-working, stressful and fun-filled years. I hated that period in my career and I loved it.

He never seemed to sleep or stop thinking about getting one over the National Government. He was always impatient and in a hurry, and everything was about now. There was no pause or off switch.

I learned more about politics, the media, PR and the psyche of everyday New Zealanders from Moore than I ever gave back to him.

Having returned to New Zealand after five years as the country's ambassador to the United States and having suffered a stroke near the end, I wasn't sure how I was going to approach him about writing a book. I was never sure if I could do a proper job, something befitting his remarkable life.

He took his time thinking about it. Moore only accepted the request in the end, I'm sure, because his many ailments had left him unable to use his own hands properly. If he'd been fully fit, he would have spent those hours stuck at his new desk writing instead of reading.

Every second or third weekend over two and a half years, I'd spend afternoons at Mike and Yvonne's home in Omana, the beach suburb in Auckland's south-east. I'd regularly come armed with sausage rolls, egg sandwiches and lemon slices from the bakery around the corner — whatever the local builders from the rapidly expanding suburb hadn't bought by the time I got there.

They were interesting and enjoyable chats over coffee and savouries. Having experienced some of the giddy days observing the fourth Labour Government, I was in awe of a generation of politicians who profoundly changed New Zealand.

It was more than the saving of the country from Muldoon's near bankruptcy of it, taking a stand on being nuclear free in the middle of the Cold War, actively opposing apartheid South Africa and standing up to colonial France's arrogance in the Pacific. That period marked the changing in the country's political guard. It was the generational change every administration hopes it is.

They were adrenalin-filled days of constant news about change, driven by some of the brightest and most capable politicians the country had ever seen, and Moore was at the centre of much of that period.

Their generation — my generation — was finally in charge and they backed New Zealand to make its way in the world, breaking the shackles with the post-Second World War order of Britain and the US.

The fourth Labour Government's demise was just as spectacular, just as news-filled as its rise and, again, Moore was in the middle of it all.

I really enjoyed those afternoons with Mike. But it presented me with a huge problem: how to tell his story.

I've tried not to be a chronicler of every minute of his life and career. Instead I've tried to pick key moments, some of which he has never openly talked about before and that were emotionally difficult for him to tell. There are the things most politicians normally never own up to — the ambition, the failures and the upsets.

By his own admission Mike sometimes struggles, particularly with names and places, since his stroke. But despite his ups and downs during our chats he was always hopeful about what tomorrow would bring — for ordinary Kiwis, the Labour Party, New Zealand and global politics.

I hope this book captures not only another glimpse of this important time in New Zealand's political, economic and social history but the essence of the man: the boy from rural Northland who once thought the pinnacle in life would be to own the local petrol station, who with no formal education went on to be probably New Zealand's last working-class prime minister, the country's highest-ranking international figure, director general of the World Trade Organization, and ambassador to the United States.

This is not a book that canvasses yet again the upheavals of the fourth Labour Government, although it has to cover some of that time. Nor is it about settling some old political scores. On a bad day Moore is happy to chronicle many of the slights and injustices against him by some former colleagues. On a good day he is reflective and generous and we both agreed the book should lean that way.

The book probably has some interesting inside oil for those who follow New Zealand politics. But that's also not its purpose. It is a book that is sometimes sad and introspective but hopefully, and more importantly, is uplifting. Because, ultimately, that is Moore's story.

It is a story mostly about an extraordinary New Zealander, someone whose life personifies what we all hope our country is about: that you can get ahead regardless of the colour of your skin, who your parents were, where you grew up, what school you went to, who your god is, whether you wear a dress or trousers or who you fall in love with.

The struggles in life aren't actually about identity but are economic; they are what our parents' generation used to call 'class'.

And all it takes to break that class barrier is hard work, intelligence, character and, critically, institutions (which Labour created) like public health and education that level the playing field to make it an egalitarian place for all. These are the things Moore dedicated his life fighting for so other less fortunate kids could get an even break.

Most of all I hope the book captures a lot of the love that is in Moore's heart: for his mother Audrey and his wife Yvonne, the Labour Party and the ordinary Kiwis he has spent much of his life representing and toiling for.

1

Tuna Town

'My mother's side, the Goodalls, were god-botherers.

'I didn't figure it out until much later but one of my great-grandfathers was one of the first people to come to Christchurch. I wish I knew that when we moved there to stand in Papanui — I could have avoided the carpet-bagger label. They had a pub in Kaikoura and he was a policeman too.

'My mum was a Labour Party person, but I didn't discover this until many years later when someone interviewed her about me. She was pro-union and a shopkeeper. It showed strength of character, I think.

'I don't know about the Moore side. A guy came to see me around 1974 and said: "I'm your father's brother." I told him: "Don't sit down, f-off. Where have you been? My mother was a widow with three boys, where were you?" He should have looked after my mother. I regret saying that now. There might have been other problems; who knows?

'Because I didn't know my father, I tended to invent things when I was young. Nowadays I don't know how much of it is romance and how much is true. I think his family were Irish, but I don't know. People have told me he was a drinker, gambler and was violent, but I don't know. He was called a communist by some, but I don't know.

'[My brother] Kerry was five years older. I have a bit of time for him. He joined the army young. He did UE, carpentry, drafting and surveying. He did really well.

'I've got some pictures of him in Parliament. He's not smiling in any of them. I hadn't noticed that before. He was a soldier, very much in favour of the war in Vietnam. He was pissed off that he couldn't go because he was married. He's changed his mind now. Everyone has.

'My brother five years younger, Shane Thomas, he's had mental illnesses for many years. For 20 years I'd go and pick him up from the hospital. Over the years I'd pay for things for him.

'It's been a very, very distraught relationship with Shane. I remember seeing the *Truth* newspaper billboard when I was an MP and it said something like: "Why I hate my brother" and going into the dairy to buy a copy I was so embarrassed. I quickly went back to the house and lay down. I didn't know what to think.

'But, actually, people have been good about that. Everyone seems to have someone in their family who's having troubles. Quite frequently MPs would come up to me to say Shane's been in touch or they'd heard something, but they weren't taking it any further. Mental illness had such a stigma around it not that long ago.

'I couldn't wait to go to work when I was young. I do regret not staying at school. They're paying you to read the books you read anyway. If I'd somehow managed to stay I don't know what I'd have ended up doing.

'Many in Labour are critical of the involvement of teachers in the party but not so long ago one of the only ways the sons and daughters of working-class people could get an education and be paid was to go to teachers college.

'Mother had to battle after my father died. She did it tough, really. She had three young kids to look after by herself. She wouldn't go on the benefit. She kept the shop going and going and going. It kept losing money. And so her way of helping was to send me to Dilworth School in Auckland.

'I hated it at the time, but Dilworth did prepare me for life. Dilworth is an interesting concept: richest school in the country for the poorest kids in the country. Its view on education is right — small class sizes to prepare kids for further education or jobs, discipline and self-reliance.

'But I was so lonely. I ended up being a bit of a hero to some of the other troubled boys at Dilworth, running away and telling the headmaster to f-off and all that. To think what a selfish prick I was.

'I didn't appreciate until much later in life the gift Dilworth gave my family. The school took the pressure off Mother and enabled her to get back on her feet and it taught me one of the most important things in my life, the love of books.

'After three years Mother remarried and I desperately wanted to be part of the new family so went back north. Moerewa Primary was a rough school. It was about 80 per cent Māori then. I was quite big for my age at Dilworth.

But when I arrived there, they were huge bastards.

'George Turanga Webber was a disaster. He and Mother didn't get along. He'd use his fists occasionally. Marrying Webber, Mother's life got harder. She got up early to milk the cows while he went off to the freezing works. I used to do the calves in the morning and the night to help her. Kerry had left by then.

'It was in Moerewa where I met my first MP, Mat Rata. I learned two things that day. We had napkins. I didn't know what they were for. Mother put them out for Mat. And I learned what an MP was. I thought he was fantastic. I then wanted to be like Mat.

'He was talking about standing up for poor people and how you could only make change through politics and the Labour Party. I was young, but I got it. He was on our side. He was a charming bastard and a good man. I was enthralled by his stories.

'His selection was at a marae and in those days, anyone could come to the meeting, Labour Party people, National Party people, anyone.

'He was peeling the potatoes for two days at the marae and they never asked him to speak. And then they came out and said this young fella is good — him.

'Mat had been a seaman in Australia during the '51 waterfront lockout. The union boys said to him: "Matty, we need you to head across to New Zealand. When you go, take this suitcase. Don't open it and when you get off the boat there will be a riot and that will distract the police and you'll be put in a car and away you go." Matty said: "No problem, no problem." He didn't think to open the suitcase.

'He got off in New Zealand and there was a riot and things were flying, he's put in a car and under a blanket, they drive off to a hotel and they go to a room and the suitcase is opened and it's full of money from the Australian unions. He could have gone to prison if he'd been caught.

'People thought he was very brave, but he knew nothing of it. Afterwards, wherever he went people would look at him and say: "'51, you're alright." He wouldn't talk about it. Real heroes don't talk about it.

'So at his selection a couple of old union guys said to him, "We know, '51," tapping their noses. Mat was a hero and he didn't know it. Many years later we used to laugh about it together.'

****

It occupied about 20 metres of the frontage of the main street at the 'Junction', the action end of the town.

For as long as the young Moore could remember, OC Godfrey Service Station was a place of excitement. It was at the eastern end of Gillies Street, just as you drove into Kawakawa coming up from Whangarei, and on the same side of the street as the Moores' house.

It was a dark blue building with two entrances either side of two petrol pumps that were right up on the street. The tyre bay was on the right and the garage on the left. There were stickers and painted signs on the building that said this was not boring Kawakawa but another world — 'Authorised Ford Dealer', 'Michelin Tyres and Tubes', 'Ford Batteries'.

He had no idea what they meant, but Moore remembered seeing the advertisements for OC Godfrey's in the newspapers his father left around: 'modern equipped garage and lubritorium', 'electric and acetone welding', 'lathe work'.

Green Brothers and Johnson, almost across the road from his house, had three pumps on the street and you had to drive through the building to the workshop. But it wasn't the same as 'Joe' Godfrey's place at the 'junction' of Queen, Commercial and Gillies streets. At that end of Gillies Street was the fire station and across the dusty street two large wooden buildings, the Post Office and the Junction Hotel. There were always people around.

Many of the trucks going to and from the freezing works and dairy company in Moerewa, just west of Kawakawa, would stop at Godfrey's for fuel or repairs, along with the travelling salesmen and those working along State Highway 11 at Opua in the nearby Bay of Islands. The men would often sneak across the road for a quick beer before going on their way.

Only a few minutes' walk from home — past the butchery, fruit and veg shop and Royd's pharmacy — Moore would often stand as close as he dared and gaze at the different vehicles and the men who would scurry about their important business, swapping stories with the young guys in overalls.

The clinking of the pumps, the revving of engines and the constant hammering — noise, smells and fumes never seemed to stop. He'd try to remember the make of the car models.

Late in the afternoons he'd often see the men rushing into the Junction Hotel before six o'clock closing. They'd hurry there from around the district. The Kawakawa Taxi Service's four cars would park up nearby to ferry many of them home afterwards.

The men would also wait — many laughing and staggering — for the 6.30 pm train from Opua to Otiria (near Moerewa) to come slowly through Kawakawa so they could jump aboard. The local bakeries would also come out with trays of bread and pies to sell to the men leaning out the train windows.

But it wasn't the commotion of the people that caught Moore's attention, it was Godfrey's. It seemed an exciting world. It seemed a fun world. It seemed a man's world. It seemed another world. Moore would sometimes wonder what a boy would have to do to work there, even own it.

Michael Kenneth Moore was born in Whakatane on 28 January 1949, the second of three sons to Audrey Evelyn Goodall and Allan George Moore.

Allan was born in Mauriceville, just outside of Masterton, in 1913, the son of Frederick George Moore and Hilda May Johnston, some of whose family had come to New Zealand from Florida in the United States.

Family legend had it that Allan had served in the Royal New Zealand Navy in the Second World War, being stationed in Fiji part of that time until being medically discharged because of chronic asthma. Neither the New Zealand Defence Forces nor the RSA has any records of him.

Audrey was born in 1922, one of three daughters and six brothers, to Kenneth Bryn Goodall and Grace Caroline MacMahon. Kenneth was a West Coaster who eventually settled in Whakatane and met Grace who had grown up in Hamilton.

The Moore family moved to Kawakawa in the Far North when he was a few months old. It was a busy country town, like many were in 1950s New Zealand, and was based around the Allied Farmers Freezing Company (AFFCO) freezing works and the Bay of Islands Dairy Company in nearby Moerewa, which used to be the home of flax and timber mills.

The Northland Express train regularly passed through, from the Bay of Islands to Whangarei, and then there were connecting services to Auckland.

Kawakawa was originally a coalmining town, with a number of shafts thought to still be under the township. The mine had donated land for the school, the RSA and churches.

Like most of Northland, the majority of the population in the district was Māori. The surrounding area is considered the cradle of the Ngāti Hine people and was discovered by Hineamaru, a descendant of ancestors of Northland's Ngāpuhi iwi. Many of the battles and scars of early New Zealand are etched into the surrounding area, including the remains of the Ruapekapeka Pā, the site of a famous battle with British troops.

Despite the heavy Māori influence in the area, like with most of New Zealand then, Pākehā tended to live on one side of town and Māori the other. It was mostly Pākehā Kawakawa and Māori Moerewa, although the latter was stratified again — Māori, Māori and poor Pākehā and the 'white coats' or Pākehā managers.

For many of the Māori who came in from surrounding Northland for the jobs, their settlement was a series of former army huts between State Highway 1 and the railway line behind the freezing works. Many locals referred to it as 'Tuna Town' — after the Māori word for eel — and the name disguised the abject poverty many local Māori lived in.

It was romanticised by some because of a local Māori whakatauākī, or proverb, that talks about the eel's struggles to come in from the Pacific into the Bay of Islands and up the Kawakawa River:

'Taumārere herehere riri, Te puna i Keteriki, Te rere i Tiria' ('Only by cooperating and working together can they successfully scale the waterfall, Tiria').

Allan was thought to be Northland's first auctioneer and ran a second-hand furniture shop on Kawakawa's main street, which was also the family home. It was demolished and replaced by a modern building in 1990 and now houses the Ministry of Social Development just down from probably the town's most well-known attraction, the Hundertwasser tourist toilets.

Audrey was the one in the family with the social conscience, often delivering pamphlets for causes including the Labour Party. During the 1951 General Strike she broke the law by delivering union pamphlets around town as she took baby Mike on a stroll in his pram. She hid the pamphlets under the two-year-old.

She was a tall, slim and broad-shouldered woman who was confident, funny and often dominated a room. She could hold an audience of men and women with her storytelling.

Their family shop was built around the 1880s on the banks of the flood plain of the Kawakawa River and the meandering Waiomio Stream, with the Moores living under the store on the slope. It was originally Bob Reyland's boot and shoe repairs and sales shop, with the flat land by the stream used as stables for horse-drawn coaches.

Moore literally grew up on the wrong side of the tracks.

Kawakawa was originally built going north to south along Albert Street from the flat river area up a hill on the south side of the town. The railway track crossed Albert Street. But in the 1890s a fire destroyed many of the buildings along Albert Street and when the town was rebuilt it was around the railway track on the flat next to the stream. All of the houses and most of the shops — except for the Moores' — were built on the south side of the track on what became Gillies Street to avoid the regular flooding on the other side.

In winter the weeping willow trees out the back of the Moores' shop and house would often clog up the stream and it would flood, leaving the living area in water. The boys would regularly join their parents in stacking the furniture before Allan would drill holes in the floorboards to drain the house. The toilet was a longdrop in the backyard, so rising water levels would often leave sewage strewn everywhere.

But the stream and the river would also provide Moore and his two best mates Terry Bayley and Bryan Gregory with hours of entertainment. They would catch tuna — eels — with their sticks with a piece of string and hook tied to them from the middle of the three bridges crossing the Kawakawa River on the town's boundary.

Sometimes they'd go to the outskirts of Kawakawa to their mate Raymond Lemon's farm where the river became a swamp and the water was still and clear and you could easily see the fat tuna. With a bit of practice, the boys knew how to reach into the river and flick the tuna onto the bank with one scoop-like motion.

They would sell them outside the Star Hotel for half a crown each to the half-cut patrons, in competition with local kuia, with their moko on display, selling crayfish. To this day Moore remembers how to gut and skin an eel, sock-like, in three motions.

The Star, which was built in 1876, was a two-storeyed wooden building similar in style to many pubs in Northland. It was about 100 metres down the main street from his home and Moore would often sit cross-legged out front on the boardwalk.

The boys had a 'fort' in nearby bushes, which were always a great place to hide from school. With their spare coins from the eel selling, Moore and his mates would sometimes watch films at the Kings' Theatre, which was almost next door to the Star, on a Saturday afternoon.

Moore thought it was a magical building. It transported him to exotic places and times. The boys loved anything to do with war and for good movies like *The Bridge on the River Kwai* they would hide under the seats at the end so they could watch the next session.

Moore's earliest memory of Kawakawa is of the Queen and the Duke of Edinburgh's visit to Northland in December 1953, a few weeks before his fourth birthday. All he recalls is standing on the side of the main street in the heat and how a water truck sprayed the dusty road minutes before 'someone flash' drove by in a big car and everyone cheered.

There was also a group of people in hospital beds who'd been wheeled down the hill from Kawakawa Hospital to be at the roadside at the end of the street. The people in the car waved. He didn't know what all the fuss was about.

He knew no different, and life in Kawakawa seemed fun but unremarkable up until just before Moore's seventh birthday. His father, who had asthma most of his life, died suddenly at the age of 42 from a heart attack. He'd been driving his truck over the bridges between Kawakawa and Moerewa when it happened.

A few weeks before school was supposed to break for the Christmas holidays, a woman walked into Moore's class, whispered to his teacher and he was asked to go home because his mother had a message for him.

The pair trudged the short distance home down the hill, past St Thomas Anglican Church, down the long series of steps the local kids called the 'stairway to heaven', past the library and across Gillies Street to the shop and house. All Moore could think about walking home was whether he'd get to eat the lunch in his bag. At home he was greeted with a hug and the news from his stoic mother.

Moore tried to get around to the front of the store to get in to see his father, who had been laid out on a table, but the door was locked and he couldn't see anything face up against the glass shopfront door. He wasn't sure what being dead meant and wanted to talk to his father.

He wished he had more memories — fond ones — of his father. Irish, drinking and violent are adjectives others used to describe Allan to him later in life.

While his memories were few, they were a strange collection and stark.

One is of his father cutting off the fat and gristle from his rump steak and passing it to him to have. For years later Moore would think rump was the height of luxury in cuts of meat.

The other is getting a beating, instead of the sympathy he expected, from his father after he severely cut his left foot on a broken bottle walking the passage between their shop and the next-door building. The narrow pathway was littered with whisky bottles that had been thrown out the window. Moore would later turn the bad experience of the lifelong scar — his 'shark bite' — into a feature attraction with other boys.

He also used to show off a light scar on the left side of his face from his nose to his chin caused when he fell down the stairs in the shop and broke a bottle he was drinking from onto his cheek. It was the wound from a bottle fight, he'd tell the other kids in the playground.

The only memory of Allan that brings out a smile in Moore is travelling for a long day in a truck with his father to Auckland to sell used bottles. Crawling over the hills and along the rough roads, it was a father and son adventure.

A Catholic, Allan agreed with Audrey that he'd name the children if they were boys and she, an Anglican, would name them if they were girls. After Allan's death the three were baptised as Anglicans in the nearby church of St Thomas. Besides, the Catholic church was just out of town in an area called 'Irish Town'.

Audrey was a widow in her early thirties and struggled running the shop and looking after three boisterous boys. Older Kerry could fend for himself, and Shane, who was barely two years old, was the baby of the three and was troublesome.

So, Moore was farmed out to the home of his mother's best friend Olga Gregory and one of his mates, Bryan, who lived in Old Mill Road a short walk through the bush from school.

Over the next six months Moore also went to other homes and was a temporary pupil at three more primary schools in the area.

With each change of school his files would be lost so teachers would cut him a break from schoolwork for a few weeks. It also meant missing out on dental nurse checks.

Opening and closing the shop, running the books, feeding the always hungry boys, it all became too much for Audrey. The business was losing money, but she refused to close it and go on any form of benefit. She was no longer her cheerful self. At church one Sunday a parishioner told her about Auckland's Dilworth School.

Founded under the terms of the will of an Auckland farmer and businessman, Irish-born James Dilworth who died childless in 1894, the school was established to educate fatherless boys or those who had 'fallen on straitened times' from the old Auckland province (the upper North Island).

Opened in 1906 using Dilworth's old farm homestead and outbuildings in the heart of Epsom, it funded scholarships for the boys from investment income from the original £120,000 left in his will.

Audrey talked to the local Anglican minister and they applied for Moore to be a boarder at Dilworth. The two came to Auckland in mid-1957 for an interview with the Dilworth Trust Board in the ornate Dilworth Building at the bottom of Queen Street.

It was the first time he'd been in an elevator and the quietness and wooden-panelled walls and leather seats of the Board's offices were intimidating. Moore was accepted in and granted the usual probation period of three months.

When Moore attended — from September 1957 to December 1960 — the school had barely 150 primary and secondary pupils and had begun to replace Dilworth's old farm buildings and create modern facilities. He entered standard two, what's now called year 4.

Dilworth School was the grand educational experiment of its time. Dilworth believed that the only limitation to a person's ability to succeed was their education. Even destitute boys could be saved by the school's strict codes of old-fashioned discipline and hard work.

It would definitely straighten out the young Moore, give him a leg up in life and give the exhausted Audrey an opportunity to get her life back on an even keel.

Moore described Dilworth's ethos many years later as an unwavering belief that 'Tory gentlemen could be created out of any little shits'.

Dilworth had a strong military tradition with its first headmaster, Colonel Arthur Plugge, having served at Gallipoli and at the Battle of the Somme in the First World War. Many of its teachers when Moore was there had served in the Second World War, including his headmaster, Brigadier John Conolly.

Hitting ill-disciplined boys wasn't a problem for many of them, and the big sweeping driveway out the back of the school was dug out by the naughty boys, like some cruel joke about prisoner of war labourers. They would sieve soil through giant screens for the driveway. The teachers called it the 'Burma Road', but none of the boys got the joke.

Moore's memories of Dilworth are distinct — itchy grey shorts, long socks, tie and cap, compulsory cold baths before 7 am, making his bed and doing chores before breakfast, huge cold wooden dormitories, forced prayers and severe canings. He learned to spit and polish his black shoes at Dilworth, something he became obsessive about for the rest of his life.

Swimming lessons at Dilworth, in the reservoir of the old farm, were just short of sink or swim and involved a master walking along the edge with a pole with rope tied around a learner.

This was not Kawakawa. This was not catching tuna. This was not sitting outside the pub talking with the local kuia. This was not playing in the fort. This was prison.

Moore often ran away. He'd head up the nearby Mt St John or Mt Hobson on either side of Great South Road with books from the library while the school went on searches for him. He'd enjoy reading his books lying in the unmown grass on the north face of Mt Hobson, overlooking Newmarket as the sun went down.

Some nights he would lead raids on the library to see how many books they could grab and hide under their beds.

Sometimes he'd even walk the uncomfortable seven kilometres from Dilworth to his mum's cousin 'Aunty' Doreen Langton's house in Arthur Street, Onehunga where she would give him dinner and a cuddle before driving him back to school.

Once he tried to jump off the returning train at Whangarei only to have another older pupil, Richard Royds, also from Kawakawa, haul him back into the carriage. He'd swear at his teachers before being caned. He wasn't afraid of the cane, but he hated it.

He became a bit of a hero to some of his classmates for what they saw as boldness and courage in standing up to authority and conformity. Once he complained to the headmaster on behalf of the boys about the treatment they were getting from one of the matrons. His stature among the boys increased when the matron left some time later.

Moore would fight against the system even though he knew it was futile. To some he seemed confident. He seemed to revel in the notoriety he had, but barely beneath the surface he was deeply homesick and sad. Instead of travelling around the school with a gang of classmates attracted to his reputation, he often kept to himself. The library was his refuge, the books his escape.

Moore quickly learned that his letters home complaining about the school had been censored by teachers so as part of his escapes from school he'd make sure he passed a post office to send unread letters to his mother.

Audrey didn't write to him as much as she had wanted as she struggled to cope with life as a widow. The ones she wrote were short but talked about brothers Kerry and Shane and were covered in 'x' marks for kisses.

Dilworth boys were only allowed out once a month to see family, but Audrey couldn't make it down to Auckland to see him or attend school events. However, she constantly organised with the school secretary for payments for him to bus or train home every time there was a long weekend or holiday.

His Dilworth reports are revealing. After only three months at school Headmaster Conolly said of Moore that he was 'content to do the bare minimum of work' but that he 'appears to have much latent ability'.

By the end of his second year he is struggling or average in most subjects but comes first equal in standard three history and geography, with his teacher remarking: 'This is what he can do when he is interested.' The headmaster describes his work as 'erratic' but that he is 'a cheerful, likeable lad'.

His interest in history and geography continues in standard four, coming second in his year. But he struggles in other subjects where his lack of basics from Kawakawa — or slackness in class — catches up with him. Nevertheless, his teachers are optimistic and say he has a good memory and that he should be able to apply himself to other subjects.

Form one, or year seven, in 1960 is when Moore goes through a particularly emotional and difficult period at Dilworth. Audrey remarried in late 1959 and calls herself Mrs Webber. Moore is given special permission to attend the wedding.

His reports in 1960 talk about 'work not learnt', 'this needs hard work', 'inclined to be careless' and 'fair, could do much better'. By the end of the year Conolly is describing Moore's attitude as 'too flippant' and 'not working to capacity'.

It's at this point that Audrey pulls him from Dilworth. In a letter to Conolly in December 1960 she says she has 'come to the decision to allow him to discontinue' the following year.

'I have taken all year considering and considering, but Michael's apparent unhappiness does not seem to abate.

'My husband and I have talked to him . . . but all our understanding of his problems and upsets does not seem to make him any happier at the school.

'It is a big blow to me because I know he is getting a wonderful education, discipline, etc but I feel that his emotional needs must be considered too.'

In a short and to the point reply, Conolly writes: 'I think this is a wise decision as I do not feel that a boy gives his best if there is any unhappiness. We have often found this to be the case when one member of the family is at boarding school and the others are at home.'

Moore heard there was a leavers' assembly so invited himself along because he, too, was departing and sat at the back of the hall. After speeches the departing senior boys were given a suit or a pair of trousers. His name was never called.

Moore hated Dilworth then but is fond of the school now, citing it as the most positive aspect of his otherwise distraught childhood. It gave him gifts he only appreciated later in life. He understands now, too, that it was the time in his life that was difficult more so than the school.

On a trip back to the school more than 30 years later, Dilworth staff proudly showed Moore around their updated facilities. In the military barracks-like clean dormitories Moore commented how nice they were compared with his day but how sad that none of the boys had photos of their mothers on display.

Unknown to him at the time, Dilworth also taught Moore one important thing — a love of books and reading, something that would stay with him and change his life.

After three years Audrey had got on top of her life, getting rid of the failing second-hand shop and having remarried local Labour Party activist, leasehold farmer and Moerewa freezing works fitter and turner George Turanga Webber. He had an older son, Barry, who was best man at the wedding, and a daughter, Treasure, from a previous marriage.

Labour had played its part again in Audrey's life. 'Aunty' Doreen, who was a party member and was to later marry a Wellington Labour MP and Kirk Government Cabinet minister Henry May, had met Webber, who was from Umawera near the Hokianga Harbour, at a Labour conference. She suggested he look up her widowed cousin in Kawakawa.

Webber had stood for Labour in the Rodney seat in 1957 and lost to National's Jack Scott, later a Cabinet minister in Holyoake's Government, and would later stand in Hobson, in 1960, coming third to National and Social Credit.

Moore was 'released' from Dilworth and excitedly headed back to what he thought would be a far more settled and comfortable life on a farm in his new family.

He didn't mind the early mornings to help with milking the cows because Dilworth had taught him how to get up before dawn. Coming home after school seemed a treat, too, and Moore would regularly sit down in the evenings doing newspaper clippings and folding Labour pamphlets for his stepfather.

Being away from home at such an early age and surrounded by male influencers had made him think a lot about his mother and yearn for an ordinary family life. Back in Northland, on a farm with his mother, Shane and a new father, he hoped for some normality and to be like everyone else.

He soon realised, though, that Webber wasn't going to be the father he'd dreamed of. He could see his mother was unhappy and it wasn't long before he felt the hand of Webber.

Once Webber told Moore to do a task in the paddock and he refused, half joking and half defiantly saying to the man: 'I'll drop you like a hot turd.' It was a phrase Moore had heard in the schoolyard and wasn't quite sure of its meaning. It didn't matter — Webber swung around with a fence batten and hit him square in the back, levelling Moore.

Moore had no one to turn to, not even Kerry who had just left home. Dawdling some distance behind, Moore followed his brother into Moerewa to watch him leave town — and their lives he thought at the time — for the army. 'See you later, fatso,' Kerry said to his brother as he got on the bus.

On his first day back at school in Northland, this time at Moerewa Primary School, he quickly learned about reputations and how they can precede you in life. He was the boy from a fancy Auckland school and Moore sensed the mood in the playground at lunchtime. At Dilworth he was reasonably big for his age, but among the local Māori boys he was just another little Pākehā kid.

So, out of character, he joined the rugby match being played. Moore was never good at sports and avoided it where he could because of his troublesome left leg which had been in a brace for four years due to a bone disorder doctors later thought might have been as a result of polio.

Moore knew he had to make an impression in the match to get on side with the other boys, so targeted the biggest player, Thomas Rawiri, and summoned up all his courage and tackled him as he waltzed past other flailing arms.

Everyone on the field froze. Rawiri put the ball down, slowly got up and whacked Moore for his efforts. But that tackle and his determination gave him a reputation and got him into the school rugby team, which wore sugar sacks as jerseys, for a couple of years.

He wasn't tall but he was solid and not afraid to defend himself if needed. Unlike some other loners who were constantly bullied, this image gave Moore the luxury most of the time to be able to sit by himself with his books during lunch breaks.

His old friends from earlier Kawakawa days, Terry and Bryan, would help Moore escape the sadness of home. They would often walk the five or so kilometres along the railway track to meet Moore in Otiria or Moerewa.

Bryan's mother Olga was also best friends with Audrey — many used to think they were sisters — and they worked together in the local TAB and bakery.

The boys were the tightest of friends, as only pre-teens can be, causing trouble and covering for each other. Moore was the even-tempered organiser of the three.

Once they chopped down a pine tree in Bryan's backyard. It took the three of them two days hacking away at the half-metre-wide trunk with tomahawks for it to fall, hit a travelling car and block State Highway 1.

It didn't take long for the local police to determine Bryan was a likely suspect. They handcuffed him all day to the leg of a desk in the Kawakawa Police Station so everyone could see and laugh at him and teach him a lesson. Despite this, Bryan never grassed on his accomplices.

But the three didn't learn from this experience. Instead, they built a giant slingshot attached to two trees on Terry's property near Kawakawa Hospital and shot fruit and vegetables across the road. They were eventually caught after firing a rotten pumpkin at a passing car.

On another occasion they untied 'Tiny' Sigley's punt — a long flat boat — on the Kawakawa River used as a duck-shooting platform and paddled it all the way to Opua and caught the train back to town.

The three friends would spend a lot of time on the Otiria farm, which was opposite a local marae and had a five-metre-high waterfall on it. During the summer the boys would spend hours jumping from it.

To be even more daring they'd sometimes ride their bicycles off the waterfall until on one occasion Bryan had to dive into the water to rescue Moore after he didn't emerge from a jump. He had become entangled in the frame of the bike at the bottom of the pond.

The gang broke up when the three were in the third form of Bay of Islands College, with the Gregory family moving to Auckland. At college Moore enjoyed geography and history but was told to do a technical course which gave him one pass in the fifth form School Certificate exam.

While he enjoyed his books and Dilworth had taught him to do his homework on time, he wasn't studious. He also wasn't part of the rugby crowd, so missed many of the Saturday-night parties.

Instead he would often go into the bush to shoot slug guns at birds with Terry and his older brother John at the weekends and learn to drink flagons of beer with other teenage boys to get away from the boredom and sameness of everything.

He ended up doing what many of the other Northland teenagers did at the time — hoon around the back roads of the Bay of Islands in cars, laze around at the beach, pretend to be tougher than they were, learn to smoke and drink beer to excess that they got older brothers to buy.

While they were ever hopeful and turned to Moore for his humour and clever words, few girls showed them any attention. They were going nowhere with their lives, but it seemed a great place to be.

It was through Webber that Moore would meet his future mentor and one of the key influencers in his political career, Matiu Rata, a Rātana preacher from the northern settlement of Te Hapua who was standing in the March 1963 by-election for the Northern Māori seat.

Rata was standing against the popular National Party candidate, former Māori Battalion officer James Henare, and met with Webber and other local Labour people at their home as part of his campaigning. Good-looking with his swept-back dark black hair, gently spoken and with a suit and tie on, Rata was the most impressive person Moore had ever met.

He spoke beautifully and kindly about people, and of the urgency in dealing with Māori issues and local housing and poverty. Moore, who was by now a normally easily bored teenager, sat silently listening to it all. He was pleased to hear Rata scraped home by less than 450 votes.

At the end of his fifth-form year in 1963 Moore left school aged 14 — he would be the official leaving age of 15 in January. There was plenty of work around.

The dairy company by this stage was the second largest in New Zealand, producing 6000 tons of butter and 700 tons of buttermilk powder from 1200 suppliers a day. AFFCO had more than 700 employees and Opua had recently been opened as an overseas port.

He'd had what he thought was a street-wise upbringing. But the freezing works in Moerewa, where Webber helped him get the job, was an eye-opener. Every bit of the beast was used — the meat, hair or wool, bones, offal, blood and casings — and much of the work was manual and highly skilled.

But it wasn't the blood and guts that shocked him. Instead it was watching the social interactions of the men, some of whom would bet their pay packets away unopened before getting home to their families.

No one had any pride working in the casing department where he was stationed, helping gather the skins for sausages. It was the lowest job in the works. At the time Moore had no idea what he was doing. The rumour — or so the older men told the young boys — was they were bundling penis-shaped offal into what would then be used in the manufacture of condoms.

Moore and the other Pākehā at the works were the minority and there weren't any race problems. That thought — that Māori weren't the cause of race problems — stayed with him throughout his life. Moore later described his gang at the freezing works as 'Ngāti AFFCO'.

There was always an undercurrent of violence at the works. At lunchtimes Moore would often sit in the smoko room reading books to avoid eye contact and the possibility of confrontation. One of the freezing workers union delegates had put out a box of left-wing literature and Moore devoured it.

He witnessed a few fights which were always allowed to go so far until some of the older men intervened and pulled the combatants apart. Moore was involved in one himself for using the hose too close to a workmate. But despite the different allegiances in the workforce, they were a band of brothers and it was their tribe against the bosses.

The casing department was easy work except for a large clock slowly ticking the minutes away in front of him. He often looked up at it, hoping the day would go by quicker.

You can tell someone is a freezing worker simply by their smell. The smell of the works — the damp, fatty, cooked meat and warm excrement odour — stays with you, almost like an imprint, despite any amount of washing of clothes or skin.

The only fashion truth was their white gumboots. With the tops turned down Moore and many of his workmates thought they looked flash enough to impress women when worn around town.

Over time Moore came to understand that for all the blood, guts and smell this was New Zealand's most important industry. He also learned that the boss did not care for his workers and they repaid him with interest.

Everything that was good and wrong with New Zealand was encapsulated in the works and formed the basis of a lot of his political thinking later in life.

In 1964 the family moved from Northland to Tauranga for a few months before going to Auckland and settling in the predominantly Pākehā working-class South Auckland suburb of Papatoetoe, a place that had grown after the Second World War with returned servicemen's housing.

Moore briefly went back to school, attended Papatoetoe High, where he struggled with sixth-form physics and maths. They were unknown languages to him, and he soon left to be a bricklayer's labourer and then a builder's labourer at Cox and Dawes.

He lasted a year in that before getting a job in a small Otahuhu printing firm, Underwood Printing, and becoming a printer's apprentice and, through that, joined the Printers Union.

It was a profession he had a fondness for: ink, words and printing presses leading to the assembly of thoughts and ideas. The creativity of it all seemed powerful to him.

The owner of the print shop, Barry Underwood, treated him like a son. The two talked often about current events and Underwood would encourage Moore to pursue his political interests and was happy to give him time off to do this. He only charged Moore at cost for all the political printing he got done.

Moore kept his links to the profession by staying a member of the Printers Union for many years after he became a politician. This love of ink led him to become chairman of Labour's media committee, which at its height published five magazines and employed five journalists, all funded through advertising.

With a job and some money, Moore hooked up again with his old mate Bryan Gregory, who was now a builder in Auckland, and Bryan's girlfriend Karen (who later became his wife). Auckland was a rapidly growing city in the 1960s and there was fun to be had for young people.

It was during this period in his life that Moore also learned about the failings of New Zealand's health system. Even though he'd worn a brace on his left leg much of his childhood and was often in pain, surgery on it was considered non-urgent and he had to go on a long waiting list. His mother used to tell him not to worry; the pain was just from him growing and it would eventually go.

In a time when a good worker's wages, with overtime, could be about £10 a week, Moore used his £60 in savings and paid for an operation in a private hospital to have some of the bones in his leg fused together. Walking became easier; although still awkward it was much less painful afterwards.

It struck him how unfair this all seemed. Rich people had choices because if their need was not urgent, they could go through the public health system and if it was they could opt out via private provision. Working people, on the other hand, had no choice but to rely on the public system which was at the whim of the funding from the government of the day.

2

'A nice boy'

'In the early days I was so impressed with the people I'd meet in the Labour Party. I always thought they were important. And it used to be Mr Moyle and Mr Kirk and then after two or three times they'd say, "Call me Colin, or Norm."

'I thought I was lucky the Labour Party had me.

'I was keen as hell when I joined Labour. I used to go to the other side's meetings and mess them up until Colin Moyle, who was patient and a good teacher, told me to stop doing it because it gave the Nats publicity. Then he said: "Oh, okay, only do it occasionally."

'Warren Goff and I went to a Young Nats meeting once and they were talking about apartheid South Africa. We got some of them all riled up against the Holyoake Government and staged a mini walkout. We signed some of them up for Labour afterwards. Hell, it was fun.

'I used to spend time talking with John A. Lee in his bookshop. He was a rebel and had interesting stories about Savage and the first Labour Government. That appealed to me. But he was a terrible racist.

'The good thing about the Labour Party in those days was you'd have a branch meeting and you'd have disagreements. It was alright. Nowadays things are so tight, everyone has to agree with each other.

'I was one of the few people in the party back then that hadn't been to university. It's good people going to university. Higher education is good. But there's got to be more to you than that. It's like having a trade's certificate. So what? But I do regret not going to university.

'Professor Bob Chapman was a hero for many of the university lot. I remember going to a student party of his and bringing along two flagons of beer and someone put them away in the cupboard.

'We had a great movement back then — lots of young and talented people. The working-class kids and the middle-class kids.

'People would give up their jobs and campaign somewhere in the country, finding some way to make a living. People devoted themselves to the cause. People were passionate. I think that's one of the great changes. When was the last time someone gave a year of their life to the cause?

'The fights in the party back then were mostly about the communists. There wasn't a day that would go by when the communists weren't thinking of a way to do over the Labour Party.

'They split our votes up. Every electorate had stories about Comms telling our people not to vote, then when the Tories won, they'd say: "See, Labour's got you nowhere." The second phase for the Comms was the populist front where they joined Labour, took over positions and told our people what to do.

'Kirk was very good against the communists. This was at the time of the Cold War and this stuff was serious. These guys had an ideological point of view. And in pursuit of that anything you did was okay.

'Others also tried to use Labour. The protest movements always wanted our involvement but on their terms. They'd then turn up to Labour conferences and dump on the party. They're never there for you normally. If people sell the raffles and are involved in the party throughout the year, they're entitled to have a go at you. But I used to think that those others could just f-off.

'Norm Douglas was the president in my early days. That generation liked young people. They liked it when you got stuck into them. Hughie Watt was deputy leader and was a good guy. I used to give him so much shit. But then he'd come up to you afterwards and say: "Hey, well done. You got in the newspaper with that issue."

'It was exciting to be in the Labour Party. I felt we were on a mission to change New Zealand and the world.

'Jim Anderton, Michael Bassett, Roger Douglas and others had produced the *Red Book* to reinvent the party's constitution and get rid of the unions. They talked about modernisation, and some of their arguments were right.

'But I thought it was really a power bid by Anderton and his crowd to take over the party rather than to reform it. Anderton wound up a lot of the young people and got them to march out of the party. He tried to get me, but I spoke against him. He marked me down then.

'Being part of Socialist Youth opened my eyes to the world. My Singaporean mates Chong Yong and Alfred didn't have much money so we rented this tiny room in London. One of us had the bed, the other the mattress and the other the sheets. They were exciting times: international politics was changing really quickly.

'I had been well known around the party and John Stewart approached me to stand for Eden. I thought if I don't win this, I'll come close and make my reputation out of that.

'I thought one of the new seats being created in South Auckland was where I'd eventually run and win. In those days you had to run in a Tory seat to build up your reputation. So, I thought, why not?

'I went full-time that year. Occasionally I'd go back and do a night shift for Barry Underwood. I had a Trekka, probably the only person in New Zealand who did, that Barry helped me buy. Wheels went like this, slightly wonky. Painted it up "Mike Moore for Eden" and just drove it around. It was very unusual.

'The Nats had this widow called Mrs Kidd. She was very good. I was respectful. "A nice boy" she used to say about me. I wasn't too sure if she was taking the piss out of me at the time.

'I came up with this new way of door-knocking and Warren and I just created this election machine. It was very manual and labour intensive, but it was great. I sold the idea to a couple of other campaigns too.

'We had a dedicated team in Eden who had so much energy.

'We got up to 20 street-corner meetings a day. We had two sets of speakers. I'd speak for 10 minutes and move on. You'd just rotate the speakers. We got good crowds. Sometimes people would get annoyed. "Piss off Mike, you've been here four times — you've got our vote." When you're in a winning campaign it's just fantastic.

'People just came from everywhere to help. Everyone just wanted to change the world; it was very exciting.

'Very early on election night I knew we were going to win government. There was jubilation everywhere.'

****

Flatmates either become your friends for life or they're people you tell stories about to others for years to come.

Brothers Warren and Phil Goff would become both for Moore. The three shared a flat in St George Street, Papatoetoe in 1970. Moore and Warren had been flatting together since 1966 in Papatoetoe — first in

Portage Road and then in Wyllie Road — and were joined by Phil, five years their junior, when he'd been kicked out of home and had initially crashed on their couch.

Moore and Warren had become great friends, having first met at the inaugural Labour Party Manukau Youth branch meeting. In fact, they were the only two who had turned up.

Moore had volunteered to set up the branch for local MP Colin Moyle who in response to his constant requests to help suggested Moore go and sign up members. Moore had put an advertisement in the local community newspaper for a midweek evening meeting and only Warren, who was a student teacher and would later work for the Post Office, turned up.

After waiting a while to see if anyone else would turn up, the pair went off to the pub and became inseparable after that. They talked constantly about the politics of the day and ended up flatting together.

The flatmates weren't quiet and had pulled off the legendary feat of convincing their neighbour in their Wyllie Road property, an elderly retired woman, to regularly pick up the beer bottles strewn in their backyard and to mow the lawns for them.

The St George Street flat wasn't a particularly tidy place, except for Phil's room which was prim and proper bar the *Playboy* centrefold pinned on the wall above his bed. The local takeaway saw a lot of their business. Moore and Warren took it upon themselves to educate Phil in all matters of politics.

For Phil's twenty-first birthday Moore got him volume one of Michael Foot's biography of his political hero, Welsh working-class British Labour Party MP Nye Bevan who helped establish the National Health Service. Goff was given volume two as a wedding gift many years later.

Moore and Warren saw Phil as a mix between their pet political project and the annoying little kid who followed you around in the playground. Deep down they wished they had some of his traits of discipline and focus.

Moore had joined the Mt Roskill youth branch of Labour in 1966 and quickly became active, writing articles regularly — from the need to establish a new form of juvenile court to lowering the voting age to 18 — for various party publications.

Labour represented the struggles of working men and women and, like him, believed that governments with principles and values could be part of the answer. Understanding National was easy for Moore — they don't believe in anything other than power for the sake of it. And a person who doesn't believe in anything has no soul.

He was brought up to believe that Prime Minister George Forbes' United Party coalition government with Gordon Coates' Reform Party in the early 1930s was the cause of the Great Depression and that 'Saint' Michael Joseph Savage had saved New Zealand.

His political education was on doorsteps, far away from lecture theatres. He rounded this off by spending many hours talking with expelled Savage Government MP and author John A. Lee in his Auckland city bookshop, Vital Books.

Through the Printers Union Moore was elected to the Auckland Trades Council as its youngest member, at 17 years old. He recalls being in a smoke-filled room late one night, where members were sick of all the whining and bickering between the communists and members of the Labour Party, putting up his hand and being elected. There was no cloak or dagger involved, more tired people wanting to get home.

One of Moore's first demonstrations was that year, too, against the visiting South Vietnamese Prime Minister Air Vice-Marshal Nguyen Cao Ky who was in New Zealand gathering support for the war. Demonstrating with a group of like-minded people, shouting slogans and waving placards excited him and made him think about the power of an idea to motivate individuals to collectively achieve something.

It was a period of turmoil in New Zealand and Labour. The party had lost the 1966 general election. The Vietnam War was at its height and a whole generation of activists was joining Labour.

Many of the older guard in the party, some of whom had seen Savage, Fraser and Nash governments, felt threatened by the university-educated and professionals joining. Many of the new members thought they could run Labour better and expected to be listened to.

There were two informal groups: the mostly older working-class and trade union socially conservative group and the mostly younger middle-class liberal students and academics. Despite his youth, Moore belonged to the former and he, too, didn't much like what he thought were those from the ivory towers. Few, Moore felt, seemed to show respect to their elders, the MPs and elected party officials.

Many were from the University of Auckland's Princes Street branch and were, he begrudgingly admitted, talented and smart. He was on the peripheries of the branch and its people, and while they were happy to have him around, he never felt comfortable in their company.

They didn't seem that much fun or interested in the daily struggles of ordinary New Zealanders, he kept thinking.

He was instinctively more conservative than many of their counter-culture views which he thought were more about them rebelling against their parents than wanting to progress the lives of others.

They said they hated American influence in the world and despised the country's global influence, yet they unquestioningly embraced its modern cultural symbols — clothes, hairstyles and music. Like them he hadn't met an American yet, let alone been to the country.

Moore felt more comfortable in a necktie than their tie dye. He knew they thought he was a square. He didn't care. He thought some of them were self-indulgent and spoilt.

He was interested in their alternative views but couldn't countenance what he thought was the arrogance of their argument: that the way ordinary people were living was wrong and that only they knew best.

He saw an attack on ordinary Kiwis as an attack on him. He was ordinary like the people he grew up with in Northland, like his family and mates, like those on the steps of the homes he door-knocked in South Auckland.

They seemed deadly earnest and wanted to constantly debate policy and put forward remits on everything. He thought of them as 'resolutionaries'. Their inspirational leader was political studies and history Professor Robert Chapman who Moore didn't really get to know like many of the other young party members.

While he was out in the new suburbs of South Auckland organising for Moyle and signing up members, they sat in the university quad dreaming of overthrowing the world.

For Moore the first real clash of these two groups came in 1967 after the party's Auckland regional organiser Jim Anderton and other prominent young members wrote a series of remits for the 1967 party conference called the *Red Book*, which took its catchy title from China's Mao Zedong's *Little Red Book* of aphorisms.

While also revolutionary in nature, the *Red Book* was hardly left wing in content. Instead, it advocated changing Labour's constitution to lessen the influence of the trade unions. The aim was to also streamline party structures and make Labour a more centrist party.

Moore, who proudly told everyone at the time that he was a 'union man', saw this as a right-wing attack on Labour and rejoiced when Kirk and Party President Norman Douglas crushed the move. The workers had put the academics in their place, he thought.

In April 1969 a new position of youth representative was created on the party's ruling body, the national executive, and with the strong support of the trade unions he became the youngest ever member of Labour's governing entity at 20 years old.

He beat Michael Hirschfeld, the son of a Wellington businessman, on the third ballot 261 to 237. He didn't know it at the time, but it was a portent of future contests Moore would have with the changing character and membership of the party.

As a member of the national executive Moore now had a nationwide stage and went on regular tours of parts of provincial New Zealand, giving speeches and helping with campaigning. Instead of flying to Wellington for national executive meetings, he would often cash in his plane tickets and catch trains and buses on a slow journey to the capital so he could visit party members.

He soon realised he had a talent for politics and enjoyed his conversations with ordinary party members, many of whom were older and had known some of his early union and Labour heroes.

In 1968 Moore was an organiser for Labour's local body campaign in Manukau City and in 1969 worked with trade unionists like Fred Anderson and Rex Jones on the election campaign of Manukau City Councillor and businessman Roger Douglas, one of the *Red Book* authors, when he stood for the Manukau seat (Moyle having moved to the new nearby seat of Mangere).

Moore thought he didn't like Douglas because of the *Red Book* but really didn't know him that well and it would be many more years before he really understood the man. He was prepared to put aside his views on Douglas's politics for the chance to be involved in his first general election campaign. During it, Douglas became his first teacher in the art of organising for selections, rolling opposing delegates and stacking branches with favourable people.

Douglas scraped home in the general election by fewer than 900 votes.

But at a national level, Kirk failed to win in 1969 — losing by six seats and falling 1 per cent of the vote behind National — despite predictions that he would beat a tiring Holyoake.

Having been part of the campaign, the 20-year-old Moore came to the conclusion that National had the money, news media and patronage, and just knew how to win elections. He realised that Labour had to stop moaning about the gap between the party organisations and radically lift its game to compete.

He also learned another lesson — respect your opponent. Holyoake had cleverly given the impression of renewal in his government with Cabinet reshuffles and worked on his public image.

It was a good time in Moore's life. He was working his way up the party's ranks, had got to know many influential politicians, had worked on campaigns, had a great boss who supported his political interests, had bought a sports car and had some savings.

He thought that if he was to run for Parliament sometime in the near future, he had to learn more about the world. He hadn't been to university but was fascinated by the international books he'd read. It was time for his OE.

Instead of following other Kiwis to the bars of London in 1970, Moore went on a four-month trip to Singapore, Malaysia, India, England, Holland, Belgium, Ireland, Sweden, the Soviet Union and France.

The following year he spent two months in Australia, Indonesia, Singapore, Malaysia, Japan, South Vietnam, Korea and Taiwan. But these weren't sightseeing holidays. On his trips he visited left-wing politicians and political parties and attended conferences. In Brussels he attended a socialist international congress for the first time. In South Vietnam he met US troops. In South Korea he visited a socialist leader in prison.

He spent all his savings and returned in debt. His trips taught him how politics was literally a deadly serious matter in some parts of the world and the importance of democratic institutions to the proper functioning of a country. Along the way he picked up many campaigning techniques and made lifelong friends.

It was during this period that he developed his admiration for what was to be later known as the 'Singapore miracle', that combination of workers, business and government working together to accelerate what the free market or central control couldn't achieve alone.

He came to admire the visionary leadership of the father of Singapore, Lee Kuan Yew. Lee was, in many respects, the politician Moore wished he could become — a mix of modernity and pragmatism with the Confucian values of order, balance and family.

Despite being stopped once and asked to have a haircut — 'they seem to equate long hair with drugs and they seem to think that like Samson my strength lies in my hair' he told the media at the time — he was fascinated by the rapid social and economic development of the country.

On stopovers in Singapore he made many student friends through the Singapore Socialist Club. Moore would often speak at campus meetings to students who were the first in their families to go to university. Like Moore, they were liberal in their outlooks, patriots at heart and in a hurry to improve their nation.

People like Loo Chong Yong and Alfred Loh would travel with him to socialist youth meetings internationally. The three were kindred spirits and would become lifelong friends. Despite their outward conservative appearances, they too came from humble beginnings and shared Moore's idealism, humour and mischievous streak.

Moore's travels opened his eyes to the genuine power of politics to progress a country. Politics, he witnessed, was more than having a turn at managing a nation. Politicians, in the right conditions, could lead a country to significant change for the better but sometimes for the worse.

His eyes were opened and he was keen for other aspiring politicians in Labour to have that experience. So he asked the Labour leadership if he could join them up to the International Union of Socialist Youth, which was part of Socialist International of which the party was already a member.

Moore was given a firm 'no'. Undeterred, he went to a conference anyway and signed Labour up as a member and got himself elected as the Asian vice president. This then entitled him to free air tickets to go to International Union of Socialist Youth conferences around the world.

Instead, he gave most of his tickets to other young party members, many of whom were to later become MPs, to allow them to travel. He would later joke that few socialist youth around the world knew what the real Mike Moore looked like.

In 1972 he helped organise an International Union of Socialist Youth conference in Hunua, South Auckland, the first time the organisation had been out of Europe. It was a catalyst for more young people to join Labour.

A number of people in the party had been watching Moore's progress and some suggested he stand for public office. A good starting place, they suggested, would be local government. If he made a name for himself there, he could look to run for Parliament.

Local body elections were being held in late 1971, so Moore put his name forward for the Papatoetoe City Council. He'd briefly been to the local high school, his mum and stepfather lived locally and he'd done a lot of party work in the area. It was a well-respected council with a mayor, returned serviceman Bob White, who was popular and had a good reputation. Papatoetoe would be an easy stepping stone to perhaps running in the 1975 or 1978 general election, he thought.

But Papatoetoe would teach Moore the first rule of campaigning, one that would stay with him for the rest of his career: all politics is local.

For a 22-year-old, he was worldly in his knowledge of the issues of the time — the Vietnam War, the Arab–Israeli conflict, apartheid South Africa and nuclear testing in the Pacific. Moore knew he was superior to his opponents, who only knew about issues in the suburbs, and tried to show this at candidates meetings and when he was out door-knocking.

He seemed to know more about the Ho Chi Minh Trail than the Great South Road. He sounded like he was running for President of the United States, and he sounded out of touch and pretentious.

Moore was thrashed — coming seventeenth in a field of 20 with 1803 votes. The humiliation was compounded by the fact that his stepfather George Webber, who had also stood, beat him by 39 votes.

It was Moore's first real political setback. Papatoetoe was invaluable, though, and with blunt feedback from some locals in the party he understood the political lesson.

The upside of the experience was that he'd continued to show his commitment to South Auckland, a place he thought his political future would revolve around. The rapidly growing suburbs of working people who had jobs in the railway yards and freezing works in Otahuhu and the factories of Penrose would mean plenty of future Labour seats as boundaries shifted and new electorates were formed.

Moore already had a small power base and that would grow over time as he worked the area and progressed his career in the party hierarchy.

In early 1972 the chairman of the Eden Labour Electorate Committee John Stewart approached Moore to discuss an opportunity.

Moore had met Stewart in 1969 when he was beaten by high-profile academic Professor Keith Sinclair for the Eden nomination. Moore used to travel to as many selection meetings as he could to meet party members and learn.

Stewart was a social worker and a returned serviceman, having been wounded in the Second World War.

While others were congratulating Sinclair on his nomination at the selection meeting, Moore went over to commiserate with Stewart and wish him well for the future. Stewart, who had also unsuccessfully been Labour's Eden candidate in 1966, had remembered Moore's kindness when thinking about who to get to run in 1972.

While flattered by Stewart's suggestion, Moore wasn't sure. Eden had been in National's hands since 1946 and while it was gradually becoming marginal was prone to boundary changes.

It was an electorate of mixed demographics. Nearer the city it had Mt Eden Prison and parts of the original settlement of Auckland, to the west and south it headed to the Labour stronghold of Onehunga and homes built by the Savage Government, and to the east was a slice of National's Remuera that was called the 'blue ridge'.

It was mostly a mix of blue-rinse older National Party people in the leafy suburbs and many middle-class professionals, university and teachers training college students and academic liberals closer to the city. None of them were his kind of people. He wondered how he could relate to any of them.

He sought the counsel of Labour's deputy leader and neighbouring Onehunga MP Hugh Watt.

Even if he could pull off the unthinkable and win, Watt warned, the seat would be impossible to hold longer term. And to make it more difficult for him, Watt then told Moore he could have his safe Onehunga seat once he retired in either 1975 or 1978. The 23-year-old had plenty of time on his side.

But, on the other hand, Watt said, it might be a good experience running for Eden, give him some more national exposure and further sharpen his campaigning skills.

Stewart asked Moore a second time and other locals continued to encourage Moore and told him that unless he ran for Parliament, all he'd be left doing in the 1972 general election was running someone else's campaign. He'd already done that for Douglas in 1969. Why not do it for himself in 1972, and maybe help Kirk get Labour back into power for the first time since 1960?

If he'd learned one thing from working on Douglas's election campaign, it was the need to not take anything for granted and to be thorough about the selection process.

High-profile academic Brian Brooks was being lined up by some for the Eden nomination. Brooks was something of a hero in Labour circles nationwide for successfully suing rising National Party star Rob Muldoon for defamation earlier in the year. He would be a difficult opponent because of his reputation.

With the help of his flatmates Warren and Phil, branches were being established in the electorate and key positions being filled by people friendly to Moore. They were stacking branches. But it probably wouldn't be enough to win the nomination.

Moore decided he needed to get Brooks out of the race. He met with Brooks and told him he was a hero to Labour people for what he'd done to Muldoon. He told Brooks that the Labour movement couldn't afford for him to be the Eden candidate and lose to National.

It would be a dent in the party's reputation, whereas Moore possibly losing to National wouldn't mean anything nationwide. Brooks seemed to buy the argument and withdrew his nomination. Moore is still embarrassed to this day about what he did.

Moore worked on his selection speech for three weeks. With his script and pen in hand, Moore practised his selection speech sitting on the end of Phil Goff's bed in the flat while he lay in it with his girlfriend — now wife — Mary. The speech focused not so much on what the Holyoake Government had done but what it hadn't: the lost opportunities for New Zealand.

'I make no apology for the fact that I am a young man. I place commitment, consistency, ideas and ideals above pure volume of years,' he told the selection meeting in the Lyon Memorial Hall in Takapuna.

'I don't apologise for the time and effort I have spent with this organisation, a time when it was not "with it" to be a party man, nor do I regard it as time wasted or a misspent youth . . .

'The fabric of our society is under scrutiny . . . we are witnessing the end of 12 years of conservative rule, 12 wasted years when we have seen our pensions system destroyed by inflation and become a mere subsidy for living, 12 wasted years in which this National Government somehow has even managed to reduce the size of the average home and double the number of mortgages needed to build it.'

He was nervous giving the speech. At least the little cardboard prompts he created to hold to hide his shaking hands worked. It wasn't the best, but it demonstrated he'd be a worthy candidate. Besides, it was almost a forgone conclusion given he had the affiliated trade unions behind him as well as having stacked some branches.

It took Party President Bill Rowling and the panel only about 10 minutes to decide that Moore should be the candidate. Eden wasn't a nationally targeted seat for Labour and few gave Moore a chance.

His victory celebrations were short-lived. The small group of young people, many from working-class backgrounds, he'd attracted to Eden quickly formed the nucleus of his campaign group, with Warren managing it all.

Future local body and national politicians were part of the dedicated team: Phil Goff, Jack Elder and Glenda Fryer. Even well-known Auckland University student protester Mike Rann, who wasn't in the party but would later become a South Australian Labor Premier, was caught up in the euphoria of a young candidate standing for Parliament.

They all thought he was the generational change New Zealand politics needed. He wasn't your usual politician: old, stolid, speaking about yesterday's issues, entitled and Brylcreemed. He was young, smartly dressed, good-looking, great company, funny, related to everyone, charming, full of ideas and energetic.

The team didn't inherit much from the party in Eden. Its headquarters was above a meat company on the corner of Valley and Dominion roads and was covered in dust and strewn with pamphlets from previous unsuccessful campaigns.

More frighteningly, the local party had no money. So they sold donated vegetables and fruit, old suits, books and any kind of bric-a-brac they could get their hands on.

Moore's campaign team had a mixture of idealists and those who wanted to change Labour, New Zealand and the world. They did more than the usual erection of billboards and delivery of pamphlets. Their idea of a fun evening together was to go out door-knocking for Moore and Labour.

Some were party members; others were caught up in Moore's campaign. Some were even from the expelled Trotskyist Socialist Action League and proudly wore their 'Socialists for Labour' campaign buttons everywhere.

Moore had a hatred for communism but was happy to have the 'Trots' on his side rather than being a disruptive influence, something that would come back to haunt him three years later at re-election time when the *New Zealand Truth* newspaper had an 'exposé' about him being a 'closet Marxist'.

Moore knew more about campaigning than most candidates but was keen to learn anything new. He had dissected the 1969 election results and noticed that Roger Drayton, who had a reputation as one of the party's best campaigners, had won what was then the marginal seat of St Albans as a newcomer by about 900 votes. So he flew to Christchurch and spent the day with Drayton picking up many ideas.

The only piece of Drayton advice Moore rejected was the idea of wearing a hat when he was out door-knocking, so that he could take it off in the company of ladies. It might have been appropriate for a 44-year-old former RNZAF squadron leader to wear on a cool Canterbury evening, but it would look creepy to have a 23-year-old printer knock on your door with one on in Auckland's balmy weather, Moore thought.

Moore gave up his job and campaigned full-time, living off his savings and moving back in with his mother in Papatoetoe to save money. As he progressively ran out of money, he sold his possessions, including his prized stereo but stopped when he had only his typewriter left.

His young team were media savvy and came up with local issues to run regularly in the community newspapers. Moore stayed away from the big national and international issues and focused on the poor roads and leaky school buildings in the electorate.

One of the highlights early in the campaign for the excitable team was drafting their first press release — which they agonised over — and then having it picked up by what they considered the bastion of the Tory media, the *New Zealand Herald*.

They stayed up into the wee hours of the morning outside the *Herald*'s Auckland inner-city offices just to see if their story was in the 6 June edition. They screamed and punched the air when they read about Moore alleging that hundreds of votes in Eden would be made invalid because of administrative chaos in the seat.

While Kirk wasn't interested, Moore did persuade some MPs to help. Hutt MP Trevor Young, who had been involved in the temperance movement, visited church ministers, Grey Lynn MP and former wharfie Eddie Isbey factory workers and Manukau MP and former company executive Roger Douglas businessmen's meetings.

National's candidate wasn't selected until many months later. Mary Kidd was a 58-year-old mother of two and widow of a doctor. She was the only National or Labour woman candidate in all of Auckland that election.

Moore couldn't bring himself to dislike Kidd, often describing her on the campaign as a 'very gracious woman'. She described him at public meetings as 'a nice boy', which Moore didn't like but could do very little to fire back at.

Moore and Goff spent many hours worrying about what voters would think of a young man up against a widow and a mother and whether or not to attack her. But she was polite and respectful of him and conducted a clean campaign, so nothing happened.

Kidd had replaced the high-profile retiring John Rae who had been Holyoake's minister of housing and local MP since 1960. Rae was almost beaten by Sinclair in 1969, having lost on the night by 35 votes only to overturn the result with special votes later to win by 67.

Moore and his team methodically door-knocked key parts of the electorate. Moore knew it was his best hope of winning, which he desperately wanted to do to prove everyone wrong.

There had been little nationwide media interest in his selection and Kirk and Labour officials didn't put Eden on their list of possible wins. Kirk also had no plans to visit the electorate to generate media coverage. While this annoyed some in Moore's campaign, he knew Kirk's time was precious and needed to be prioritised for the more winnable seats.

As well as effort, Moore also knew his campaign had to be smart. He introduced to Labour — and perfected — two techniques that had never really been used and are now the cornerstone of party campaigning: phone polling and 'get out the vote' canvassing.

Moore had seen in the US and Europe how phone polling could be used to give a snapshot of the public mood at a particular time and how it could be tracked over a period to see how a candidate or party was performing. In the evenings Moore had volunteers phone polling Eden to see how Labour and National were doing and whether the electorate knew of him.

The first polls weren't encouraging. Labour was behind and few knew who Moore was. But as the campaign went on, the improving numbers gave Moore hope. He knew he and Labour were getting traction.

'Get out the vote' canvassing Moore had picked up from Britain. Labour's door-knocking efforts had since Savage's day been based on trying to convince people to vote for the party. It would often involve long conversations on doorsteps. It was highly inefficient and its impact questionable.

Moore turned Labour's approach to door-knocking on its head forever. Canvassing now focused on identifying whether the household had people who were strong Labour, strong National, Labour-leaning or National-leaning voters. In addition, canvassers asked voters what they did for a job and what issues mattered most to them.

Moore then colour coded this system onto little cards and put voters into 13 different issues categories. He would then systematically write personalised letters to people in Eden based on the issues he knew could encourage them to vote for him and Labour. These letters went out at regular intervals. By today's marketing practices it was a standard audience segmentation exercise, but in 1972 New Zealand politics, it was genius.

On election day an army of people on phones would call the strong Labour and Labour-leaning voters to remind them to go to the polls. They would even offer car rides there through campaign volunteers.

Labour scrutineers would then sit in each of the polling booths and tick off the strong Labour and Labour-leaning voters who'd cast their ballots. Those scrutineers would then pass that information on to volunteers who drove around the booths three times during the day to take back to election headquarters. Those voters would then be checked off against the canvassing data and those who had yet to vote would then get reminder phone calls and house visits by more volunteers until they did.

An unpublished partially completed poll by a market research firm two weeks out from election day had a swing to Moore of 4.5 per cent. People found it hard to believe and dismissed it. Warren and Moore didn't. Their polling was similar.

They knew exactly where everyone was, what they did and roughly how they felt about the election. They had known for some time that if they executed their election-day plan well they would win.

Three weeks out from polling day, 20 mostly young volunteers gave up their jobs to join Moore in the electorate full-time. There was no publicity about this fact and National had no idea of the extent of Moore's ground team, which regularly worked 18 to 20-hour days.

On election day around 200 volunteers turned up to help. It was a major logistical exercise for Warren, but it maximised Labour's vote in an electorate where every ballot would make the difference.

After the polls closed party members and volunteers gathered at the Balmoral Intermediate School hall. One part of the hall had a television set tuned into the coverage, while another had people standing around a radio listening to reports. Seats were falling to Labour, including those held by National Cabinet ministers, but Moore tried not to be confident for fear of jinxing the situation.

At about 9.30 pm Kidd came to the hall to see Moore and concede. She praised him and he was humbled. Moore introduced her to the crowd: 'There's a very gracious lady here to announce the result,' he said.

The hall was silent momentarily and then cheered as she started to say: 'Michael Moore has won Eden by 947 votes . . .'

3

'New Zealanders look to great things from you'

'At one of my first caucus meetings Norm Kirk stood up and told us we needed a Cabinet that had a balance between the North Island and South Island, Māori and women. "Our future is in your hands," he told us.

'My heart was pounding at my first caucus meeting, I was so excited. Kirk was the first New Zealand-born Labour prime minister and he was the second youngest one ever. Labour's campaign theme had been "It's time" and it was.

'We had the Cabinet vote. I was wide-eyed, just happy to be an MP. I made a couple of bad decisions. You had people going around with pieces of paper. I wasn't a member of any of the groups. I generally went with Roger Douglas and Michael Bassett and the young crowd. I didn't vote for Norman Douglas and I should have. I voted for Phil Amos. He was useless.

'Kirk was inspirational, though. We had to fight the bureaucracy; they were our enemy, he said. I've inherited a bit of that from him. He thought they were Tories. He disliked people with higher educations, which was sad.

'The manifesto is the manifesto is the manifesto, he'd say. He put it down on the desk. He used to carry it around with him everywhere. But it ended up being a problem for him. Circumstances changed for that government and he should have broken some of his promises.

'The first thing Kirk did was the Christmas bonus for pensioners. It wasn't in the manifesto. He just made it up. The pensioners needed it and it was pure populism.

'Kirk was very conservative working class and had he lived would have eventually clashed with the young people coming into the party. But there's always been generational clashes in Labour.

'For my maiden speech I paid for a bus to bring people down from Eden and to stay the night. The speech wasn't spectacular. My brother Kerry was there. Shane was not. I suppose it was a proud moment for Mother.

'I should have been made prime minister back then, I thought I knew everything.

'We made a huge mistake and it's only in hindsight but during the oil crisis we should have shoved everything off the table. It was a genuine excuse. Norm Kirk, Hugh Watt and Bill Rowling as far as I could see did all the thinking. Kirk was different. He didn't like many of the people in his Cabinet — a bit like Lange later — he was going to do things himself. Kirk was very lonely.

'Warren Freer, Hugh Watt, Arthur Faulkner — people who weren't threats — he'd get advice from. Kirk was paranoid about threats.

'We young ones were used by him, too, to smash his opponents down, to force them to keep promises. He would send one or two ambassadors to see us young guys to say don't you let the Cabinet get away with this or that. We were willing to be manipulated. It was a weird environment but very stimulating.

'Then you had Rob Muldoon come in.

'He was scrappy. On one occasion he'd been involved in some fisticuffs with protesters in Auckland. Back in the House the Whips told us not to say a thing. The bell went off in Parliament and I couldn't help myself and screamed out: "Round two." Everyone fell about laughing.

'Muldoon was ruthless. He played the race card. He'd send Islanders back to the Pacific and offending Māori back to their marae. He hated the media. He knew everything — a bit like Trump. But all this stuff resonates with working-class folk.

'I remember Muldoon laughing at me in the House about how I had to withdraw a private members bill about protecting coastal land. He called out: "Been cut off at the knees by your own party." I said, "That might be true, but I'll still be taller than you." I loved it that I was a pebble in his shoe.

'We didn't see Muldoon as a threat, though, because Kirk could deal with him. If Kirk had stayed around, I'd like to think he would have dealt to Muldoon. The country would be a very different place; our history would be very different.

'We didn't realise how sick Kirk was. He was this imposing character, but there was a fun side to him too.

'One night a bunch of MPs — Mat Rata, Joe Walding and some others — were drinking and singing in one of the offices. Joe was looking out the window and all of a sudden he sees flames shooting out of the roof. They set off the alarms and call the fire brigade and run out of the building. It was a false alarm. What Joe thought was a fire was the setting sun reflecting off the roof.

'The next day they get a call from Kirk's office to come and see him and to bring a bottle of Scotch each. He says to them: "You've been on the piss, haven't you? You pushed the alarms, didn't you? There's a recording at the fire station of your voices and it's recognisable that it's you and you and you."

'"What can we do, Norm?" they said. "Each of you give me your bottles of Scotch," he said. "What, as compensation for the fire brigade?" "No, for me, I've got the tape recording," he said.

'Christ, we were a stupid government. We were popular for two years then crash. The oil crisis did it. Inflation got a boost so we put restrictions on and before we knew it we were back to where we started.

'But foreign policy was great. When the frigate went to Mururoa I was at Devonport and I was so proud of Kirk. No one ever did that to a colonial power back then. Then there was the Springbok tour. We were going into areas we knew some of the public didn't like, but we did it anyway because we knew it was right.

'I'm not sure what Kirk actually thought of me. In his biography he says two communists got elected to the party executive. I was one of two elected to the executive back then. So, he must have thought I was the communist and Anderton was the right winger.

'I was at my parents' place in Papatoetoe when it came across the TV Kirk had died. So I drove into the electorate and lights were coming on, in the pensioner flats too. I popped into a few of them — I didn't know what to do.

'We put a book in my electorate office and people streamed in to sign it. They wanted something to do. I knew immediately then that Rowling would be leader.

'After the funeral I went to Watt to tell him I couldn't vote for him. I told him his time had passed. He was a good friend of mine. Hugh said: "Keep that to yourself — don't tell Francie because she likes you."

'The leadership contest was very dignified. There wasn't any lobbying. I voted for Arthur Faulkner for deputy then switched my vote to Bob Tizard. That was a terrible mistake. He was a scrappy little bugger and I thought he might take it to Muldoon.

'I thought Rowling was good, but you could feel it in the streets that we were unpopular. Inflation was up. Prices were up.

'I remember talking to Douglas and saying: "Christ, what's Cabinet going to do at Budget time?" He said: "I've got something special on." And on Budget night he went bang — it was a baby bonus. It made things worse. We had to borrow more. The compulsory superannuation stuff was great, though.

'I was working even harder in the electorate. I took as much leave as I could. I was signing letters to everyone for any reason I could think.

'Then there was a movement that I go stand in Onehunga. I thought about it. Watt was very supportive. He said he'd come back from being high commissioner to London to help. But I thought I was the Prince of the Labour Party and thought if I lost Eden I would easily come back later. I also thought I could possibly pull it off in Eden.

'Most of the people didn't think we were going to lose. Arthur Faulkner came around on election day in 1975 and said he couldn't wait for the day to be over so he could be back at the desk on Monday.

'We ankle-tapped every vote we could in Eden. We had more money and people than we had in 1972. I'd just married Yvonne and we were always in the papers. But it still wasn't enough. If the swing against Labour was what I had in Eden, Muldoon would never have been elected.

'Labour people were proud of those who lost. We were heroes. I got letters from all around the country saying come and stand in our electorate. There wasn't hatred. It was a different sort of people joining the party in those days.'

****

Moore's 1972 Eden result shocked Labour and many political observers around the country.

The final count had Moore winning by 788 votes, having turned out more than 9000 voters. New Zealand's youngest ever MP had won 48.2 per cent of the votes cast.

It was a night of overwhelming emotions, with Norm Kirk winning in a landslide with a 23-seat majority and more than 48 per cent of the votes cast. Not since the 1935 election had there been such a turnover of MPs.

Moore had campaigned full-time for seven months and dramatically lifted the local party membership from around 25 to 500.

Labour's campaign caught National off guard — they thought they might win the seat by about 1000 votes. There was little nationwide news coverage of Moore's campaign because few even in Labour expected him to win. He was, they thought, just running to prepare for a serious campaign in 1975.

In all, Moore and his team had knocked on more than 10,000 homes, delivered more than 180,000 pamphlets, including 1500 personal letters, written in longhand, to swing voters, put up 265 hoardings, and held more than 150 public meetings.

On election night Moore and the team celebrated long and hard at the school hall. But not before Moore and his local electorate committee, within an hour of his election, sent the new prime minister a telegram demanding the immediate withdrawal of all New Zealand training troops from Indochina.

They were intoxicated by Labour and Moore's win and wanted to change the world — immediately. It was to be the first of many thorns in the side of senior Labour MPs from the new, young and brash MP.

The celebrations continued the next day at a supporter's home and Moore and others talked enthusiastically about the new government and all that had to be done. Moore was continuously on the phone dealing with well-wishers and talking with his new colleagues about going to Parliament.

He was already being lobbied for his vote for Cabinet places but wasn't focused on the new game being played. He was running on adrenalin; a mixture of hung-over, tired and excited. So much was going through his head: people to thank, continuing to celebrate with his supporters, what he had to do as an MP.

Moore flew down to Wellington with another first-time MP, Waitemata's Michael Bassett, and slept in his sleeping bag at a friend's flat.

Many have vivid recollections of that first day at Parliament. As the new MPs gathered outside the building next to the giant marble staircase and in front of what's known as 'the rubber door', shaking hands and slapping backs, many members of the Parliamentary Press Gallery came down to introduce themselves to the new intake.

Some of the MPs were in awe of the names they'd only read about, heard on the radio or seen on television. For most Labour MPs the news media fell into one of two broad camps: part of the Tory establishment or liberals who wanted to change the world. Moore understood their importance to his career but like some of his colleagues was initially suspicious and reticent.

The other memory was Moore meeting Muldoon for the first time. Moore had already determined that he would deliberately target Muldoon, the ruthless, quick-witted and feared star of National, and make him the equivalent to Moerewa Primary School's Thomas Rawiri, enemy number one. Moore had nothing to lose — everyone would expect Muldoon to get the better of him, but if he could inflict some wounds he'd be noticed.

Muldoon was meeting and greeting the new MPs when he saw Moore and came over to introduce himself. 'You must be Mike Moore,' Muldoon said as he stuck out his right hand. Moore grabbed it, shook it firmly and — cleverly, he thought at the time — replied: 'And who are you?'

There was a moment's stunned silence before the Labour MPs roared with mocking laughter at Muldoon. Moore was cocky and calculating, but many repeated the story to others. He was already making his mark.

Initially he was shy and kept his distance from colleagues. But he was quickly drawn to the excitement of being a new MP and being in the governing party.

There was a strong feeling of camaraderie, particularly among the young and new Labour MPs. Moore and a group of them lived in apartments in a Ministry of Works building a short walk away from Parliament on Hill Street near where the new motorway was being built in Thorndon. There were always drinks and a card game in one of the flats.

Moore's office was on the ground floor of Parliament with some of this group, while the other new intakes were in offices in a building where the Beehive now is.

As the baby of the caucus, Moore was allocated a seat in the House right at the back near some of the National MPs and just in front of Michael Bassett, and veteran MP and former rebel Norm Douglas from Auckland Central.

Traditionally, maiden speeches are non-controversial and discuss an MP's upbringing and background and what attracted them to politics. They're an insight into an MP and their political philosophy.

Moore ignored that tradition in his on 27 February 1973. There was not one word about his family.

In front of a busload of supporters who had driven down from Eden, including his mother, he used his maiden speech to attack National, saying it had given the country 12 years of 'defeatism at its worst and escapism at its most obvious'.

He targeted Opposition Leader John Marshall and again focused on National's ambitious deputy Muldoon.

'This house is truly representative. We have members from all vocations and backgrounds. What other room in this country embraces such differences of political thought and background and where else can you find individuals with such political differences sitting side by side? I refer, of course in particular, to the leader and deputy leader of the Opposition.'

Moore said he was proud to be a member of a political party that wanted more than just a better standard of living. Labour was far more ambitious than this.

'We seek a different set of values. We sought parliamentary office not as an end but as a means of legislating for the ideals we hold so dear.'

He attacked National for making social security neither social nor secure, blindly supporting the Vietnam War, talking about equality while supporting apartheid South Africa, proclaiming independence yet following other countries' foreign policy, putting people into prison for homosexuality and sending people into mental asylums as the answer to the drug crisis.

Labour had won because many New Zealanders had come together 'in a coalition of conscience'. New Zealanders had voted for a government 'with New Zealand attitudes and with a political conscience that only the Labour movement could provide'.

He urged a new way of thinking about the development of industries and how the principles of cooperatives and employee investment in companies should be encouraged. Farmers had long ago determined that cooperatives for freezing works, fertiliser manufacturing and the dairy industry was advantageous. Māori also had cooperatives for land use and there were cooperative department stores.

'These organisations are invariably cooperative to the suppliers . . . but somewhere along the line the role of the employee has been ignored. What are his rights? What say in the direction of his industry does he have?

'Some may say he has no rights there, because he can leave at any time, but if he has no rights, he cannot be expected to have any responsibility.'

Work councils, where employees had a say in their companies as in some European nations, should be encouraged.

He gave notice in the speech that he saw the economy differently from many of his Labour colleagues.

'Let us recognise that multinational companies, international capitalism and internal monopolies threaten the economic freedom of this country . . .

'In the past some people once proclaimed that the way to a better society was by state involvement in crucial industries.

'In some areas this is vital, but this did not end profit enterprise or public poverty.

'Too often even now in state-run enterprises the attitude by employees to their management is no different from that in private industry. Nor, in fact, is the attitude of the management any different. State capitalism has solved little. We should be bold, and with apology to no one, seek out new solutions.'

Many inside and outside the party noticed the speech.

The following speaker in the House, justice minister Martyn Finlay, complimented Moore on his 'spirited, substantial and articulate contribution', saying it augured well for the future and how he eagerly looked forward to hearing him again.

The news media noticed, too. A *Sunday News* editorial in early 1973 said Moore was an impressive new MP.

'Eden MP Mike Moore deserves his newfound high standing in the Labour Party. He has already shown enormous drive and enthusiasm for his role as a politician. Congratulations Mike. New Zealanders look to great things from you in the future.'

Sunday News, then a national newspaper aimed mostly at blue-collar male readers with its page three photos of scantily clad female models, had a huge circulation and became enamoured with Moore.

'Mike Moore is the comer of the New Zealand political arena. In just one term in Parliament he has shown qualities which have made hardened political observers take notice. Qualities which, some believe, could ultimately win him leadership. Who exactly is this young backbencher who challenges Rob Muldoon to public debate? What are his aspirations for his party? And for his country?'

It was great for his profile but terrible for his standing with his caucus colleagues. In less than 12 months he was already starting to annoy Cabinet members and the older MPs.

In September 1973 he gave a speech at an Engineers Union conference that was reported in Wellington's *Evening Post* newspaper complaining about the country's industrial relations system. The headline screamed: 'MP Warns: Things Not Going Well For Labour'.

'The system must change,' Moore was quoted as saying. 'The government will fall and unions will be weakened if it doesn't. The government must act and act quickly.' Moore also criticised the apprenticeship system.

In Parliament the Opposition seized on the apparent divisions within Labour. The government was caught flat-footed and hadn't agreed a line on how to deal with Moore's comments.

Kirk and labour minister and Deputy Prime Minister Hugh Watt came under sustained questioning from National and struggled.

Kirk said Moore's speech had been inaccurately reported and waved around a telegram he had from someone at the conference to confirm that. Watt contradicted Kirk, saying Moore had, in fact, made the comments but that they were his personal opinions and not those of the government's.

It was a disaster and Moore had embarrassed the prime minister and deputy prime minister. At the following caucus meeting Moore got a dressing-down from Kirk. His friends felt sorry for him, while his enemies smirked.

But Moore wasn't deterred, and the experience only emboldened him to be better planned in what he did. He continued to get the headlines.

After barely a year in Parliament, he gave a powerful and widely reported speech in the Budget debate about how the justice system, like democracy, should be representative.

There were no Māori judges in New Zealand, he said. Only 2 per cent of magistrates, 2.5 per cent of justices of the peace, 4.2 per cent of the police force and 4.5 per cent of probation officers were Māori. Yet 40 per cent of the prisoners were Māori, while Māori were about 10 per cent of the population. He said the justice system seemed stacked against Māori with 56 per cent of Māori defendants not having legal counsel appointed as against 13 per cent for Europeans.

He further argued there were no women judges or magistrates and fewer than 10 per cent of justices of the peace.

Moore also agitated for the loosening up of New Zealand's libel laws, complained about the proliferation of 'motorways that go nowhere', wanted electoral laws changed so parties were publicly funded and couldn't 'buy' elections, wanted tougher privacy laws for the public, and advocated for a surveillance unit to check on the efficiency of government departments and report to Parliament annually.

As well, he garnered lots of local publicity in his community media — from putting up notice boards in pensioner flats and giving Christmas gifts to the elderly, to opposing building on the slopes of Mt Eden. His colleagues used to joke that no Christmas was complete without a story about Moore helping pensioners. For a first-time politician Moore quickly developed a nose for issues that resonated with the electorate and captured the media's attention.

Even the fervently anti-Labour newspaper the *Truth* saw Moore as a politician on the rise and gave him a column opposite his chosen adversary Muldoon. He used it every week to relentlessly slam National.

In late 1973 he went for a well-publicised tour of Auckland's inner-city and central suburbs with justice minister Dr Martyn Finlay in a police car to look at trouble spots first-hand. But for a few drunken youths, they saw nothing.

He then convinced transport minister Basil Arthur to ride with him and Auckland commuters at rush hour on the 5.15 pm Three Kings bus through the electorate. It was a great publicity stunt and Arthur agreed that Auckland should have a rapid rail system to deal with its urban transport woes.

The problem for the government was that the only promise they could give about the issue was that it would be looked at when local government structures were reviewed under a Local Government Bill due before Parliament later that year.

Moore wasn't seen so much as a maverick in his first term but more an MP in a hurry who wasn't afraid to tread on toes. He was clearly ambitious, a trait MPs are supposed to feign indifference to.

He happily accepted invitations to speak at trade union gatherings and party functions. He'd already created a fan in Palmerston North MP and associate foreign affairs minister Joe Walding who would describe him to others as a future leader in the mould of Kirk. But it was a compliment that would, later in his career, draw derision from some in the party.

Moore also quickly established a reputation for funny interjections during debates and question time in Parliament and would often tag team with Bassett, just sitting behind him, near the back of the House in baiting National MPs.

But it wasn't long before some, including those in his own caucus, gladly saw Moore taken down a few pegs.

Moore tripped himself up over a private members bill, the Coastal Moratorium and Management Bill, that he'd devised with the Environmental Defence League.

The Bill was designed to protect sensitive coastal areas from property development. Homes and baches had been springing up around the country without any proper planning or infrastructure being put in place. It was sensible legislation, but the Opposition labelled it as Moore and the government trying to nationalise coastal land, and much as he tried, he couldn't get the correct information out and win back the debate.

While most of his caucus colleagues had been supportive of the Bill, the moment it hit trouble few would stand up for it and Moore. The issue was becoming an embarrassment for the government, and Moore eventually withdrew it from the House.

It was not only a lesson for him about the power of shaping the perception of issues and how National were good at doing that but also about how showing initiative isn't always applauded by your colleagues.

Moore wasn't deterred or afraid to take on sensitive issues, however. He openly talked — when most others saw it as a taboo — about mental health being an issue for communities. The more affluent and materialistic society became, the more isolated and alienated people were. He said part of the answer was recreating 'a sense of community'.

He advocated for stronger regional government and continued to press for partnerships between trade unions, businesses and government.

He introduced another private members bill, the Right to Confidentiality Bill, which aimed to safeguard confidential information of doctors and social workers, including from the police who had recently raided an abortion clinic in Remuera and taken away patient records.

Moore was also starting to think strategically. The Values Party performed credibly in 1972, taking almost 2 per cent of the vote, and the environmental movement would only get bigger. He had seen through the Save Manapouri campaign the power of that movement to engage ordinary New Zealanders.

Moore thought that instead of fighting Values head on, Labour should try to embrace some of the party's environmental thinking. At the very least it would shore up some of Labour's younger voters. He hoped that one day Values could have a relationship with Labour like the socialist Fabian Society did, promoting reform through a particular lens.

While many of the ideas Moore promoted had merit and would eventually lead to changes in law and thinking in future governments, his timing was sometimes awry. Ideas would capture people's imaginations and then flicker and die. Timing would later become a common complaint about Moore. He would often describe it as: 'It's wrong to be right too soon.'

Moore's career was almost scuttled in July 1974 when the *Truth* had a front-page exclusive titled: 'MP cares for cop killer'.

One of the party members in Eden ran Aroha House in Avondale, a home for newly released prisoners. Moore had financially supported similar groups in Auckland and was a member of the Periodic Detention Committee for Auckland. So he occasionally helped released prisoners get back on their feet.

Moore had two rooms and offered his flat in Eden as a temporary place to stay for the released prisoner Bruce Douglas McPhee, who had served 11 years for killing two policemen in Lower Hutt.

When asked about the controversy he didn't hide what he'd done. 'I've always been interested in prison work, in trying to help people adjust when they come out,' he told the *Truth*. He wanted to help McPhee find a place to live, a job and to adjust to the outside world.

'It's something I intend to keep on doing, because I believe in this sort of work.'

But the incident cemented in the minds of some in the public the charge National always made about Labour — it was soft on crime and was more interested in criminals than the police and victims.

Behind the scenes Kirk had called him into his office and, pointing his sausage-like fingers at Moore, told him to kick the man out, shouting: 'Are you a social worker or an MP?'

He reminded Moore that Eden belonged to Labour, not him. But Moore stood his ground and like a teenage boy talking to his father he belligerently said he would live his life the way he wanted.

Kirk continued the tirade, saying that by becoming involved in politics he'd surrendered his personal life. He should refocus his energies away from trying to be a glorified social worker solving everyone's problems to being a parliamentarian who influenced and changed laws that had real impact on people's lives.

Thankfully, the man moved out of the flat of his own volition without the need for Moore's intervention. But it didn't stop the National Party having fun, grabbing copies of *Truth* newspaper's billboards and sticking them around the electorate.

At times Moore felt Kirk was picking on him deliberately, looking out for the smallest of infractions trying to correct his waywardness. It got under his skin.

He was almost reduced to tears once in caucus after an angry Kirk turned on him because he felt the party's newspaper, of which Moore was in charge, wasn't supportive enough of the prime minister. Later, Kirk phoned Moore and in a conciliatory tone said he hoped he'd learned his lesson.

While the *Sunday News* liked publishing stories about Moore's achievements, the *New Zealand Truth* was on the hunt for any that could put him in a bad light.

Moore understood the importance of spending time in the electorate and was conscientious about that. The party had an Eden electorate headquarters on the corner of Mt Eden and Ellerton roads that had meeting and social rooms in one part and doubled as a flat for

Moore on the other side. They held card afternoons for the local elderly and barbecue and social evenings for party members.

Belonging to a political party also had to be fun, Moore believed, to attract young people. The local party gradually grew to have 10 branches, including dedicated youth, women and teachers training college ones.

Moore was energetically active in the seat, which he always regarded as marginal. He'd help organise outings for local pensioners to the Mercury Theatre in the city, Guy Fawkes night barbecues for locals and their families, and annual Labour Day outings and picnics to the Michael Joseph Savage Memorial. He even gathered grapefruit and other unwanted fruit and vegetables in the electorate to give away to others who couldn't afford produce.

He spent much of his spare time in the electorate meeting constituents, community groups and businesses. One who he befriended was Willy Dereany, a dispatch manager at Sonny Elegant Knitwear in Dominion Road.

Willy, a Croatian, and his wife Rosie, an Austrian, had emigrated from the rubble of Europe after the Second World War. They chose New Zealand as their new home after seeing a movie with singing Māori, thinking they were going to be new settlers on some distant tropical islands.

After arriving in Wellington in 1950 they spent time in an internment camp in Pahiatua before coming to Auckland. They didn't have much, but Willy got a job as a glazier before going to Sonny Elegant Knitwear.

Willy and Rosie would regularly invite Moore to their Blockhouse Bay home for dinner. The local Member of Parliament, the man always in the newspapers, was treated like royalty.

Willy admired Moore, describing him as 'determinated'. Rosie was a great cook — although it took him some time to get used to the then unusual garlic-infused European cuisine — and it was a novelty for Moore to be in a stimulating, warm and loving family environment.

Having seen the evils caused by politics in Europe, neither Willy nor Rosie had strong political views. Nevertheless, Moore felt at ease in their company.

The Dereanys had three daughters, with the eldest, 19-year-old Yvonne, having just returned from a year travelling around Europe in late 1973. She was preparing to go to Auckland Teachers Training College.

It wasn't long before the two started going out. It was an unusual relationship because Moore was travelling a lot and when he was back in Auckland often had party or constituency business to attend to.

The two had been seeing each other on and off for about 18 months when one evening in April 1975 Moore called in to the Dereany home to see Yvonne. He'd given up on the idea of going to a party branch meeting, which seemed unusual to Yvonne.

Moore then sat for two hours on the couch with her watching television, before asking Yvonne: 'Would you be opposed to marrying me?'

Moore wasn't used to going out on a limb. He'd learned through often bitter experience in life to give himself a back-out or escape route.

He thought Yvonne was stunningly good-looking. But more than that, he was excited by her free spirit, her courage to speak her mind, her social conscience and her ability to see issues differently to him. He felt refreshed being in her company.

Moore had had girlfriends in the past — young women from Northland, friends of friends and those in the party. But he always tried to stay aloof, distant and uncommitted for fear it would get in the way of the political career he wanted.

None of that seemed to matter with Yvonne. He felt an attachment to her, a sense of belonging like it was all very normal. Even in his rare moments of rational thought about her, being with Yvonne seemed the perfect political match.

Yvonne suggested they maybe live together, but Moore didn't think it was proper.

The couple celebrated by waking up Willy and Rosie and drinking champagne.

Most people they told were overjoyed. Yvonne's Uncle Zarko wasn't happy though. He'd always thought Moore was a Māori and a communist — two things the couple always found hilarious, never disabused him of and used as a running joke — and was opposed to the marriage. But Uncle Zarko was later generous to the couple, giving them the height of luxury in 1975, a Philips K9 colour TV, as a wedding gift.

Moore couldn't believe how lucky he was. But he still had huge doubts about himself and whether he was partner material. Moore hadn't been around too many successful families. His mother's 1959 second marriage was unhappy and would later turn out to be a failure. His relationships with his brothers Kerry and Shane were always distant and sometimes strained.

The trade union movement and the Labour Party had been his substitute parents and family and you couldn't call them normal, he thought.

But what gave him confidence and put him at ease was seeing Willy and Rosie and the unbreakable bond of love they had with their daughters. He was sure Yvonne would fill in the gaps and make up for his awkwardness in relationships.

Their engagement was front-page news, as most MPs were already married. They became the light and entertaining political news to counter the serious parliamentary goings-on.

In between the engagement and the wedding in July, Moore was elected the party's first junior vice president at its annual conference in Wellington, beating former Labour Women's Council head Sonja Davies.

Moore was also now starting to show up in public opinion polls. A *Sunday News* poll scored Moore more heavily than high-profile justice minister Dr Martyn Finlay among Labour voters as a future leader. He was the government's 'most impressive' politician, the newspaper said.

While the polls made him unpopular with some of his colleagues and provided entertaining fodder for the Opposition, his career and personal life had never been better.

A huge crowd of well-wishers turned up outside St Alban's Anglican Church in Dominion Road for what the *8 O'Clock* newspaper had the night before described as 'The wedding of the year'.

Inside among the guests were more than half the government. The 30 MPs, including Prime Minister Bill Rowling, Deputy Prime Minister Bob Tizard and seven Cabinet ministers, and the President of the Federation of Labour Tom Skinner, had something to celebrate after a poor start to election year.

The wedding was a pleasant distraction from the hard realities of government. Not since September 1974, a few weeks after Kirk's death when Labour got a strong bounce in the New Zealand Herald-NRB polls to be 50 per cent to 40 per cent, had the government been in front of National. That July, National was in front 51 per cent to 40 per cent.

Originally Moore and Yvonne asked their great friend Mat Rata, the Minister of Māori Affairs and a Rātana preacher, to marry them. While not overly religious, Yvonne was a Catholic and Moore was an Anglican. Very soon the wedding plans became unnecessarily complicated so to try to broker the peace they had Rata and Catholic and Anglican priests officiate.

They were, unusually, married on a Sunday afternoon. But that had to do with logistics — the Dereanys wanted the wedding reception across town at Trillo's near the Auckland Harbour Bridge for the 250 guests and it had been booked out for a year. But it did mean the politicians could attend because there had been a candidate's conference in Wellington on the Saturday.

Yvonne's 15-year-old and 10-year-old sisters Elizabeth and Sonia were the bridesmaids, while Moore's 21-year-old brother Shane was best man. Members of the Tongan and Māori communities performed for the guests at the reception and the couple were driven away in a car with a 'Mike Moore's a good MP' sticker on the side window.

As with many weddings, the Moores had their minor dramas — the hāngi supper, which came in a truck from Otahuhu, arrived late and Shane fell into the harbour near the function centre with all their honeymoon trip tickets and his brother's wallet in his pocket.

With the general election only months away, the couple honeymooned for two weeks in the South Island before returning to share a villa in Grange Road, Mt Eden with Warren Goff and his wife Nina.

Moore and Yvonne had been inundated with cards and letters wishing them well and took out advertisements in the local newspaper to thank people. Yvonne was popular in the electorate, particularly with women and the elderly.

They both knew re-election would be difficult in November so agreed to take advantage of all the good publicity while it lasted.

They produced leaflets with wedding photos and invited senior citizens in Eden to a free outing, including transport, to the Symphonia Theatre in Dominion Road as a way of thanking them for 'their expressions of goodwill prior to the wedding'.

Moore knew the tide had turned on the government. He believed four major events played their part to undermine the government and allow Muldoon to divide the nation.

It had started with the 1973 oil crisis, created when the Organisation of Arab Petroleum Exporting Countries put an oil embargo on countries that had supported Israel during the Yom Kippur War.

This saw the price of oil rise from US$3 a barrel to nearly US$12. As a country totally reliant on imported oil, the impact on the New Zealand economy was immediate and was felt by consumers.

The government's cancellation of the proposed 1973 Springboks tour had also divided a rugby-mad country, particularly provincial New Zealand. While Moore strongly backed the decision, he knew Labour candidates in the smaller towns would find it difficult to defend.

The relationship between Māori and other New Zealanders came to the fore with the third Labour Government. It had started well with Kirk going to Waitangi in 1973 and walking onto the Treaty grounds holding the hand of a young Māori boy. That image and Kirk's speech helped sell a message to New Zealand of a nation of respect and unity for everyone.

Kirk also changed Waitangi Day to New Zealand Day and changed it from a provincial holiday to a national one.

Moore was in awe of Kirk. He thought it was a significant step forward not only for race relations but also in capturing the mood of the country and the desire at the time of New Zealanders to forge their own identity away from Mother England.

But in 1975 when the government passed the historic Treaty of Waitangi Act, which established the Waitangi Tribunal to look at grievances against the Crown after 1975, Rowling wasn't able to carry the argument as well to the public.

This was followed later that year by a group of protesters, led by an almost 80-year-old kuia, Whina Cooper, marching from the Far North to Wellington to present a 60,000-strong petition to Parliament calling for an end to the sale of Māori land.

Race relations looked a mess and Moore was shocked at how Muldoon was exploiting it.

The fourth event was the sudden death of Kirk in August 1974. It had been a shock to New Zealand, the party and Moore. Most knew Kirk wasn't a healthy man — he pushed himself hard and drank a lot. But no one expected this.

New Zealand's first charismatic leader, perhaps since Savage, the announcement of his death was the country's John F. Kennedy moment. People recalled the moment they heard the news. A popular and idealistic leader who filled the nation with optimism was cut down unexpectedly in his prime.

Moore's eyes welled up hearing the news on television at his mother's home in Papatoetoe late on the night of Saturday, 31 August. In shock he jumped in his car to drive back to the electorate.

As he cruised around Eden lights went on in houses, in retirement homes and in pensioner flats. Tears streamed down his face as he drove, not wanting to stop and talk to anyone. He didn't know what to do, he didn't know what to say.

Some of Moore's colleagues, the media and Opposition MPs had previously joked or taunted Moore that he'd modelled himself on the working-class non-university-educated trade union man Kirk.

It was true that Kirk was one of his heroes. Most of the time, he was in tune with Kirk's thinking. Yes, he'd got under his skin many times, but it was like what boys did with their fathers. Moore was sometimes scolded but mostly encouraged and occasionally allowed in to share a drink and a laugh.

Kirk was such a dominating presence in the caucus, corralling his flock. Now he was gone, with no final words of advice, just as when Moore's father suddenly died.

The following days were a blur for Moore. Kirk lay in state in Parliament for three days before a funeral service at the nearby St Paul's Cathedral. The next day, on 5 September, another service was held at the Christchurch Town Hall before he was buried in his hometown of Waimate.

Everything seemed grey about the day. It was raining and cold. Most of the government's MPs boarded a Royal New Zealand Air Force flight bound for Christchurch, but the weather was so bad the plane couldn't land. Wellington was now not much better so the flight diverted to Auckland.

It was hardly the send-off Moore hoped for his hero but the sad petering out of the day which included the mad dash of the funeral motorcade from Christchurch to Waimate to bury Kirk before sunset. The day seemed to encapsulate the third Labour Government's fortunes.

The whole government seemed in mourning for the rest of the term and Kirk's successor Bill Rowling didn't have the strength to overcome that. Rowling didn't have Kirk's charisma, oratory skills, common touch or political cunning.

In contrast, he seemed mild-mannered and timid, and his squeaky voice wasn't suited for the new medium of television. More importantly, he was no match for Muldoon's cruel put-downs and humour, quick wit, sharp political analysis and television presence.

He'd variously called Rowling 'a sheep in sheep's clothing', 'a modest man with much to be modest about' and 'a shiver looking for a spine to run up'.

They were similar lines used by British Conservative Opposition Leader Winston Churchill to describe post-Second World War British Labour Prime Minister Clement Attlee. Nevertheless, the news media lapped it up.

Despite the mood of the country in late 1975, Moore held out hope for Eden. Unemployment was low, hospital waiting lists were coming down, there was a boom in construction, Labour's new ACC scheme was proving a success and more money was going into education. Moore had worked hard in the electorate, had a strong local and national profile, and his party organisation had been built up since 1972.

National had to advertise for a candidate and chose Aussie Malcolm, a 34-year-old social worker turned advertising man, as its candidate. He was polished and ambitious.

But before the campaign got under way, a small group from the party approached Moore about changing electorates and running in the Labour safe seat of Onehunga which had been vacated by Hugh Watt, who had gone to London as New Zealand's high commissioner after he missed out on the leadership to Rowling. Watt was supportive and promised to come home and campaign for Moore.

It was tempting. But Moore had invested a lot of emotion into holding Eden and believed jumping ship now would send a signal to the wider electorate that he had little confidence in Rowling winning the

1975 general election. He also figured that if he lost Eden his popularity would mean another seat would easily come his way in 1978.

Moore told Rowling what had gone on and that he'd stay in Eden as a vote of confidence in the prime minister. Rowling said he wouldn't forget it.

Barely a month out from the election, the *Truth* newspaper dedicated two pages to Moore being in cahoots with New Zealand's Trotsky-ist communists, having originally 'won' Eden with their help and trying to take over the Labour Party.

Truth completely ignored Moore's history of hating the communists. Unlike some of his colleagues, Moore had always distrusted the communists and always opposed any of them speaking at Labour Party conferences.

They were the ones who would discourage working-class people from voting Labour and then turn around and complain about National always winning. They were the ones who would often run candidates in elections to try to split Labour's vote. They were the ones who during the Vietnam War protests would infiltrate the marches and go to the front with their banners pretending they'd organised the events.

Most of the communists Moore knew weren't working-class men or women but middle-class guilt-ridden individuals trying to deny who their parents were.

In the middle of the Cold War and when earlier in the year public servant Bill Sutch had been acquitted of trying to pass government secrets to the Soviet Union, labelling someone a 'Trot' or a 'commie' was a serious matter. To sue for defamation would take money and, more importantly, time he didn't have.

Moore knew it would stick and possibly impact upon his campaign. It just meant he had to double his efforts.

Warren Goff was his campaign manager again and had been working full-time on the re-election since June. This time they had double the volunteers and the local party's regular fundraising meant Moore had a war chest.

The campaign had been canvassing and polling for some time and regularly produced its own free local newspaper, *Eden News*, which was delivered across the electorate and had stories of how hard Moore was working in the seat and how Labour was delivering for New Zealanders.

He had a well-organised street-corner meeting team and was well received by residents. But unlike in 1972 National had a group of young men driving around in cars trying to disrupt some of them. They would park at a distance and scream abuse until a couple of the burly builders who were in Moore's team walked towards them when they would quickly drive away.

Moore felt good about his campaign. Everywhere in the electorate he drove around in his New Zealand-produced Trekka car, which was painted like a mobile billboard promoting its local MP, he got a good reaction.

His meetings were well attended and Moore's polling in Eden showed he had a 90 per cent approval rating, although voters still preferred National over Labour. All in the inner circle of his campaign team thought he'd win. He had a huge profile and had worked hard in the electorate. Labour would probably lose government but Moore would scrape home was the thinking.

It was becoming clear to Moore in the lead-up to the election that little direction was coming from Labour headquarters. Nationally the party seemed in disarray and this led to what Moore thought was the ill-fated 'Citizens for Rowling' campaign, which had its genesis in Eden.

Moore's campaign knew that to win in 1975 they had to stop voters going back to National and the best way to do that was to seem non-political. They came up with the idea of getting non-Labour people and neutrals — local dairy owners, local council workers, local teachers — to say in a series of newspaper advertisements that they were behind Moore. Former journalist David Exel, who was working for the party, had heard about the idea and wanted to use it nationally.

Moore was happy for head office to take the idea for Rowling but was disappointed that other than Sir Edmund Hillary it ended up having mostly academics, writers and artists supporting the prime minister.

In contrast, Muldoon had All Blacks, successful businesspeople and achievers behind him. Labour looked like it was supported by the elite and National looked like ordinary New Zealand battlers were behind them.

Moore understood at that moment that this could be a turning point for the modern Labour Party. Muldoon seemed to understand ordinary New Zealanders better than Labour. It was this group of what should have been Labour voters — 'Rob's mob' as they came to be known — that would form the core of his popularity for almost the following 10 years.

National was cleverer than Labour and Moore knew it was over for the government when he saw their television advertisements, which were creative, entertaining and focused. For Moore and others, the 'Dancing Cossacks' advertisement, which only showed twice on television, stood out. It seemed to epitomise all that was right in National's campaign and all that was wrong in Labour's.

The 'Dancing Cossacks' was part of a series of advertisements on issues and cleverly attacked Labour's compulsory superannuation savings scheme. Animated by Hanna-Barbera, the producers of popular children's cartoons like *The Flintstones*, it positioned Labour's scheme as Soviet communist in nature.

The advertisement featured a red wash of colour across the screen, dancing Cossacks and Russian music. It said the scheme would lead to the nationalisation of all companies and farms, and that women, the elderly and those on social welfare would miss out in retirement. In a nation enthralled by the recent arrival of colour television, the advertisements were devastating.

Labour, in contrast, had worthy newspaper advertisements with long-winded headlines — 'The rest of the world invited New Zealand to a depression. Labour refused to go' — followed by a page of words and ending in the slogan 'Trust Labour. It's working.'

Muldoon was pithy and to the point, pledging to restore the economy and giving people 'New Zealand the way you want it'. Rowling also gave National the agenda, agreeing through the news media that the handling of the economy was the dominant election issue.

At a local level Moore knew 1975 was going to be very different from 1972. At his campaign launch on 11 November at the Maungawhau School hall persistent hecklers drowned him and guest speaker justice minister Martyn Finlay out a number of times.

By mid-afternoon on election day Moore knew he had lost. He and Goff started diverting some of their resources to nearby electorates who were still in the fight.

Despite the efforts of the flood of volunteers, Moore lost by more than 1300 votes. While the number of voters in the electorate had grown significantly since 1972, the turnout was down more than 12 per cent.

Moore had almost 43 per cent of those who turned out voting for him, compared with more than 48 per cent in 1972.

It was a night of tears as Moore spoke to his supporters. He told them that Labour would be back but that they all needed to organise for that to happen.

He was determined to do the right thing, as Kidd had done three years earlier, so Moore and Yvonne drove over to Malcolm's election-night celebrations to congratulate him.

When they arrived a group of jubilant National Party supporters surrounded their car, hitting it on the roof and screaming personal abuse at the couple. Moore was punched by someone after his speech to Malcolm's supporters. The crowd was threatening and angry and Moore had to be escorted out of the Balmoral Hall National headquarters. It was as if Muldoon had liberated a lot of ugliness.

After returning to their supporters, Moore and Yvonne spent the rest of the night hugging, kissing and consoling them.

The only upside of the day was Moore had won the electorate sweepstake on the result, the only one who had bet against himself. He had predicted a loss by 400 votes. He knew he'd now need the $40 prize.

4

Second in command of a one-man dredge

'I lost Eden and the phone just didn't go. No one in the party said: "I might have a job for you."

'I started to get desperate. It was very tough. People forget Muldoon was scary back then and many didn't want to get offside with him.

'I noticed an ad in the paper — night watchman on a dredge, Saturday to Monday. The guy I went to see was a very good Labour guy at the harbour board. He said the best job he could give me was on the dredge.

'The Nats thought it was a great laugh. The Prince of the Labour Party was second in command of a one-man dredge, they'd joke.

'The media loved the idea — the more misery I was in the better the story. I didn't realise this at the time. I thought it was a good job. It burnished my Labour credentials.

'The dredge was good. I had to ring someone every two hours. I said to the guy after a while: "Why do I need to do that?" "To keep you up," he said. So I said: "But I'll keep you up too." He said: "Yeah, let's not bother."

'After a while I saw a job for a social worker at Oakley Hospital and got it. I ran the two jobs for a while to make some money. I think I was chosen there for political reasons. I could help people get jobs and work out their benefits. There was also a political battle going on about mental health institutions: conservative versus liberal.

'I learned a lot from that time. People were locked up under ministerial direction. In those days it was a ministerial decision.

'One guy said to me once: "I haven't seen anyone in five to ten years. My family lives in Mangere. Can you take me out there?" So I did and after he was back he slashed himself with razor blades he got from home. I didn't see him get the razor blades.

'Overall I think it's a good thing we've let people out of institutions. But there's a good proportion that need these places — not to be out of sight of the public but because they need them as sanctuaries.

'I kept thinking about politics and Eden. Could I have won it again? Probably. Could I have held it? No.

'A group in Eden started organising against me. So I was going to have a contest to get the nomination again. I wasn't going to do that after all I'd done. I don't know to this day why they did that to me.

'Then came the Mangere by-election. I didn't need much encouragement. I fell over myself going for it.

'I'd seen Lange around Auckland. He was a good guy. If I had legal problems with constituents, I'd go see Lange. When he gave his speech in Mangere, I thought geez he's good. He's going to go places.

'I then went for Papatoetoe, but Moyle wanted it. Then the usual story happened with head office conspiring against me.

'Eddie Isbey ended up getting it. He didn't even know how to dial Papatoetoe. I told him he had to dial 2. I had to go around and wake him up to go canvassing. I got sick of it in the end.

'So when they say I'm not a Labour man, that'll be the bloody day. I wouldn't sacrifice myself now.

'I finally worked out that Rowling and all these guys weren't my friends, they were my opponents.

'Then I got cancer for the first time. I couldn't get a break. I thought I can't let people find out about that because then I'd be really stuffed. I had surgery and then radiotherapy, but I was back at work pretty quickly.

'I hadn't given up looking for a seat, but it was getting pretty rough. So I looked around the country and there was Papanui. No one seemed to be going for it that was senior.

'I found out by door-knocking that Kerry Burke and Russell Marshall had been ringing around the locals for a young guy called Clive Matthewson.

'Then the cancer came back for a second time. I had surgery and chemotherapy. For some of the treatment they had to cut my foot. So my foot was slopping around in blood in my shoes as I went around door to door to talk to party members in Papanui about the selection. I wasn't going to let them or the bloody cancer beat me.

'I never had a cabal doing work for me. Douglas, Bassett, Prebble — none of them travelled around with me. I just did my own thing. I suppose I was naive. I never had my own network. People have always said I was street wise. Perhaps it's the way I looked. But I never had my own gang.

'I didn't have a job in Christchurch. We did some crazy things. We got some kūmara from up north, packaged them up and sold them to make money. There were times in the year we couldn't take the troops to the pub to thank them. It was a rough ride. Then Yvonne got the job in TV and the Hotel Workers Union gave me some money.

'Every day for a year I'd get up and get out at 9 and be back at 6. I was always signing letters. Papanui was good to me. It was very different to Eden — very working class. We didn't put a pamphlet out for four or five months. We didn't have the money and I didn't want to be in people's faces, being the outsider.

'Running through the election I felt crook again. My eyes were big and black. The exhaustion came in waves. And so I won the election, but I was so sick. The cancer was back for a third time.

'After the election I had chemotherapy and it was bad. I flew up to Nelson and met Rowling. He was good — well, he couldn't be anything else, could he? I didn't go to Parliament. I didn't talk to anyone.

'There was a vote for the shadow Cabinet. I didn't vote for myself because I didn't think I'd be back.

'Throughout those three months I was sick as a dog. It was so much different then. They bombarded me with something like nine treatments. They gave it right through in case the cancer had spread. You get sick and then you get well. It's up and down. Every now and then I'd come right and listen to Parliament on the radio and wish I was there. I was bloody angry. I was angry about everything.

'I was told later that a Christchurch MP had phoned people in the electorate to say that if anything ever happened to me that they had a possible candidate to fill my role.

'One day many years later an MP approached me after many drinks to say that when he heard I'd lost my seat he cheered, when he heard I had cancer he applauded. He said he was sorry and apologised. That's the kind of place Parliament can be.'

****

Members of Parliament find out who their real friends are when they lose their seat. The 26-year-old Moore was soon to discover this truism.

After the Eden defeat the newly married couple survived on Yvonne's bare savings as a teachers college student and his cashed-in parliamentary superannuation. They had to rely on Yvonne's VW Beetle as the Trekka had been lent to party members for a trip to Wellington and they had crashed it.

Moore started applying for middle-management jobs he'd seen advertised in the newspapers. He had, after all, been a Member of Parliament helping promulgate laws, debating important matters of state, and dealing with members of the public and the news media. He had skills most middle managers wouldn't have after a lifetime of work.

But most jobs he applied for he didn't even get the courtesy of a rejection letter.

So, he changed tactics. He went back to what he knew. He applied for a printer's job at the Auckland Regional Authority, only to be humiliated by a National Party local authority candidate who interviewed him.

He then applied for a job at the freezing works in Otahuhu. The interview was polite enough, but he missed out again. Union officials offered to go on strike for him because they'd overheard bosses laughing about how they'd rejected Moore for a job.

He finally thought he got a lucky break when Keith Hay, the housing developer who he'd met as an MP, called asking to see him. He didn't know much about building houses, but he knew his way around government departments and the council. But instead of a job, Hay gave him a bible and offered to pray with him.

Work eventually came as a night watchman on an Auckland Harbour Board dredge. It was a simple job — make sure no one messes with the dredge when it's moored at the wharves over the weekend. It meant staying on the dredge from Saturday afternoon until Monday mornings and checking in by radio telephone every couple of hours.

Many former MPs would have seen the job as beneath them and humiliating. Moore knew it wouldn't stretch his potential, but he saw the positive in it. He was being paid to sit around, read, think and organise on behalf of the party.

New to marriage and politics, the change was also a shock to Yvonne. She was sure her husband was going to be re-elected, he was so well known. She was still baffled as to why it didn't happen.

They were short of money and getting desperate, and Yvonne was determined to make the best of their new circumstances.

Very soon Yvonne joined him on the dredge for the weekends and would bring their electric frying pan and portable TV, to go with Moore's books and note pad. Friends and party members soon joined them and their weekends were filled with card games, debates about the state of the country and political organising.

The couple didn't have much money but there was plenty of laughter, little stress and endless discussions; it was an enjoyable way to start a life together. Losing Eden might have been a blessing in the end because he ended up learning to not take himself too seriously.

Later that year Moore saw an advertisement for a social worker at Oakley Hospital, a secure mental institution. It was full-time work, better paid and sounded more interesting. As an MP he'd been interested in mental health issues and had practical experience with his younger brother Shane who had been diagnosed some years earlier with schizophrenia.

Moore got the role and became a social worker, even though he received no training for the job. He instantly proved useful to many of the patients. As a former MP he understood the system and how to navigate it to help patients with accessing benefits and housing.

He and Yvonne helped many patients restart their lives on the outside, getting second-hand furniture and helping them move into new homes in other towns. Some succeeded at restarting their lives, many didn't.

It was a largely depressing job. It was sometimes rewarding but mostly not. Some of the patients were sexual offenders with little hope of rehabilitation.

Most of the staff were well meaning, although, like Moore, under- or untrained, and many of the treatments seemed from another era. Moore saw first-hand the impact of hormone therapy and electric shock treatment on patients.

There were cases of rape, molestation and suicide. It broke his heart.

There were, however, some lighter moments like when he 'escaped' with some patients, without approval, to see the recently released movie *One Flew Over the Cuckoo's Nest.*

In a scene in the movie Jack Nicholson's character R.P. McMurphy takes his charges on an excursion — fishing — and when confronted about what they're doing introduces his charges as from the state mental institution: 'This is Dr Cheswick, Dr Taber, Dr Frederickson, Dr Scanlon (the famous Dr Scanlon), Mr Harding, Dr Bibbit, Dr Martini and Dr Sefelt.'

On the way back from the movie Moore bumped into a party member who recognised him and asked what he and his companions were doing. So he introduced the patients just like in the movie. They got back to Oakley without incident.

But working at Oakley, or on a dredge or anywhere else, was not the new life Moore wanted. He had stayed in touch with the issues of the day while he and Yvonne tried to get some semblance of normality back in their lives.

During this time, he kept up his interest in international affairs and became friends with Father Walter Lini, the New Hebrides independence leader, and ended up paying for and smuggled up to him the first Vanuatu flag.

This only whetted his appetite for getting back into Parliament.

Eden was a possibility, but longer-term boundary changes were likely to make it difficult. Unbeknown to him until after his election loss he'd also managed to upset a group of local party members who he described as wealthy people who lectured others on the joys of socialism from their flash homes.

One of the branches had also been causing Moore problems about his conservative views on abortion. People with single issues had started joining the party which until that period had been a broad church of mostly conservative working-class 'Micks, Marxists and Methodists'.

Moore and electorate chairman John Langdon had also fallen out in the wake of the 1975 defeat.

Most of the Eden party members were respectful and kind. But it was this group, the party's hierarchy and some sitting MPs who he felt had become standoffish and even ignored him.

He thought he'd paid his dues by winning a marginal seat for Kirk's Government.

Getting reselected for Eden in the 1978 general election wouldn't be easy. He knew that if he was to return to Parliament, he would have to make his own luck. Being a former MP and current vice president of the party granted him no favours, he quickly realised.

A number of seats would be coming up for the 1978 general election and even though National was in its first term and unlikely to shed much support, boundary changes were likely to favour Labour in some electorates.

So, he started casting around the country and turned his attention back to a part of the city where he'd spent a lot of his early political career — South Auckland.

South of Mangere Bridge was rapidly growing in the 1960s and 1970s as Auckland desperately built houses and shopping centres for the growing number of workers for the airport and the many factories in Penrose, Otahuhu and Manukau. If the party organised well, much of the south could become heartland Labour, he thought.

A new seat was going to be created in Papatoetoe where his mum lived, he'd briefly been to high school, had flatted and where he'd done a lot of organising for Colin Moyle and Roger Douglas in the 1960s.

The energetic Moore helped set up Labour's party structures in the area, signing on members and canvassing many of the streets. Papatoetoe would probably be a safe Labour seat and a great springboard for his career.

But Labour politics and Moore's life were never simple.

One evening in November 1976 Muldoon savagely attacked Moyle in the House, claiming he'd been questioned by police for homosexual activity over a 1975 incident involving an undercover police officer.

Moyle struggled to explain himself publicly and Rowling seemed to make misstep after misstep in handling the situation. To try to end all the speculation, Rowling suggested a special inquiry, which Muldoon promptly agreed to.

In early 1977 Moore received a call one evening from a senior party member saying Moyle was going to resign and that he should nominate for Mangere because he'd win it easily. Moore naively thought the person was being generous and was trying to help his career.

Soon afterwards Moyle did resign but with the intention of putting his name forward again for the by-election. He would put himself before his constituents, who in his Labour stronghold would easily re-elect him and silence Muldoon.

Everyone assumed it was Moyle's seat to take again, so Moore kept his distance. But within a couple of weeks there were murmurings that others would challenge Moyle.

Auckland lawyer David Lange, who had come third in the National stronghold of Hobson in 1975 and had run on the Labour ticket for the Auckland City Council, and former Hamilton West MP Dorothy Jelicich were said to be interested. Moore thought if it was going to be an open contest that he, too, would throw his hat in.

Such was the hatred among Labour members for what Muldoon had done to Moyle that the key to nominating for Mangere was to be sensitive to local members. Putting your hand up first or too quickly could be seen as crass.

Once again, Moore's ambition would be interpreted as something else. He had been looking after Moyle's seat while his old friend gave himself time to think things through.

Moore nominated for the seat and it was quickly seen as him double-crossing Moyle. It was compounded to devastating effect by an *Auckland Star* front-page story and 'Bromhead' cartoon in February 1977 that had him backstabbing the Mangere MP while saying 'I'm right behind you, Colin'.

Under the headline 'Moore moves to take Mangere vote', he is quoted as saying he owed it to Moyle 'to see him first before I put in my nomination'.

Moore said party members from around the country had put 'unbearable' pressure on him to stand and he stood by an earlier statement that he would not stand while Moyle had the support of the party leadership and the local electorate.

'I believe this is one way to find out for sure whether he does have that support. We're a democratic show and this will tell where the support lies — one way or the other,' Moore told the *Auckland Star*.

With a strong field quickly gathering, Moyle withdrew his candidacy and publicly turned his back on Moore by supporting Jelicich.

His short political career had taught Moore not to be put off by critics. He put aside the hatred and did what he had learned to do best — organise.

He door-knocked party members in Mangere, many of whom he knew well as local party electorate secretary for Moyle. Getting their three floor votes would be critical to winning the selection because relying on a speech on the night to do that wouldn't be enough. He put a face to his name.

While Lange had grown up in nearby Otahuhu and was the son of a well-known local doctor, Moore felt confident. He'd been far more active in the party and union movement in Auckland, had been a high-profile MP, had done his time by winning a marginal seat and held a senior office in the party. Surely, head office would take all that into account and select him for this safe seat?

Head office sent a strong selection panel to Mangere for the night: New Zealand Council member and future Dunedin North MP Stan Rodger, party elder and former trade minister Joe Walding and party General Secretary John Wybrow.

Moore's pre-organising had paid dividends. The three party members elected before the meeting to sit on the selection panel all favoured Moore.

It was thought that Rodger loosely favoured Lange, Wybrow on instructions from party leader Bill Rowling was to support Jelicich and then follow Rodger's lead, and Walding wanted his protégé Moore.

After drawing straws, Moore was one of the early speakers out of the more than 18 nominees.

It was a good speech about what Muldoon and National were doing to the country but not one of his better ones. It seemed enough, though, to outshine the others — bar the last speaker.

That was from Lange who was introduced as having 'the longest wait of anybody'. And seemingly on cue like a TV comedian, Lange said: 'Yes, and the greatest weight as well.'

The more than 300 who had packed out the Mangere Intermediate School hall roared with laughter. Yvonne and Moore looked at each other. Moore whispered: 'He's got it.'

Lange received a great applause at the end and fresh in the minds of party members in the hall he won the straw vote from the floor, which is used to give the selection panel guidance.

The six-person selection panel retired to a room behind the stage of the hall. It didn't take the panel long to eliminate all the candidates but the three pre-race favourites: Moore, Lange and Jelicich. When it was clear that only Wybrow was behind Jelicich, she was dropped.

There was a deadlock now between Moore and Lange and the discussions went on for some time. Moore had the three locals on the selection panel on his side, along with Walding. Lange had Rodger, probably Wybrow and the morally important straw vote.

Sitting outside, Moore and Yvonne knew it would be a close-run contest. The longer the panel were out the more pessimistic they became. As the probable favourite, with the three locals and Walding on his side, Moore knew that they must be having to stare down head office.

It was generally agreed among the panel that either Moore or Lange would make a great MP for Mangere.

To break the impasse Rodger asked the three locals who they thought their much-admired outgoing MP would support. The *Auckland Star* cartoon would come back to haunt Moore. The three locals knew the answer all too well. Seeing this, Walding and the three locals didn't oppose Rodger's idea that they name Lange the candidate.

While he thought it might be coming, the news was like a punch to the stomach for Moore. He and Yvonne congratulated Lange, shook the hands of the other candidates and many of their local supporters and quickly retreated.

He felt personally slighted by the party hierarchy, and the only consolation was he was excited to see a breath of fresh air in Lange. Moore had met him a number of times around the party in Auckland but didn't really know him.

On the Mangere selection night, he saw an extraordinarily gifted orator with a great wit who he thought could light up an otherwise dull party.

It was important for Labour after the controversy of the Moyle resignation that it won the Mangere by-election well. MPs and party members from around Auckland descended on the seat. Moore also took annual leave from Oakley to go canvassing for Lange and to try to repair any ill-feelings in the local party towards him.

The efforts worked magnificently for Lange but not so much for Moore. On polling day more than 64 per cent of eligible voters turned out. National's Clem Simich, from the other side of the city, and the six other candidates didn't stand a chance and Lange won by more than 4500 votes, much more than Moyle's 1975 majority.

Moore now turned his attention back to his original plan for the

1978 general election, the new seat of Papatoetoe. It was a good second choice for an electorate and he was determined not to have another Mangere. Phil Goff was the local electorate chairman and he went back to demonstrating his commitment to Papatoetoe and local members.

But Moyle also liked the seat, which neighboured his old one and used to be part of his larger electorate, and he thought it was ideal for his comeback. There was little love lost now between the two old friends.

Once again Moore organised supremely and had the three local votes, which included Goff, Otara West branch secretary Hugh Jarvis and Fire Brigades Union delegate Geoff Sommers. Party President Arthur Faulkner, party General Secretary John Wybrow and party Area Secretary Geoff Braybrooke were the head office votes on the selection panel.

Moore, who spoke second, and Moyle, who spoke fifth, probably gave the strongest speeches out of the six nominees in front of the 400 packed into the Papatoetoe Intermediate School hall.

One of the candidates, Jill Amos, the wife of former Kirk Government education minister Phil Amos, gave her speech via a tape recording because she was in Tanzania.

Moyle was considered the head office candidate, although it wasn't absolutely clear they wanted him given his recent controversy.

The panel were out more than two hours, taking the meeting into the early hours of 6 August 1977. The three locals were strongly behind Moore, but it was clear head office was against him. Goff, Jarvis and Sommers were politically experienced and would not budge despite the efforts of Faulkner, Wybrow and Braybrooke to dissuade them.

Eventually Faulkner came out to tell the crowd that had remained that the selection was deadlocked and would be referred to Labour's New Zealand Council meeting in Wellington later in the month to decide what to do. He told party members it had been 'one of the most difficult considerations I have ever been involved in', the *New Zealand Herald* reported.

'It seems pointless to pursue this matter through the night.' He described the 'straw vote' from the meeting as 'not decisive enough to be of any assistance', which seemed strange given that Moore had the three local votes.

Moore was in a rage and many locals were hurling abuse at the party officials in the chaos. Locals reported overhearing senior party officials — who later became parliamentary colleagues of Moore's — gloating that they'd vetoed him. Some party members had offered to 'go punch them out' for Moore.

As party junior vice president, Moore went to the New Zealand Council meeting as of right. Before the meeting he spoke with Rowling who promised to get nominations reopened.

In the background, unknown to Moore, a deal was being stitched up for seat-less former Auckland trade unionist Eddie Isbey who since 1969 had been the MP for Grey Lynn which, because of boundary changes, was being absorbed into Auckland Central in 1978.

Isbey had been beaten earlier in the year by Richard Prebble for that nomination and by Ralph Maxwell for Waitakere. Some union officials were urging that Isbey be given Papatoetoe.

Isbey had been a wharfie in Auckland from 1954 and had been president of the New Zealand Maritime Union — a wealthy and powerful Labour affiliate — for 11 years before entering Parliament.

The New Zealand Council agreed with Rowling's suggestion that nominations be reopened for Papatoetoe but that a new nominee in Isbey also be invited to stand.

Moore smelled a rat, a double-cross coming. He knew Isbey from union circles and liked him. He thought of him as a smart but mostly ineffectual man. He didn't have the nickname Eddie 'Was-bey' for nothing.

While looking around the New Zealand Council table at what he considered traitors and cowards, Moore quickly calculated that if there was another stalemate in Papatoetoe between him and Isbey that another candidate could come through the middle.

Moore wondered who was being lined up. He knew it wasn't Moyle. Could it be Jill Amos who some thought head office had wanted all along? Maybe that was their plan.

Isbey couldn't be their real candidate. They hadn't gone to all this trouble just for Isbey, surely?

Their game plan must have been about engineering another stalemate using an unsuspecting Isbey to create the inside running for their real horse, Moore thought.

Moore wasn't sure what to think or who to trust around the table.

To everyone's surprise, Moore stood up in the New Zealand Council and moved that Isbey be the candidate.

The fact that what he'd done was unconstitutional wasn't lost on Moore, but it was also conveniently overlooked by the rest of the meeting. Dumbstruck, the meeting gladly accepted Moore's motion.

Moore left the meeting feeling sick. He'd been done over again by the party hierarchy, he thought.

He phoned his mother to explain what had happened. She was furious and after a period of thinking of ways to overturn the ruling agreed to his request that she organise an urgent meeting of the electorate at her house that evening.

In an angry meeting Moore told the local party members what had happened, how it was not the outcome he wanted but how having Isbey, who was a good Labour man who would make for a strong local MP, was better than having an unknown imposed on them from head office.

Against his better judgement Moore calmed the electorate down rather than wind them up for a battle. An all-out war with the party hierarchy wouldn't help him win a nomination in another seat, wherever that might now be.

Moore personally took Isbey around Papatoetoe introducing him to party members, friends and local opinion leaders. Isbey went on to win Papatoetoe in 1978 by more than 1500 votes and hold it for three terms until his retirement in 1987.

Where to now? Someone suggested all the way down in Gisborne. Local Labour MP Trevor Davey had lost in the 1975 Muldoon landslide by about 1300 votes and it might be winnable in 1978. It was another marginal seat that swung regularly between National and Labour depending on what happened to the rural–urban boundaries.

There was also the possibility of New Plymouth or Whangarei. A report even surfaced in the *Truth* newspaper in August that his old friend Hugh Watt had nominated for his old seat of Onehunga in the hope of laying the groundwork for Moore.

A number of other electorate committees had written to Moore, seeing what had happened to him in Mangere and Papatoetoe, suggesting he consider their seats. It was flattering.

But he couldn't think with a clear head, so much had happened so quickly. And, more importantly, by this stage Moore was exhausted. He'd campaigned non-stop for about 12 months for Mangere and Papatoetoe, all the canvassing, cottage and town hall meetings with locals, recruitment of members, fundraising, planning and thinking.

Moore was never afraid of hard work and he'd dealt with plenty of rejection in his life. It seemed like he'd been in a semi-permanent haze for months. He'd drag himself up each morning, often living off coffee and cigarette breakfasts as Yvonne rushed off to teachers college.

He'd regularly fall into bed after midnight, having just got back from a party or local members meeting somewhere in Auckland, with only a sandwich or sausage roll along the way.

He looked terrible and Yvonne convinced him to see his doctor. After a medical examination he was given the all-clear. But Yvonne didn't believe it. She knew him better than anyone and he was more tired than usual.

So Moore went back but this time to Yvonne's doctor. He got Moore into a specialist later that day and then into hospital the next. He had testicular cancer.

It was early days and the cancer, called a germ cell tumour, was in the sperm-forming cells within the testicles. His tumours were 'seminomas' which tend to grow slowly and stay localised and don't spread.

In 1977 little was known in the public about cancer and the different types. It was a disease that people simply died from.

Moore could use his sickness as an opportunity to retreat, recover and reset his political career. It was a legitimate excuse to take a break from politics and aim for the 1981 general election.

But he knew that that's what his enemies would have expected, would have wanted from him, and vowed that not even cancer would stop him from getting back to Parliament. This wasn't a reflection moment, just another hurdle to overcome.

He didn't want his enemies to use the situation so he kept it secret.

He thought that his comings and goings from hospital would eventually get out, so he phoned people in the party he knew to be gossips and mentioned that he was having problems with a twisted bowel and was getting treatment. He and Yvonne only confided in her family.

He knew that if it became public he had cancer he would never get a nomination for a seat anywhere. Local party people, let alone the voting public, wouldn't want an MP they thought might not be around long.

Moore had surgery to remove the cancerous growth and then as an outpatient had radiotherapy for three months. His treatments included enduring long discomforts while a blue dye was circulated through his body and having a wire down his throat to monitor its circulation.

Surprisingly, the treatment didn't knock him around much and he was back at work at Oakley within weeks. Yvonne would take him to his morning treatments, then drop him off at work before heading to teachers college. So long as the cancer hadn't spread, the prognosis was good.

Despite the regular treatments, after a few months Moore was feeling better and his strength slowly returned. After a period of rest and clearing his head, he turned his attention back to politics and, specifically, what seat he should try for.

Most of what he'd tried politically, up to now, had failed. He'd been diligent and worked hard. But he knew he wasn't part of the in-crowd and calculated that no matter what he said and how much he tried to fit in they would ultimately reject him.

It was time to get a seat and show them all. It was time to get more serious about the task. In late 1977 Moore jumped on a plane for Wellington to spend time with Labour MPs and those who negotiated electoral boundaries for Labour. He was particularly keen to understand the likely population changes across New Zealand for the next 30 years.

A picture became clear to Moore in his early discussions with MPs. A major rewrite of the electoral boundaries was coming because of the 1976 census and many were concerned about their fates.

In the 1978 general election there would be 92 seats in Parliament, five more than 1975. But there was a significant rejuggling of almost half of the seats with 22 electorates abolished and 27 created. All this change should create an opportunity for him, he quickly calculated.

He thought that, in the increasingly news media-driven political world, an electorate in a city with television studios would be important. He wanted a 'Boeing seat', an electorate served by jets because that meant more regular, fast and reliable services to Parliament and other places. And he wanted to be in a place where there were young people, teenagers who were idealistic, wanting to change the world like him and had the energy to help him do it.

A group of local party members in the National-held seat of Papanui were keen to see if Moore would move to Christchurch to help them unseat six-term MP and Muldoon friend and Cabinet minister Bert Walker, who had a high profile nationwide for his tough stance on social welfare and Domestic Purposes Benefit recipients.

One of the Papanui group, an organiser with the Canterbury Hotel Workers Union, Rod Lingard, made the approach. Lingard and Moore knew each other from Labour Youth days.

Unusually, Lingard had become involved in the union via the party and not the other way around. The Hotel Workers, which had about 100,000 members nationwide, was one of the more influential trade unions affiliated to Labour and happily wielded its card votes at party conferences. But they were also a conservative trade union and were attracted to the energy and values of Moore.

Lingard, who would later work for Cabinet minister Phil Goff in the fourth Labour Government, got Moore down to Christchurch to meet and talk with union officials and local party members.

Papanui was a safe National seat with an almost 3000 majority, but with the planned boundary changes — which included going into the Labour stronghold industrial area to the north of Belfast — it was perhaps down to around 500 on paper. With a strong ground game someone like Moore could unseat Walker, local electorate chairperson Marianne Shaughnessy told him.

As coincidence would have it, Moore had bumped into a group of Labour Youth from Christchurch at the party conference in Wellington in 1975. He talked to them when most of the other MPs were otherwise preoccupied and had invited them down onto the conference delegates' floor to sit with the team from Eden.

The two were Shaughnessy's grandchildren, and they had subsequently raved about Moore to their grandmother after the conference. For once, his reputation preceded him positively.

Christchurch was a strong Labour and trade union city, and the party was in reasonable heart.

Labour's incumbent MPs, Avon's Mary Batchelor, Christchurch

Central's Bruce Barclay, Sydenham's John Kirk, Wigram's Mick Connelly and Southern Māori's Whetu Tirikatene-Sullivan, had high profiles and had withstood the 1975 Muldoon landslide. There was talk that well-known Christchurch City Councillor and lawyer David Caygill was also likely to stand in St Albans with the upcoming retirement of MP Roger Drayton.

It was still unknown who in Labour would go for Papanui because Walker was such a high-profile MP. There had been talk at one stage of trying to attract a lawyer by the name of Geoffrey Palmer. The locals kept encouraging Moore.

But he also had to convince Yvonne to up-roots to another city, away from her family, friends and upcoming career as a teacher. She had just finished being a trainee teacher at Maungawhau School in Mt Eden and graduated from teachers college at the end of 1977.

Yvonne had been offered a job at an intermediate school in Otara as an arts and social studies teacher and was excited. It was the first step in her career goal of being a secondary school arts teacher. She was not happy about the idea of moving from Auckland and didn't speak to him for a week.

With the help of Lingard, Shaughnessy and her husband Tim, and Labour Electorate Committee Deputy Chair Brian Gargiulo and Secretary Roger Pike, Moore was kept busy visiting key local party members and was mostly well received.

From the moment the news broke in Christchurch on 4 November 1977, the local newspapers were dismissive of his candidacy.

Four days later a story with the headline 'Mr Moore unlikely' appeared in *The Press*. The story said Moore's political comeback via Papanui had become a major talking point in the local party and it didn't look promising.

Anonymous Labour sources were quoted saying the electorate was conservative and didn't suit an Aucklander who was 'an opportunist with a big, brassy Ronald Reagan approach'.

'He is being described as a spoiled boy who is trying to use us. Others have asked why, if Aucklanders reject him, they should be expected to pick him up,' one source is quoted as saying.

'How would Aucklanders feel if they were offered some reject from Canterbury?'

The news story then editorialises: 'But if the reliable Labour sources quoted are any guide he could well have made the wrong choice. It is not just a question of an outside candidate being unacceptable, but merely a young man from north of Taupo with the wrong sort of image for Christchurch.'

While his local party backers told him to ignore it, the local media coverage worried him deeply.

It was going to be an upheaval to move to Christchurch, Yvonne was unhappy and would have to find work and, once again, he thought he wasn't popular.

Moore went up against more than 10 nominees on 18 November including former Christchurch civil engineer and Wanganui Labour Electorate Committee member Clive Matthewson, former Christchurch Mayor Neville Pickering, former Papanui candidate and city councillor Mollie Clark and women's movement leader Judy Waters.

Moore had spent a lot of time meeting and talking with local party members. His view of the world — focusing on ordinary New Zealanders and their families and creating wealth for the country — appealed to many.

They also admired his work ethic — he canvassed more than any of them did — and that he had a record of winning a marginal seat. The locals were tired of losing to Walker and were keen to knock off an ally of Muldoon's. Many became convinced that Moore could do that and swung behind him.

The selection meeting seemed like a repeat of Mangere and Papatoetoe. Moore had the three locals on the selection panel on his side and easily won the straw vote from the floor after a strong and humorous speech. But he knew that the head office representatives on the selection panel, Party President Arthur Faulkner, General Secretary John Wybrow and Joe Walding, could provide problems.

Moore turned up smartly dressed in a cream suit, white shirt and dark tie. He wanted to look like an MP in waiting.

He was upfront about having few local connections and didn't hide it.

'It's rumoured that my mother once stopped in the electorate to buy an ice cream at a dairy in 1948 — and I was born the following year,' he told everyone to great laughter. The humour got many over the fact that he was an outsider and, worse, from Auckland.

The selection panel was out until late and Moore and Yvonne prepared themselves for the worst, again.

Moore started formulating in his mind what he'd say to the media and what he was going to do with the party's national executive. He was going to say how undemocratic the party was, how it needed to overhaul its selection processes, and how the hierarchy no longer represented the interests of working-class New Zealanders and needed to be cleaned out. Serious reform was needed.

But Faulkner came out eventually and, in many people's memories, begrudgingly announced Moore was the winner.

There was a huge cheer and with tears streaming from her eyes Yvonne threw her arms around the neck of a motionless Moore.

Unknown to Moore until many years later, Yvonne had called Wybrow the night before and warned — or rather threatened — him to let the locals decide her husband's fate and not to play any silly head office games around this selection.

Moore had actually won and was still processing the fact that he hadn't lost when he went over to shake the hands of Faulkner and Walding.

With an unemotional look on his face, Moore told the pair he didn't want the seat. He had only run in Papanui to test how far the party hierarchy would go to stop him and that he was now going to tell the party faithful and the gathered news media that they 'could stick their nomination up their arses'. He wasn't interested.

As the crowd cheered, Moore walked up to the lectern and then turned to look at Faulkner and Walding and paused. They stared back blankly.

'I used to work on a dredge,' he said, 'and its name was *Horonui*.'

'That means landslide — we'll start canvassing on Saturday in Belfast,' he bellowed out as the crowd cheered and applauded again.

He gave Faulkner and Walding a long glance as he stepped down from the podium and was immediately engulfed by well-wishers, triumphant like a winning boxer leaving the ring. He almost forgot to enjoy the moment, so mixed up were his emotions at almost not overcoming yet another set of obstacles in his career.

He told *The Press* newspaper after the selection that the locals had chosen him 'because they wanted someone who would fight' and to deal with the out-of-town criticisms said: 'There are only two cities in New Zealand worth living in — Auckland and Christchurch.'

Moore and Yvonne had little money and debts to pay but packed up what few possessions they had into their VW camper van and drove to Wellington to catch the overnight ferry to Lyttelton. In Christchurch they slept in the van in the backyard of the house of Moore's brother Kerry and his wife Lorraine.

Yvonne busily applied for teaching jobs across Christchurch and despite the teacher shortage kept missing out until she was reminded that she was the wife of a Labour politician. Fortunately, the Hotel Workers Union came to Moore's assistance, offering him a temporary researcher's job so that they had some income and the local party helped with petrol costs.

Getting selected and campaigning are two different things, although many candidates don't realise that. Moore was experienced enough to know. In the months after gaining the selection in early 1978 he put a lot of effort into creating an organisation on the ground, signing up members and fundraising — the ammunition of any campaign.

Very soon local party membership began to grow. Moore took a party membership book with him everywhere.

In the first few weeks he got his closest local party members to do a quick but small confidential local telephone poll to gauge the mood in Papanui. It was disastrous. Labour was well behind National and Moore was seen, at worst, as a reject from Auckland and, at best, some flash Harry from up north. In contrast, Walker was seen as an in-touch conservative local Canterbury gentleman.

Within days Walker was quick to criticise Moore's selection and continue to position him as an outsider.

'Is the calibre of possible Labour candidates from this area so low that they have to import a man from the north of the North Island to contest this electorate?' *The Press* reported.

Letters to the editor in *The Press* described Moore as an 'Auckland Marxist' and how Labour's hierarchy had ignored the rank-and-file local party members.

There was a strange mood in the electorate, Moore thought. Muldoon and his economic policies were increasingly unpopular, but would people trust him and Labour?

This was borne out when Bruce Beetham won a by-election in the usual National stronghold of Rangitikei in early 1978 which gave Social Credit a fillip nationwide, including in Papanui.

Social Credit had a librarian as its candidate and the Values Party its high-profile leader Tony Kunowski. Moore had a real fear that the third parties might split his vote, allowing Walker to win again.

By now Yvonne had found work, as a presenter on the new children's television show being produced out of Christchurch called *Romper Room*. She had wisely applied for the job using her maiden name, and in a time when employers wanted to know if women were married she had said her husband was a social worker.

On the interview day Moore dropped Yvonne off a block away and waited for her there in fear that someone would see them together. Once short-listed, Yvonne told them who she was.

Being 'Miss Yvonne' was a fun and well-paid job that used her teacher training. They would film all five shows for the week on a Wednesday 'as live' which meant getting it right the first time. The show also gave the couple great profile and she created many contacts and learned many media skills that would later help her husband.

Yvonne was happy and had settled into their new life in Christchurch. She and her sister-in-law Lorraine had become best friends. This put Moore at ease and had removed a huge level of stress from his life.

During the Papanui selection process his cancer came back for a second time. It was even more important now that he keep it a secret. He wouldn't put it past some in the party hierarchy to try to reopen nominations for the seat.

Even a hint of that would be disastrous for him and Labour in the electorate. His political enemies within Labour were more of a worry than anything Walker or the National Party would do.

As well as surgery to remove part of his lung, this time he had chemotherapy. Memories play funny tricks with the mind. He has vague memories of lying in bed in hospital, hearing the clinking of the food trolley and the smell of the tea stewing in giant pots. The thought, let alone the smell, of brewing tea was something that for many years later would make him gag.

There was a lull for a few months in the campaign. They had little money to do anything anyway.

When he felt better, Moore devoted himself to the campaign. He went back to his Eden playbook and taught those in Papanui how to canvass the electorate using his system.

Using detailed canvassing data of the electorate he was able to map where his supporters were and sent letters to tradesmen, women at home, teachers, blue-collar workers, doctors and small business owners.

The locals had never seen a system like it and were excited by the prospect that their hours of door-knocking would make their lives easier on election day and help them communicate well with the electorate.

Moore also got MPs to ask questions in Parliament for him to elicit information about the electorate — street lighting, drainage and roading details — which he then used for personalised direct mail. He even sent a postcard to voters from an imaginary friend who'd shifted to Australia pining to come home if only National was voted out.

He even did a fake power bill to promote Labour's idea of an electricity price differential for the South Island. It was so convincing that there were many complaints, even from Labour voters, and Walker accused him of using 'Auckland tricks' — surely the dirtiest tricks of them all — in the campaign.

For a while he was concerned that his fake power bill idea would backfire on him. But it generated enormous publicity for him and tapped into South Islanders' belief that since they generated a lot of the country's electricity it should be much cheaper for them.

But nothing beat meeting voters in person so Moore and Yvonne would go out in the evenings and weekends to pubs, sports clubs, shopping centres and school fairs.

He also had the temerity to set up an electorate office as though he were already the local MP to meet constituents and resolve their issues.

He was everywhere and his mini-street-corner meeting routine epitomised the campaign. The initiative would see a group of young supporters literally run house to house around a neighbourhood knocking on doors to tell residents to hurry because Moore would be speaking on their street corner in 15 minutes.

If no one was in, they'd leave one of his business cards saying he'd called in while they were out. Moore would then turn up in a flat-bed truck with speakers attached, stand on the back and talk for 15 minutes.

People turned out to see this curiosity, peered through their sitting-room curtains or had to hear him while watching *Coronation Street*. Meantime, the team of young supporters had moved on to another part of the neighbourhood and continued the door-knocking.

The mini-street-corner meetings presented the image of a young and energetic candidate who was out to earn their votes and not take them for granted. It generated many volunteers for him including a young man with Down syndrome in Papanui who used to turn out to stop traffic and wasn't afraid to silence hecklers.

Moore sat down with Gargiulo and others and set targets for Labour votes in each booth in the electorate. He was also thinking ahead, urging his team to focus in particular areas so that if they didn't win a particular booth on election day, they'd set themselves up for victory next time.

After starting his campaign by using every opportunity to attack Walker — which pleased many party activists given the National MP's criticisms of beneficiaries — Moore soon realised that tactic was backfiring.

Walker was seen as an old gentleman and he needed to be more respectful of his status. So Moore gently praised Walker when asked which surprised voters in a time when politicians were supposed to dislike each other.

With Moore's encouragement relatively new MP David Lange — who had been more popular than Rowling in New Zealand Herald-NRB polls since the beginning of 1978 — came to an election rally in Papanui that attracted about 300 people.

Lange was entertaining in his attacks on Muldoon and the government, and Moore was impressed by how he'd captivated the audience. Lange had got better since the last time he saw him, at the Mangere selection.

Despite Labour lacking a charismatic leader in Rowling and lacking on the policy front, Moore felt confident he'd win. It would be a hard-run contest to beat an incumbent government minister, but he knew he had the election-day system and local party organisation to win. His election hoardings were being defaced, which he took as a sign of desperation from National.

It felt better than Eden in 1972 where he was more hopeful than anything else. This time he just knew he was the better candidate. And more than that, deep down he felt that all his disappointments and hurts — the missed selections, being treated badly by some in the party, being forced out of Auckland to find a seat and his ill-health — in the past three years were going to turn around with this moment.

On election night Moore took more than 10,700 votes or almost 53 per cent of those who turned out, winning about two-thirds of the more than 30 booths. Moore beat Walker by more than 4400 votes, a swing of almost 16 per cent and the biggest in the country.

But there was a degree of bitterness around the result.

Walker had told his supporters on the night that he was confident of winning Papanui back in three years. 'We have seen Moore in the House,' Walker was reported in *The Press*. 'He talked himself out. If you look up Hansard, you'll see how he used to praise Karl Marx. When he starts around here, I think the people of Papanui will realise what he has done.'

It was very different at Moore's election-night headquarters at St Gregory's Church Hall where many felt that the Papanui victory was going to be part of a nationwide change in the government. He said he'd spent 10 months listening in Papanui and two months talking. 'I've learned a lot in the past three years. I think I learned more from being booted out than I ever did in government,' *The Press* reported him saying.

Walker didn't go around to Moore's on the night to concede, as is usual for candidates. Instead, he phoned him on the Sunday morning.

Moore, however, was generous about Walker. 'If I can leave politics with as many friends as he has, I'll be a happy man.'

Labour won the popular vote in the 1978 general election. National fell from almost 48.5 per cent of the vote to just under 40 per cent. Labour went from just over 38.5 per cent to almost 40.5 per cent. Social Credit had hurt Labour, taking more than 16 per cent of the vote, but under the first past the post electoral system won only Beetham's Rangitikei seat.

Moore was annoyed, though, that he and his team weren't being given much credit for their victory. The post-election coverage by *The Press* had a big front-page photo of newly elected Labour Lyttelton MP

Ann Hercus and her family and the editorial said Walker was a victim of boundary changes and the swing to Labour.

Along with Moore, four others (Frank O'Flynn, Joe Walding, Jack Ridley and Kerry Burke) defeated in 1975 returned, plus seven new MPs (Stan Rodger, David Butcher, Ann Hercus, Eddie Isbey, David Caygill, Ralph Maxwell and John Terris).

Moore arrived at the first caucus meeting of the new Opposition terribly conflicted, though. He was excited to be back, but he had a deep secret that he didn't know how to deal with.

A few days after the election Moore's doctor called asking for an urgent meeting. One of his regular check-ups had shown the cancer had returned. This time it was very serious, and he might have only six months to live.

His mind was working overtime figuring out different scenarios. In the end he told no one in the caucus. He decided to get through Christmas back in Auckland where he'd be surrounded by the love of Yvonne's family and start chemotherapy in Christchurch five days later. He would make an assessment after that.

For the first time he also decided to tell his mother he had cancer. He hadn't wanted to worry her the first time because she was struggling with heart problems of her own, dealing with younger brother Shane and having recently separated from Webber.

It was the most difficult piece of news he'd ever told his mother. He had tended to shelter her from his disappointments and bad news, not wanting to burden her already difficult life.

She embraced him and told him she knew something was wrong with him 12 months earlier. Shane asked if the cancer was contagious.

The Moore-Webbers never really celebrated Christmas so he was pleased to drive back across the city later to Yvonne's parents' Blockhouse Bay home.

It was a strange Christmas. The cancer stayed in the back of his mind the whole time. It seemed like this time it could probably be it.

He couldn't help but feel sad among all the great food Rosie usually made, the toasts from various relatives who'd popped in and the thought-provoking discussions with Willie. Just as his political career seemed to be getting back on track, was this the last time he'd enjoy all of this?

Back in Christchurch he discovered that Labour's Christchurch

Central MP Bruce Barclay also had cancer. Barclay was staying quiet about it and the two formed an unusual relationship based on shared treatment experiences. Any policy differences or caucus allegiances between the two were clearly insignificant compared with their current common enemy.

Moore's chemotherapy started on New Year's Eve and Yvonne snuck a bottle of champagne into the cancer ward, which the two drank quietly together.

Within three days the poison of the chemotherapy treatment was having an impact. Moore was constantly vomiting, lost most of his hair which he covered with a cap, and quickly dropped a third of his body weight. He was too weak to do anything — go to the toilet, wash, talk, eat and, worst of all, read — and Yvonne had to wheelchair him around.

All sense of dignity had been taken away. He felt humiliated and but for Yvonne he was all alone.

With what little energy he had he constantly worried for Yvonne. She had her work but few friends in Christchurch as Lorraine and Kerry had by now moved to Wellington. Rosie and Audrey took it in turns to come to Christchurch to be with Yvonne. She was also managing all his electorate work, sending letters and telegrams under his name.

The cancer had spread to one of his lungs and part of it had to be removed in an operation. Everything just seemed to get worse.

If he gave up, all the stresses and strains would go away for everyone, he occasionally thought.

When you're in a cancer ward you have many thoughts. For Moore it was a mixture of reflections on his life — not so much regrets — and the lessons from them. He wasn't angry. But he did wonder if he'd lived his life well and spent enough time with Yvonne.

He often jokes that he's not religious, he's an Anglican. Getting cancer made him wonder whether it was all some kind of divine punishment or encouragement, and for a short period he sought guidance from Bill Subritzky, a successful businessman and Anglican preacher who was well known in the 1970s for his faith healing.

Subritzky spent time with the couple in their flat and they prayed together. It felt uncomfortable at first for Moore the Anglican and Yvonne the Catholic because to pray for help only in their hour of need seemed false.

But the couple ended up getting great comfort from their discussions with Subritzky and their shared prayers.

He felt the prayers of many people, just as Subritzky had told him he had asked others to do. It didn't remove the cancer, but it seemed to lift the darkness in his spirits.

Moore wasn't so much converted during this time, more reminded of his Dilworth religious teachings and Labour's core beliefs of applied Christianity. Those concepts of goodness, care and love were actually real, he realised.

After more than six months of difficult treatments and surgery, the chemotherapy seemed to be working and his strength began to return. He would often drive out by himself to Orana Wildlife Park, a new 80-hectare tourism venture on the outskirts of Christchurch, to wander around, sit and think.

It was time to tell the truth. The rumours of his illness had become so intense that members of the public had started sending him all sorts of natural and mystery medicines in the mail to combat the cancer. A journalist had also visited their home unannounced hoping to catch a glimpse of Moore. Yvonne had to deal with a barrage of questions while Moore hid inside.

Moore later phoned him and a story appeared saying the illness might be more serious than first thought and that he might be fighting for his life. 'As far as I'm concerned there is no such thing as terminal — it's only a state of mind,' he told *Sunday News*. 'But everything really depends on the person, medical science and the good Lord.'

There was nastiness too. There were some horrible letters hoping he would die and Yvonne having a shouting match with a taxi driver about how Moore had ripped the taxpayers off.

A local Christchurch Labour MP had even secretly discussed with members of the Papanui electorate the idea of deselecting Moore in the hope that they would end up with a friendly future ally in Parliament. Rowling had even been approached about the idea but was strongly loyal to Moore and told the MP he would hear nothing of it.

Fortunately, much of this was kept from Moore while he recovered.

In mid-1979 Moore called a press conference at their Belfast flat to tell the news media about his recovery from cancer.

He said he'd been a 'bad liar' and was sorry he'd put a number of people close to him in the 'unfair' position of having to cover for him during his ordeal. Cancer was probably the most dreaded word in the English language, but he hoped his survival might bring hope to other sufferers.

In its editorial at the time, *Sunday News* said the public deserved to know if their elected representatives were in bad health but said 'it took guts' for Moore to battle cancer.

'Mike Moore has showed tremendous courage. We wish him all the best now he's ready to take up his seat in Parliament. Get stuck in, Mike.'

It was a weight off what remained of his shoulders. It was time to get back to Parliament.

5

A medical diagnosis or an opinion?

'Coming back into Parliament was very strange. Many didn't know how to react. Saying you had cancer in those days was saying you were dying. When I came back some showed great kindness and concern and others, I could tell, were waiting for me to die. The reactions crossed political divides.

'The House used to be a bear pit. You have to be forceful, quick and funny. Everyone's watching for any sign of weakness. When I got back to Parliament, I had to show I wasn't weak — even though I probably was — and do it quickly.

'Muldoon was my target and I'd had cancer so I wasn't scared of anyone. Many MPs on both sides of the House were afraid of Muldoon. He'd say menacingly: "I know about you."

'Throughout my career I think I've got on with most politicians, even my staunchest opponents. Not him. I actually hated Muldoon. He was an awful person.

'But it was like a new lease on life coming back to Parliament, I remembered why I loved it. It's one of the only places in life where you're a true equal and judged solely on your performance.

'I always got an adrenalin rush when I was standing there making a speech about something I passionately believed in. You could sense the other side knowing you were right and being afraid that you'd beat them with your argument, and your own side agreeing and urging you on.

'I think that's the beauty of the debating chamber, it's a House of Representatives of New Zealanders and it doesn't matter who you are — it's the contest of the ideas, the humour, the passion.

'But it's also a place of camaraderie across political divides. For me — and I know for many others — you knew it was a privilege to be a parliamentarian, that people had trusted you with the power to make laws to govern them with. There's also this unspoken understanding about the sacrifices required by your families and on relationships for you to be an MP and how you have to go easy sometimes on each other.

'I did a lot of reading on trade and economics when I was out of Parliament between 1975 and 1978, and Joe Walding helped me. He was a great mentor.

'Trade is underestimated. It was where I could make an impact and make a difference for the country, Joe said. There are more Labour ministers of education, housing and justice than you can shake a stick at. I thought I wanted to be minister of housing initially, but Joe sorted out my thinking.

'Joe stated the obvious to me. The country needed to trade with the world to grow. Education and health were critical for our people to get ahead, but we couldn't afford them without a growing and outward-looking economy. I could do more good for our people helping make it easier for our exporters. It was a revelation to me.

'People don't realise just how powerful the hatred against Muldoon was. The whole country was closeted.

'I became convinced that fortress New Zealand wasn't a goer any more. It was probably okay in the 1930s when 90 per cent of our stuff went to England. But the Common Market was now in.

'In Labour we were all searching around. Mind you, in Parliament we kept saying the same things. But we knew this wasn't a goer. There was a group of us starting to think this way, but we weren't cohesive. There wasn't a committee of us. We were talking and discovering we were reading the same kinds of books.

'Bill Rowling was the leader and he was fundamentally a good guy. Our 1978 election figures were good. We got more votes than the Nats. So there was a case to run again with Rowling.

'But between 1978 and 1981 all hell broke loose and that undermined him.

'We were lucky Lange was doing well publicly. The Nats were always promoting him trying to undermine Rowling.

'There was a small group of us thinking it's time for a change. And the good thing about that group was that it was a good cross section of the caucus.

'The divide in caucus wasn't generational. We had a lot of people supporting Lange — Gerry Wall, Fraser Coleman; the core of the party. But in the early days the problem we had was with those who I thought were thinking of themselves as the leader — Russell Marshall, Kerry Burke, Jim Anderton, Ann Hercus. It's about the three favourite words in politics: why, not, me.

'I looked at myself and everybody else and I thought Lange would be an outstanding leader. He was a talented bastard. I enjoyed his company. He was funny, he was generous. There weren't many bad marks against him.

'Lange came from almost nowhere. I know I wasn't ready. I wasn't suitable, I didn't know enough. Richard Prebble wasn't the right person. Roger Douglas couldn't do it — he couldn't speak on behalf of our people even though he had a very strong pedigree; his father and grandfather. We were all good but no one was as good as Lange and we all came to that conclusion.

'My ambitions weren't that strong, funnily enough. I'd been sick and I didn't know what would happen. You think about it all the time. They say you're cured of cancer then you die of something else.

'I went and told Rowling I thought we had the numbers and we were going to move on him. I thought it was the honourable thing to do. He was so angry. But I thought we were two ahead.

'All hell then broke loose in the caucus and party after Rowling pushed off our challenge. We went up to Roger's office and got some fish and chips. It was something we often did. Then we had an opportunity of a photo of all of us and I thought "Perfect".

'The way Anderton was behaving, there was going to be a special party conference and we were all going to be chucked out. It would have suited his ambitions to be leader.

'I thought it's going to be a bit sour for a while. I wanted the photo to say: "We're not moving." It told the caucus: "We're staunch with Lange — don't mess with him."

'Maybe it was a mistake, I don't know now. We were pretty tight. I don't know if Lange showed that loyalty back to us. He wasn't as tribal as some of us.

'Have a look at the photo and ask yourself who's not there? Someone you'd expect with that crowd . . . Prebble's not there. He ran for the door. He didn't want to be seen with us.

'We got so many letters about that photo. Branches were complaining about how disloyal we were and all that shit.

'We then got stuck in behind Rowling. We told Lange: "Do well and you'll be leader in time." But we had to try to win in 1981. To do anything else would have been obnoxious.

'Everything was done for Lange. He knew what was going on. He wasn't innocent. He knew exactly what was up.

'I never thought of politics as an age issue. I didn't think the older guard should move on. But I did think we had better ideas. It was an exciting time. I was starting to feel better.

'Geoffrey Palmer had come in on a by-election. He used to wear this silly Sherlock Holmes kind of hat and people didn't use to rate him. But Palmer was a deadly operator. He's more political than people think. He got a lot of what he wanted. He planted seeds to blossom six months later. He's a very strategic guy.

'I was annoyed I didn't get to be deputy to Lange, but I knew Palmer would be really good at the job. I think I ended up in a far more influential position off the back of it.

'Jim Anderton was very tight with Michael Bassett and Roger Douglas for a long time. Anderton and Douglas used to play rugby league or something together at the weekends. The falling-out was, I think, simply about Anderton wanting to become leader.

'There comes a time when you're knocking on a door that's closed. So you should look for someone who can go through, and try to help them.

'I'm saying all this now, but it's probably one-eyed of me. I should have made peace with Anderton many years ago, I suppose. I couldn't be bothered with him back then, which is probably a weakness of mine.

'Politics should be about promoting ideas to make the country a better place. We're supposed to be better than the other side and generally we are. But we can make it pretty personal on the left.'

****

It was nine more months after the 1978 general election before Moore was well enough to finally make his comeback to Parliament.

What should have been a triumphant and jubilant occasion — the return of one of Labour's up-and-comers — was more a moment tinged with relief. Rowling and Yvonne escorted a frail Moore from Christchurch by plane back to Wellington and into Parliament on 7 August 1979.

Rowling had been in Christchurch the night before to launch the Christchurch Central by-election campaign of a bright young lawyer called Geoffrey Palmer, who was replacing Bruce Barclay who had lost his battle with cancer.

Moore was returning earlier than he should have because he was eager to be back in the caucus and was concerned that the public sympathy he had might be waning.

He was gaunt and 13 kilograms lighter, had lost much of his hair, was narrow in the cheeks and had a suit that barely hung on to his shoulders and hips. Despite his attempts to be positive with well-wishers he was clearly far from feeling fit and well.

Rowling seemed genuinely happy to see him again and Moore expressed his gratitude for the calls the Labour leader had made to Yvonne during his illness. MPs and Opposition staffers came out to greet Moore and applause broke out when they saw him.

Moore told the *Evening Post* newspaper that he felt 'a bit like Lazarus' and that he would do 'whatever the boss expects me to do'. He commented to TV reporter Alastair Carthew: 'I've gone to the top of the mountain and seen over the edge.'

After the obligatory news media interviews and a few public words from Rowling, he was quickly reminded of his status when he was shown to his new parliamentary office. It was barely bigger than a coffin which, he thought at the time, was probably apt given his condition. The caucus clearly didn't expect Moore to survive so there was no need to give him a decent workspace, he thought. He was insulted and angry.

The next day he slowly walked to the debating chamber as other government and Opposition MPs rushed past him — some turning to slap him on the back or shake his hand — to find his seat in the back benches.

Moore was tired, shaking and feeling dizzy. He recalls closing his eyes and praying to God that afternoon rather than like most MPs robotically reciting with Speaker Richard Harrison the prayer to start the day. He then moved forward to be sworn in to the thirty-ninth Parliament.

Yvonne sat in Parliament's public gallery barely containing her emotions as he put his left hand on the Bible and swore allegiance to the Crown. Both sides of the House applauded.

Moore felt extremely self-conscious that afternoon. He felt the eyes of the public and the Press Gallery that overlook the chamber peering down on him. He even thought he could hear his colleagues' minds questioning his return. Did Moore still have fight in him or was he just here to draw a salary until he passed away? He was happy to sink into his green leathered seat and not be noticed for a while.

The next day he scanned the Questions of the Day. Under the Westminster system of Parliament, Questions of the Day are the Opposition's opportunity to test the prime minister and Cabinet ministers about the affairs of government. They are pure theatre of which few members of the public are aware and if they were would not care about.

But in Parliament they take on a huge significance because of their morale-boosting qualities for caucuses. An Opposition leader or spokesperson who can embarrass or ridicule a prime minister or minister is seen as capable of doing the big job themselves. The Press Gallery used to watch question time with enormous interest not only for possible titbits of news but also for its subtle nuances of competence and confidence.

The Opposition was targeting Acting Prime Minister Brian Talboys about the prime minister's current overseas trip to the Commonwealth Heads of Government Meeting in Lusaka, the costs and what Muldoon had achieved.

Quips were being made about Muldoon and Auckland Central MP Richard Prebble asked if the prime minister's chartered plane was required not because of the delegation size but because of the 'food and grog' being taken. When asked to name who was in the delegation in a follow-up question, someone screamed out 'Johnny Walker'.

Opposition MPs were openly laughing at the government.

Moore then decided he had to show everyone he was back to his quick-witted self even though he looked and felt awful. He'd already established a reputation the first time he was an MP for targeting Muldoon.

Little did he know about the chaos he was about to create. Moore rose to his feet and straight-faced asked if reports that the prime minister was 'mad as hell' when he arrived in Lusaka were 'a medical diagnosis or an opinion'.

The Opposition screamed with laughter and the government roared outrage at the un-parliamentary nature of such a question.

Talboys appeared taken aback and, after hesitating, rose from his seat calling for a point of order and, glaring at Moore, said: 'I have just about had a gutsful of this sort of nonsense from children parading as men.'

Speaker Harrison told Talboys that his language wasn't parliamentary and asked him to withdraw the comment. Talboys stayed in his seat and said he wouldn't. After Harrison repeated his request Talboys said he would only because he was being required to. But that wasn't enough for Harrison who said it must be done without qualification.

Ministers then started to gather around the acting prime minister's seat and after further discussions he withdrew his comments and asked Moore to withdraw his.

After further discussions the Speaker asked Moore, saying he wasn't imputing that he'd done anything improper. Moore didn't want to be ejected from the House (and never was in his career), so withdrew and apologised.

It might have all seemed childish to outsiders but to those in the House the acting prime minister had just been rattled by a man who'd been back in Parliament barely two days.

Before coming back to Parliament, Moore had wondered what his old friends and foes from battles past would think. As some MPs left the House after question time, a number came up to him smiling and welcomed him back. A Labour soldier not afraid of taking it to National in the House — he'd reminded everyone who he was.

But the physical stress was being felt by Moore. Within days of being back in Parliament he had a painful attack of the shingles; his immunity system was so weak. He told no one but Yvonne.

The following week, back in Parliament, Muldoon crossed the chamber to shake Moore's hand and welcome him. Muldoon was nothing but polite, but Moore knew it was the prime minister accepting his challenge.

Being back in Parliament was also tinged with reflection for him.

Having fought his way back into Parliament after many selection battles, moving cities, straining his relationship with Yvonne and beating cancer Moore wondered what it was all about. He wasn't feeling sorry for himself, just questioning whether he would make any difference given the sacrifice required.

Muldoon and his National Government were all-dominant even though they had lost the popular vote to Labour 39.8 per cent to 40.4 per cent in 1978. The mood in the Labour caucus was very different from what he remembered of the Kirk one. There wasn't the same desire and hunger he recalled. Yes, Labour wasn't the government, but the team felt beaten down by the 1978 general election defeat.

Moore was also conscious that this time he had to behave differently. People — the media, the public and the party — knew who he was and his reputation as an ambitious upstart preceded him.

He had to be different. Cancer had reminded him of his mortality. He hadn't had a religious epiphany, but he'd thought a lot about his place on earth and had a calmer view on being a politician. This reflectiveness didn't mean he'd given up on political combat or caring about the day to day, though.

For Moore it manifested itself as an imaginary helmet and body armour. Show me the battle, bugger the odds. There's a lot to do, let's not waste time talking about it.

He knew he wasn't invincible, but he wasn't afraid of anything — smoking, editors, colleagues or Muldoon. Stuff them all. He didn't know if his cancer would come back so time might be short.

He quickly found like-minded allies in the caucus. Impatient and ambitious, they were tired of the old guards' caution around Muldoon and weren't afraid of his popularity. Rowling would also often wonder aloud through the news media about reshuffles and then hesitate to make them, which only created uncertainty and anger in the caucus.

During this time Moore took counsel from his old mentors Mat Rata from Northern Māori and Joe Walding from Palmerston North. They were also uneasy about the current leadership but urged patience and caution on caucus matters. Circumstances in politics, many unplanned for, often created opportunities. Manipulating situations often didn't create openings, they urged Moore.

The life of an Opposition MP can take one of two paths, particularly if you're a backbencher with few responsibilities. You either sit around bored at select committee hearings and speaking in the House about bills you have little interest in most of the term waiting for the next election or you take every opportunity to undermine the government — polish the lino, as Moore calls it — and think about solutions to issues.

Moore fell back on his habit from Dilworth — reading, of which he had an easily accessible source. He kept the Parliamentary Library busy finding him books from Pacific history and economic development through to manufacturing and marketing.

He realised, too, that as an Opposition MP he had an opportunity — he saw it as a responsibility — to create policy debate among his colleagues and across the party to develop a platform for a future Labour Government.

To his surprise, though, many of his caucus colleagues weren't interested in engaging. They were Labour MPs and they were wedded to thinking a particular way. Labour's job was simply to stand up to the bosses and more fairly redistribute the wealth of capitalism than National was prepared to.

That was Moore's political upbringing, too, but everything he was reading was telling him that life wasn't black and white — bosses versus workers — any more.

His interest in travelling and the friends and contacts he'd created through Socialist Youth also broadened his horizons.

His political thinking was at a crossroads. Be safe and stay with many of his colleagues and the party on social and economic thinking or look for alternatives and help steer the debate.

It was in his blood to be suspicious of capitalism. He'd seen what he thought was capitalism first-hand in the freezing works as a teenager.

Ordinary men and women would work hard all week and the bosses would drive out the front gate in their flash imported cars. The only way the workers could get a share of the spoils would be for their unions to do the only thing they knew would grab the employers' attention: strike.

It was adversarial. It was the only way employment relations seemed to work in New Zealand. And the politics of it all saw Labour standing up for the workers and National standing up for the bosses and the farmers, the cornerstone of the economy.

But Moore noticed that this constant jab and counter jab between employers and employees was missing an important ingredient — whether or not industry was producing products that customers wanted to buy.

In his days in the freezing works sheep and cattle were produced by farmers because they had a captive market in Britain. Later, when the market started to disappear, production stayed the same because of government subsidies and much of the meat was ground into fertiliser.

All the while employers and workers were divorced from this and fighting about wage rates because inflation was rampant. The irony was that the more the workers ended up earning the more inflation stayed high and the more tax they paid, which ended up back in the pockets of the farmers via subsidies.

Moore was trying to get his head around this and reconcile it with his early political beliefs. He knew he needed to learn more.

Most Labour Members of Parliament enter politics to change the world. Their strong social conscience is founded in a belief that well-funded health, education and social welfare systems level the playing field for ordinary working people. Publicly funded institutions, rather than the free market, is the answer to most of the country's ills.

They are, therefore, naturally drawn to social issues. All polls showed then and now that Labour is considered the best party to deal with the country's issues around health and education, while National is best at matters around managing the economy.

In his first term in Parliament Moore was interested in housing, prison reform and mental health, a traditional Labour mix of issues.

He knew that he — and Labour for that matter — had to diversify interests into the economic sphere. Walding, who took New Zealand's first trade mission to China in 1973, often told him to pay more attention to the trade portfolio.

Walding discussed with Moore the consequences of Britain entering the European Economic Community, about the rise of Asia out of Third World poverty, and how as a producer of food the country would eventually need to move out of shipping it as a commodity to adding value to products that could be sold at a premium.

He convinced Moore that New Zealand was in a great position to prosper in the changing world so long as it backed itself.

Walding told him that few in Labour would be interested in the trade portfolio and how he could make a name for himself in the party by taking his career in that direction. The portfolio would also give him an entrée into the rapidly growing and diverse business community that was focused on exports.

Moore could, importantly, also have input into economic policy from a practical level from his first-hand understanding of it rather than a university-based theoretical learning. He could be the bridge between the two sides of the economy, the workers and the bosses.

To help with his different perspective Moore went out of his way to meet employers and he would spend much of his time writing down his thoughts afterwards. He understood the orderliness of books and writing helped him think them through. It forced on him a discipline around his research and thinking he believed would enable him to get on top of issues and his caucus responsibilities.

In 1980 it led to Moore publishing *On Balance: a Labour look at regional, community and town development*, what would be the first of 10 books over his career.

The book was about the development of New Zealand and pointed out that while many Kiwis had a pioneering spirit and belief that the country was forged out of taming the bush, it was far more planned and organised than that.

Other than Auckland, the New Zealand Company founded many settlements and Premier Sir Julius Vogel's railways and public works construction in the 1870s and Liberal Government lands and agriculture minister John McKenzie's land reforms in the 1890s actually built the country.

Moore argued that New Zealanders had always sought a collective approach and that governments undertook initiatives and accepted responsibilities for balancing the country's development. He discussed regional development and what a future Labour Government might do.

Moore's thinking about economic management was starting to emerge.

He thought regional development programmes were important, but they were pointless if the general economy was in relapse.

'You cannot inject new blood into one limb if the whole body is haemorrhaging,' he wrote.

The Swedish experience of employers and employees working together to set production targets and wages and conditions resulted in higher productivity, fewer accidents, less absenteeism and better industrial relations.

He wondered why in New Zealand cooperatives were commonplace for farm producers with freezing works, fertiliser works and jointly owned machinery, but not the factory worker.

Beyond economics he also argued that governments needed social investment to ensure local communities flourished, that local government needed more devolved to it, that historic parts of cities needed to be saved, that urban environments needed to be greened, and that technology would eventually allow people to work and study from home without the need to travel. He was developing his thinking and reaching out to a broad section of stakeholders.

But back in Parliament nothing seemed to be changing.

The new MPs saw the world differently and were open to other ways of thinking about the country's economic woes and Muldoon's prescription for it, which were hands-on and not too far off Labour thinking at the time. They also wanted change within the party. They eagerly organised at a local level and signed up members.

It became clear to Moore soon after returning to Parliament that Rowling was struggling with the new paradigm. He found it difficult to reconcile the old and the new. Caucus debates were often left hanging because Rowling couldn't, or wouldn't, agree with either the position of the old or the new. He ended up pleasing neither side and annoying both.

Moore felt the mood in caucus slowly getting worse with the old guard, and Deputy Leader Bob Tizard in particular, increasingly uncomfortable.

Lange had become a popular figure inside caucus, with the broader party membership and the news media which warmed to his humour and personality. He was a stark contrast to the prime minister and certainly the leader of the Opposition.

A New Zealand Herald-NRB poll in July 1979 had Muldoon on 18 per cent as preferred prime minister, Rowling on 18 per cent, Beetham on 11 per cent and Lange, barely two years in Parliament, on 6 per cent. Many of the new guard — but only as individuals initially — quickly saw the 37-year-old Lange as the future.

Rowling's management of caucus matters continued to annoy Moore. In announcing Labour's spokesmanships in 1979, Moore's great friend Mat Rata had been left off with no one looking after Māori Affairs.

Initially it seemed a mistake. But Rowling compounded the error by saying to the news media that Māori Affairs would be covered by Richard Prebble, who was the spokesman for human rights. This was news to Prebble and the rest of the caucus.

Moore was furious. Rata and the other Māori MPs were insulted.

In a caucus of 40 a small rumour or an inappropriate or accidental phrase or action can easily spiral a situation out of control. Paranoia is a common trait among MPs. Many learn — often through costly previous experiences — to tune in for the most minute of details and to compare it with other titbits of information they've gathered. The good ones can triangulate a situation quickly; the bad ones completely misread it.

Whatever caused it, Moore sensed that Tizard was becoming concerned about his tenure as deputy leader. A rumour spread quickly that Tizard was going to counter this by focusing the caucus discontent on Rowling by challenging him for the leadership.

While Moore was sure that Rowling wasn't the answer to the party's problems, he was definitely convinced that Tizard wasn't. Rowling would eventually have to make way for Lange, but he was nervous and conflicted about doing it now.

Meantime, a group of the new guard, including Roger Douglas, Richard Prebble and Michael Bassett, saw this as the right moment to move on Tizard. They went to Rowling to reassure him that the manoeuvrings weren't about him and they pledged to support his leadership at an upcoming caucus ballot in November 1979. He was re-elected unopposed.

But for the deputy leadership Douglas boldly nominated Lange. For the old guard in the room, there was a mixture of stunned and insulted looks. It seemed to come from nowhere.

The new guard had been lobbying caucus members on Lange's behalf and Moore pledged his support to them despite being heavied by the likes of Basil Arthur and some of the old guard. Moore didn't have much time for Tizard, who he saw as a grumpy old man who stifled rather than encouraged young MPs. Lange beat Tizard by two votes.

Moore's upbeat demeanour after the caucus vote quickly disappeared in the House that afternoon. By accident or design the reshuffling of the front bench — Rowling, Lange, Tizard, Arthur, Faulkner, Douglas, Connelly and Colman — to make way for the new deputy meant Rata was temporarily seatless.

Arriving late in the House, Rata fumbled around looking for a place to sit on the front bench in full view of the government, the Press Gallery and his colleagues. Moore tried to give Rata his seat, but the Northern Māori MP was barely containing his anger and awkwardly retreated from the chamber.

Moore tried to convince his friend in the lobby just outside the chamber that it was a mistake, not knowing what the truth was. Rata would have nothing of it. Rowling had insulted him for the last time.

The pair drank late into the night, Moore trying his best to change the mind of his mentor. Despite the best efforts of Moore and others, including Rowling apologising personally, Rata resigned in early 1980 and formed the Mana Motuhake party. He lost the resulting by-election to Labour's Bruce Gregory, a young Northland doctor.

The whole episode deeply saddened Moore. But it also quickly taught him to separate his personal and political feelings.

He had to learn to disguise his feelings towards Rata and to harden up his political attitudes towards people. He loved the man dearly, but he was running against his party in Northland and was organising candidates in the other Māori seats.

For Moore you were either with Labour or against it; my tribe or another tribe. The line was clear, not blurred, and Rata was on the wrong side of it.

Compounding Moore's melancholy was the fact that Rowling had overlooked him in his post-deputy leadership change shadow Cabinet reshuffle. A number of the other new guard had been promoted but not him.

It was also dawning on him that he wasn't always being included in conversations among the various groupings in caucus. He thought as an MP in the Kirk Government and a tried-and-tested marginal seats campaigner he'd have a lot to offer.

In Parliament casual groupings occur often through boredom or loneliness. Some Opposition MPs and government backbenchers wander around the corridors during sitting evenings looking for company or someone to share a drink with. Moore learned that in his first time as an MP and he enjoyed the camaraderie. He found the behaviour strangely similar to the dormitory of Dilworth.

Something was different this time, though. Moore was seldom invited. It wasn't an obvious slight, but he'd sometimes walk into an MP's office to discover a small group already gathered. So he determined he had to push his way in if he was to be heard and have influence.

He decided he needed to be more active in determining the future leadership of the party and joined the Lange, Bassett, Douglas and Prebble grouping. While Moore had known them all from Auckland party circles going back to the 1960s, he hadn't been particularly close to them.

He liked Lange for his sense of humour, Bassett for his knowledge of the history of the party, Douglas for his creative mind and Prebble for his strategic thinking. While they never felt like friends to him, it was a stimulating bunch to be in the company of and, besides, they enjoyed a drink and were fun to be around.

Rowling had been good to Moore when he had cancer and, unlike some in the party and caucus, supported his running for Papanui even though there was a real possibility he could have died in office some months after the general election. Moore saw him as a kind and decent man, and he was caught between loyalty and wanting a change.

Moore was to finally take a firm stand on Rowling in late 1980. Moore was coming up the parliamentary stairs to the Opposition offices with Douglas and Prebble after lunch when they bumped into an agitated-looking Bassett.

He'd just come out of the Leader's Office where on the spur of the moment he'd told Rowling how unhappy he was with his leadership and how the party was going. Rowling had dismissed him out of hand.

The four of them went into Douglas's nearby office to see what Bassett was concerned about. There he told them about the meeting and how frustrated he'd become with Rowling. They decided at that meeting Rowling had to be rolled.

They realised to do that they'd need to get to the key figures in the caucus, Yaldhurst MP and former Kirk Government minister Mick Connelly and Roskill MP and former Party President Arthur Faulkner. The group then circulated a petition asking that the leadership issue be put on the caucus agenda.

In December 1980 Moore thought it was only right that he should be upfront with Rowling about the increasing uneasiness in caucus about his leadership. He took to Rowling a list of 22 names and signatures out of the 40 caucus members who said they would vote against him in a leadership ballot. Rowling was offended and angry, given all the support he'd shown Moore in the past, and the meeting didn't last long.

The situation was threatening to spiral out of control. Party President Jim Anderton supported Rowling against the conspirators, threatening a special party conference to deal with the traitors. Some in the caucus believed Anderton wanted Rowling around long enough for him to become an MP and challenge for the leadership ahead of Lange.

Some played the abortion card against Lange — who was thought to be against it — thus rallying many of the women MPs for Rowling.

Rowling was at his fighting best. The caucus where his leadership was due to be discussed in early December 1980 was postponed a day to a special meeting on the Friday morning because he was out seeing young unemployed Māori in the provinces. He then used this to accuse the plotters of backstabbing him while he was out trying to solve some of the nation's problems.

The 24-hour delay in the vote meant Anderton, Ann Hercus and other Rowling supporters could put pressure on some of the MPs Moore had shown him would be Lange voters.

Rowling's people persuaded three, Māori MPs Paraone Reweti and Koro Wetere, and Pencarrow's Fraser Colman, to switch sides and with three Lange supporters — Island Bay's Frank O'Flynn, Palmerston North's Joe Walding and St Kilda's Bill Fraser — unable to make the rescheduled caucus meeting, the numbers changed. The contest was locked at 18–18 with Rowling's deciding vote saving his leadership.

During parliamentary dinner breaks Moore, Lange, Douglas, Bassett and Prebble would often gather in an office to discuss issues of the day over fish and chips from the takeaway shop on Molesworth Street opposite Parliament, Wellington Fish Supply, and a beer or wine. It was a regular haunt for MPs.

On the afternoon of the unsuccessful move on Rowling the group didn't want to be seen in the Bellamy's dining room and went to Douglas's office to regather their thoughts. Douglas and Bassett were sent to get fish and chips. They trundled out through Parliament's ground floor 'rubber doors' to walk across the forecourt, past the 'King Dick' Seddon statue, out the gate and across the road.

Unbeknown to them the *New Zealand Herald*'s young political journalist Greg Shand and the newspaper's Wellington photographer Geoff Dale saw them. They'd been assigned to cover the Labour leadership spill — Shand even predicting in that morning's edition that Lange might win — and had got what the rest of the Parliamentary Press Gallery had that day. But they were looking for something different from the rest of the pack.

On Shand's urging the pair had trailed the MPs. What was their secret meeting about?

They followed Douglas and Bassett to the fish-and-chip shop where Dale took a series of photos. Walking back, Dale told his colleague he wasn't sure if he got good enough photos. So, Shand suggested they hunt down the gang.

Inside Parliament they found the group in Douglas's office. Shand popped his head around the door and asked if they could get a photo of the group having their late lunch.

Moore knew Shand well from his early days in Auckland when the two worked on Labour Party publications and trusted him. Moore immediately realised that a photo of them with Lange in the *New Zealand Herald* after they'd unsuccessfully tried to topple Rowling would send a more powerful message than any press statement full of rhetoric.

Before Dale came in, though, Prebble scurried out of the room. Dale didn't want to ruin the moment and set up a shot, and hurriedly took his photos — only a handful of frames — as the group were eating and drinking beer out of wine glasses and as Lange was scanning the newspaper.

The 'fish-and-chip brigade' of agitators and plotters — and, later, probably along with Geoffrey Palmer, David Caygill and Helen Clark, the most influential group in the fourth Labour Government — was born.

After the vote, the caucus descended into chaos and Moore was demoted to the third row, finding out via the news media.

Douglas also went off to produce his own economic blueprint for Labour, 'There's got to be a better way', which was based on his unauthorised 1980 alternative budget. It put him further offside with Rowling and others.

Members of the party in Papanui were also unhappy with Moore, who they had thought was a supporter of Rowling's. Moore thought he was in real trouble with his local party members, some of whom worked for Rowling during his unsuccessful Fendalton campaign in 1960.

Moore had never said a disparaging word about Rowling to them so they were shocked to learn through the news media that not only had he voted against the leader but had been one of the plotters.

Moore apologised to his local supporters, saying he thought it was important to always be publicly supportive of whoever the leader was. Deep down he knew Lange would be better than Rowling. In future he promised to be more upfront with them even if he knew they'd disagree with him.

During all the Rowling upheavals of late 1980, Moore also had to face his biggest personal challenge after dealing with cancer. Audrey, who by now was 58 years old, divorced and living alone in a flat in Auckland, had become frail after a series of heart problems.

Though her health was quickly deteriorating she was a proud woman and didn't want Moore's help from Christchurch or Kerry's from Wellington. Shane, meanwhile, was now living in a boarding house in Sydney.

Yvonne suggested to Audrey she come to Christchurch for a holiday in the hope that they could eventually persuade her to move near them. Moore knew that if she was based in Christchurch, every time he was home there was a chance he'd get to see her. Audrey clearly wasn't well and had to take daily medicine for her heart so Moore hoped being around him and Yvonne would help her health.

But Audrey's few weeks in Christchurch were a struggle. To cheer her up on the evening of Saturday, 26 October Yvonne cooked the three of them an old-fashioned roast pork dinner, with roast vegetables, apple sauce, gravy and plenty of crackling.

Audrey enjoyed the meal, particularly the crackling, and went off to bed early. Soon afterwards came cries of pain from her bedroom. Moore immediately called 111 and an ambulance arrived within minutes. Audrey was having problems with her heart so everyone agreed to take her to Christchurch Hospital. Moore and Yvonne followed in their car.

Not long after departing Dormer Street, as they were travelling along Papanui Road, the ambulance suddenly pulled over.

One of Moore's last memories of his mother is seeing the ambulance rocking back and forth as they urgently tried to revive Audrey. She'd had a massive heart attack in the back of the ambulance and they didn't have a defibrillator.

Moore felt guilty for many years afterwards that he wasn't with her at the end when she most needed him. They later discovered that she hadn't taken her medicine that day.

A number of local Labour people turned out for the funeral in Christchurch to support the couple and it helped them cope.

Moore returned to Parliament after Audrey's death a quiet man. The goings-on in caucus often seemed irrelevant, he thought, compared with what was going on in the real world for real people.

While Labour was being introspective, a new world order continued taking shape among many younger New Zealanders who were increasingly uncomfortable with National's stance on foreign policy matters.

Labour had a history of independent non-aligned foreign policy thinking as evidenced by its stand on the Vietnam War and French nuclear testing in the Pacific. In fact, Labour's stands attracted many to the party.

Muldoon's decision to allow the New Zealand Rugby Football Union to invite apartheid South Africa to tour the country with the Springboks in 1981 created a rallying cry for Labour.

But for Moore and Labour's caucus it created angst. Everyone was firmly anti-tour, but they realised it would split the country, particularly the provincial towns that loved their rugby and which Labour needed to win the general election that year.

The tour brought out the worst in some New Zealanders and Moore hated how Muldoon had deliberately divided the country into pro- and anti-tour factions, setting workplaces, maraes, schools, congregations, families and even rugby club members against one another.

But it enabled Muldoon to squeak home in 1981 with 47 seats to

Labour's 43 and Social Credit's two. Interestingly, Labour again won the popular vote, getting 39 per cent of those who voted, compared with National's 38.8 per cent.

Social Credit's showing of 20.7 per cent (it had reached 30 per cent in popularity after the East Coast Bays by-election) ensured Labour didn't win some seats it expected. In all, 15 seats out of a Parliament of 92 were decided by majorities of fewer than 1000 votes.

In Papanui, Moore easily beat his National opponent Brian Keeley, the Northlands Shopping Centre manager who like him had left school young and done a variety of jobs, by more than 4400 votes. Moore pulled in a massive 55.4 per cent of the vote, up 2.5 per cent on the previous election. But even in Papanui, Social Credit had a strong showing — more than 2000 votes or more than 10 per cent of the vote.

Despite the nationwide sentiment and some predictions, Labour had lost again. While many put it down to the wily Muldoon, the Springboks tour or the rise of Social Credit, the fish-and-chip brigade and their supporters in caucus blamed it on a moribund Labour that lacked ideas and courage.

Moore believed that Labour had done a reasonable job at opposing Muldoon and National, but what they were proposing was little different from the past. An Opposition can't 'depose' a government unless it does the 'oppose' and the 'propose' right.

Eyes once again gazed at Rowling.

On the hustings Rowling struggled to foot it again with the quick-witted and abrasive Muldoon. He came across as sincere and caring, but New Zealanders didn't want their school teacher to be their prime minister. They wanted to be led and inspired.

Moore was becoming increasingly confident as an MP. Having won his first re-election convincingly and locking himself into his seat as a 'local', he looked to expand his interests and influence.

He had been looking at the Closer Economic Relationship (CER) agreement National wanted to sign with Australia and was keen to create a campaign against it, copying the British Labour Party's one against the Conservatives with Britain joining the European Economic Community.

Rowling didn't like the idea, let alone Moore running it, so the idea died.

But it made Moore look more closely at CER and it quickly dawned on him that it was, in fact, a great trade agreement with enormous potential for the country.

He soon realised that New Zealand was languishing economically because it was propping up dying industries with the taxes of workers to the benefit of a small group of industrialists who, in turned, kept the National Party going.

In the previous 20 years, Moore discovered that New Zealand's economy had grown by 29 per cent, while Japan's growth was almost 240 per cent, France's more than 90 per cent and Australia's 60 per cent. From being third in the world in 1965, New Zealand's GDP per head of population had slid to near the bottom of the OECD rankings.

Moore was so sure that CER was taking the country in the right direction he wrote a paper about it for the party's 1982 conference. In what some considered a prelude to a future approach to the economy, he wrote: 'CER is as important to New Zealand as the first smack given to a new born baby; it might hurt but the shock gets the system going and the pain is soon forgotten.'

But the conference rejected Moore's paper. He was talking about new economic thinking to a Labour Party still locked into debates about redistribution of wealth rather than how to create it.

Regardless, Moore's reading and thinking helped him come to the conclusion that as well as being the bully everyone knew, Muldoon had managed to bluff many businesspeople, journalists and even working people into thinking he had the economy under control.

Moore equally believed, though, that Labour in 1981 had let the country down by not exposing Muldoon with a better alternative.

He again put pen to paper to map out some economic thoughts, intertwining free trade, foreign policy and environmentalism, which he published in 1982 in conjunction with the University of the South Pacific in Suva.

'A Pacific Parliament — a political and economic community for the South Pacific' teased out some regional issues still being debated today.

The economic survival of the Pacific's smallest states, development aid, the implications of the Law of the Sea on ocean minerals and fisheries, France's then nuclear testing, the labour market, coping with multinationals and the spreading of the benefits of technology, the impact of CER, the superpower rivalries and the potential for a strong international Pacific regional block were covered.

Moore had been inspired by Norm Kirk's work in helping establish the South Pacific Forum and his desire for a Pacific Council that had been included in Labour's 1969 general election manifesto. He was also watching closely the rapid growth of the EEC half a world away.

He saw huge economic opportunities for the island nations if they could get the right investment and training to create industries. Otherwise, he was afraid those nations would be exploited by developed countries taking advantage of their fisheries and tourism potential.

He believed New Zealand and Australia should consider widening CER to include Pacific nations in a broader free trade zone. New Zealand and Australia had more in common with the Pacific than Wales and Italy did with the EEC.

Moore saw fighting for the Pacific as part of Labour's historical interest in the region going back to its first leader Harry Holland who took a mission of MPs to Samoa to investigate the bloodshed from New Zealand troops putting down the Mau movement in 1929.

Holland's stand for Samoans was unpopular in New Zealand, which saw itself then as a colonial outpost of Britain and here to oppose any independence movements.

Moore promoted the idea of a Pacific Parliament, made up of representatives from each country, to allow the region to tackle its economic, political, environmental and security issues together.

Like many on the left, Moore was influenced by the Scandinavian progressive movement. So, he proposed that the Pacific Parliament have a permanent headquarters or rotate around various member capitals like the Nordic Council, which only met one week a year with committees working throughout.

Many of Moore's colleagues were pleased he was stretching out in the policy arena, but few read his book. Their attention was diverted by issues around Labour's leadership.

The 'fish-and-chip brigade' was still at work and others joined in.

From mid to late 1982 Lange, Bassett, Heretaunga MP Bill Jeffries and Moore would have an hour-long conference call every Sunday morning where they'd discuss how they were persuading their colleagues in Auckland, Wellington and Christchurch to roll Rowling.

Rowling had had three attempts to beat Muldoon. The opinion polls and caucus unhappiness were too difficult for him to ignore or fight against any more.

So, in a specially called caucus on the last sitting day of the year on 17 December 1982 he announced he wouldn't seek the leadership in the scheduled caucus ballot in February 1983.

Over the Christmas break Tizard expressed an interest in the leadership, as did Moyle. In the end only Marshall, an old supporter of Rowling's, put himself forward against Lange, but it was no contest, 33 votes to nine.

Moore was keen to put himself forward to be deputy. He was a Lange supporter but being a member of the 'fish-and-chip brigade' hurt him. He was seen as a plotter and polarising, and not someone with the popularity among the Rowling supporters to help pull the caucus back together again. He was brash and flamboyant.

His main competitor for the role, Palmer, was seen as solid and boring, and a good contrast to Lange's style.

Nevertheless, Moore still wanted it. The original anti-Lange MPs saw the deputy's contest as a way to stay relevant and rallied their support behind Ann Hercus. Moore won the first ballot 20 votes to Palmer's 14 and Hercus's 9. With no outright majority, however, the vote went to a second round with Hercus having to drop out.

It's thought that Douglas strategically voted for Palmer in the first round because he was afraid Hercus would come second, kicking him out of the contest and creating a genuine chance for her to win.

With Hercus dropping out, her supporters pledged their votes to Palmer, and Douglas voted for Moore. Palmer ended up winning 22 to 21.

Moore likes to think Lange was honourable throughout the process, although rumours circulated that some kind of deal had been struck between the new and outgoing leader over Palmer who was favoured by Rowling.

Moore was again disappointed that a group of his colleagues had thwarted his ambitions. In a *New Zealand Listener* interview three months later, he admitted that his reputation sometimes got in the way.

'Yeah, there are people who fear me, say I'm dangerous,' he told the *Listener*.

'I'm far too impatient. I polarise. I offend people and I'm a fear object. There are people who worry about me. When people talk about me, they talk of street gutters but I don't mind that. I don't mind sticking my bloody arm down the drain hole, ripping it up to get the water moving.'

Moore was still making a favourable impression with some. *National Business Review* columnist Colin James described him as 'a restless bounding scallywag . . . a street kid of politics with as acute an instinct for how to work the machine and work over the customers as any, save the prime minister himself. He annoys, angers and delights. In a grey world he glows — and, red or green, glow is glow.'

Moore's disappointment was tempered with the fact that Labour finally had a leadership combination that could win a general election.

He admired Palmer for the disciplined approach he had to tasks and the methodical way he dealt with issues.

A deep thinker about the law and the institutions required to run a democracy, Moore knew Palmer would make a strong foil to Lange's entertaining style and be someone who would be invaluable carrying the heavy workload of government. He was the nerd that every gang had to have.

In exchange for missing out Moore demanded, and got, the number three spot on the front bench with responsibilities for overseas trade, sports and recreation, and tourism. Outside the leader and deputy, he was now the most powerful person in caucus.

It was around this time that Moore would meet a 14-year-old high school student from Christchurch who would have a profound impact on the lives of him and Yvonne.

Clayton Cosgrove was a fourth-form student at St Bede's College and was curious about some issues of the day that he was looking at in his social studies class. Cosgrove's father had met Moore a number of times through his work at the Waimari County Council and suggested his son make an appointment to pick the brains of the MP.

They met at one of Moore's Saturday-morning electorate clinics at the Bishopdale Creche and talked about current issues. Cosgrove was invited back to Moore's house that afternoon to meet some local Labour members and later signed up as a party member.

Cosgrove was a weekday boarder at St Bede's so had to jump over the closed school gates in the evenings to go to local party meetings in Papanui. Within a year he became chair of the Redwood branch.

Cosgrove was studious and serious, wearing a jacket and tie to party conferences and writing reports about them. He didn't bother with Labour Youth and much preferred the company of Moore and his team, who treated him as an adult, in the hands-on of campaigning. He was like a sponge, sucking up political knowledge.

He would spend many hours with Moore and Yvonne at their home helping draw up campaigns and plans. Moore was impressed by his enthusiasm, hard work and loyalty. Before long he would tell people — and no one knew if he was serious or joking — that Cosgrove would be his successor.

In Parliament under Lange's leadership, Moore and the new team were energised and enjoyed attacking and undermining an increasingly tired Muldoon and National Government.

Moore's organisational skills were put to use now across the caucus and party. Lange gave him free rein.

As a result, he spent a lot of time in Australia with state Labor Governments in New South Wales, Victoria, South Australia and Western Australia, as well as new Australian Labor Prime Minister Bob Hawke and his team who had successfully won a snap election in March 1983.

The Australian Labor Party was campaigning and conducting its politics at another level of sophistication.

Moore had some key thoughts about what the New Zealand Labour Party had to do.

The two most important people in the team, he believed, had to be the leader and the finance spokesperson. Without their credibility with voters, nothing would happen. Voters had to have confidence that their house and savings would be safe and that they had the right recipe for economic prosperity.

The Australians talked a lot about 'inevitability' and 'natural party of government'. Voters needed to feel that it was inevitable that Labour would win the next election and that it wasn't abnormal for them to be in charge; they were the natural party of government.

To assist those themes Moore set up a Committee of Transition, which would plan for Labour moving into government smoothly, and a Wednesday Club. The club would invite business, union, news media and diplomatic leaders to discuss issues with the caucus.

Again, it would give key influencers the view that Labour was ready for government and help break down any traditional barriers some of them might have had with the party.

Meantime, Moore's economic and trade thinking developed further as the party approached the 1984 general election. Moore, along with Douglas, Prebble and Lange, was already thinking about how a tiny nation at the bottom of the Pacific could sustain itself in a world that was rapidly trading with each other.

But he was concerned many within the party were being left behind by some of caucus's thinking. So, Moore wrote another book and it was published in early 1984: *The Added Value Economy — New Zealand's trading future: a negotiated economy based on manufacturing, adding value, further processing and tourism*.

It was based on his thinking after reading the 1980 Brandt Report on North–South issues, which argued that the best way for Third World nations to develop was not through aid but by boosting their productivity, and the Commonwealth Secretariat's report 'Protectionism — threat to international order'.

Moore argued for a fresh and radical new direction for New Zealand. Moore believed that adding value to commodities — processing, rather than raw materials — and the tourism industry were a practical alternative to Muldoon's 'Think Big' policies which required huge public borrowings.

New Zealand in the mid-1980s was in an economic and social malaise. There were regular nationwide strikes and Moore argued for a 'negotiated economy' — where bosses and workers would agree together on wages and economic output — as a way out.

This was something being successfully progressed in some northern European nations, was being openly talked about in the Australian Labor Party but wasn't gaining much traction with Moore's colleagues. Douglas humoured him about it but was focused on other macroeconomic ideas.

It would take him six more years to convince — or rather bludgeon — his colleagues into agreeing to pursue the idea.

The pragmatist and collectivist in Moore also radically for the time promoted the idea that New Zealand needed a global marketing strategy — a simple brand to present to the world to attract the growing numbers of middle-class travellers flying on quicker and more sophisticated aircraft to our part of the world.

Moore also became increasingly interested in foreign affairs as he looked at New Zealand's trading and political future under the then constructs of international trade: the EEC, CER and the General Agreement on Tariffs and Trade (GATT).

For the first time in his political career Moore felt on top of everything. The leader and front bench were working in unison, his seat was solidly his, he was allowed to use his campaigning skills across the party, and he was clear in his mind what needed to be done to fix the country.

6

The Madman Fraser file

'Muldoon couldn't put a budget together. He couldn't make it work and I think he was looking for an excuse to go to the country.

'He got himself into such a mess around Richard Prebble's anti-nuclear legislation and everything else that was going on in the economy. You could just feel the pressure building up on the government.

'While I was always anti-nuclear, I wasn't sure we needed legislation — it could simply be the policy of the Labour Government. I was afraid that once we made it law that eventually the Nats would have to agree to it and then we'd lose our leverage against them at elections.

'The snap election was great for us. We didn't have to spend weeks negotiating with Jim Anderton for things. Once it's on the party president is irrelevant.

'Lange said did I mind not being called campaign manager? He said the executive of the party didn't want me as campaign manager. I bet it wasn't. I bet it was Anderton.

'I said: "I don't give a stuff what you call me. When we win I certainly won't be recognised."

'I suggested Joe Walding be the minder for Lange. Joe was a good guy. I could talk honestly to him and Lange respected him, and it wouldn't be coming from me. Joe could talk to him. Lange didn't need saving. He was bloody good. Joe's job was to get Lange to bed every night. Lange enjoyed the company of people. I couldn't do it because I would end up agitating Lange.

'People were overwhelmingly in support of David. He was very good. And you could write stuff and he'd ignore it for a month and then suddenly he'd bring it out.

'In the Muldoon practice debate with Lange I played Muldoon because I'd spent my career attacking him. We tried attacking Muldoon, we tried everything. But we never said we loved him. Lange just put his arms around Muldoon in the debate and it stuffed him. We had thought it all through.

'Geoffrey Palmer was a significant figure with Lange. Palmer wrote the manifesto. It was vague because it was Geoffrey being Geoffrey. There's no big conspiracy there.

'I knew Roger Douglas had been thinking of radical change for some time. But I didn't know how tough things would be when we won. I thought we'd do things over a six-year period.

'In the middle of an election campaign you don't feel as much of it as you should but there was a mood for change. The money came in, party membership was huge, volunteers kept turning up you'd never seen before. That's when you know you're going to win.

'Right after we won and we met at the DB Mangere hotel, it was probably when I was at the peak of my power. Lange, Palmer, Douglas and me. Treasury wanted to see us before the markets opened on the Monday. We didn't realise the extent of the problems. We then realised Muldoon had had no choice but to call a snap election — that's what it really was all about. It was none of the stuff about controlling the House.

'Muldoon was playing silly games and I was helping David deal with him. I was listening to Muldoon on the other phone and whispering to David. Muldoon was already trying to trip us up for the next election. It wasn't so much about not wanting to give up power but about creating an even bigger mess for us to give himself the best chance of a comeback at the next election. That's how cynical he was.

'Jim McClay and some other brave senior Nats fronted Muldoon and that helped in the end.

'We didn't realise how much shit the country was in. Treasury and the Reserve Bank were very open with us. All these government entities had huge off-balance-sheet debts. The coalmines, for example, had more debt than income. It was costing a couple of hundred thousand dollars a job. You can't keep doing that.

'But we were so excited by the challenge, to be ministers. You'd go to sleep at night, a pile of papers by the side of the bed.

'As time went on Douglas got stronger, Prebble got stronger, Caygill was always strong. And I was edged out. As overseas trade minister I was always travelling and missed the conversations and nuances of what was going on.

'As the government went on I had less and less influence. I had my ties back into the party, but they were also fast disappearing. Helen and Anderton were taking over the party. I didn't realise it at the time.

'Bob Hawke was helpful to us as we clumsily navigated the anti-nuclear issue. At one point before the campaign started, we got Lange to talk to Hawke. I'd already spoken to him.

'I believed on the nuclear issue that the public don't mind you telling the Americans to get stuffed. In fact, they quite like it. But I believed you couldn't tell the Australians to get stuffed because it's a different relationship. We'd end up having no place to send our troops or have our ships dock. And if Hawke had shifted it could have been all over for us. Hawke was a good friend to New Zealand during that period and I like to think my good relationship with him helped.

'I was opposed to David going to speak at the Oxford Union because the risks were immense. I thought it cheapened our anti-nuclear stance. I thought we'd piss off the Americans, but of course there are a lot of votes in pissing people off. But he did bloody well. I was wrong. He was very good David then. I was so proud of him.

'The first term everything seemed to be going well. In Cabinet we'd start by telling jokes, getting lines for Lange's press conferences later. It was the best-natured Cabinet in the world. We roared with laughter all the time. He was very orderly too. He was very gifted.

'Douglas had spent many years thinking about things in his own mind. He had a top team around him in Prebble and Caygill. But we kept saying to him tell us so we can explain it to the people.

'Everyone felt as though they were being railroaded into decisions. But what was the alternative? Borrow another billion?

'I was treated well by Douglas. He gave me money for tourism and the trade development board. I think he tried to keep me out of his and everyone else's hair.

'I had a great office of political staff and wonderfully smart and hard-working public servants like Gray Nelson and Andy Anderton who constantly saved me from myself.

'The job meant I met some fabulous New Zealanders. The guy I really admired was Tom Clark who was involved in the round-the-world yacht races. I said to him: "Let's have a go for the America's Cup." He said: "Don't be stupid. We can never win that."

'A week later he comes to my office and says I'm not up to it, but there's a guy with balls like an elephant, he doesn't know the difference between a yacht and a yak, and he's outside — Michael Fay. He comes in and I say: "Michael, no f-king money." He says: "I don't want your f-king money." I said: "Good, we can now talk."

'In the end we put in a couple of hundred thousand to help promote New Zealand through the event in Fremantle. Fancy that, the government and the private sector working together.

'After 1987 I also wanted to be minister of science, defence and fisheries.

'Phil Goff came up to my office and asked what was happening about the Cabinet positions. So we went next door to Palmer's and we had to barge our way into his office. Who should be there with him but Roger Douglas and a Treasury official with cards on a table working out the Cabinet.

'I only ended up with trade. I took it as a deep personal insult. Whether it was Palmer settling old scores I don't know. So I deliberately kept away after that.

'I was kind of in denial about David and Roger's relationship breaking down. Denial is a thing I do quite well. It's a product of my upbringing, I think. I just didn't believe it would happen. I just thought things would get better, David would pick it up.

'I deeply believed at the time we could get them together again. But the relationship had snapped. I thought it was more personal than policy differences between David and Roger.

'We could have held it together, but it would have required David behaving like a prime minister.

'I used to think David was a better person than all of us. He was a practising Methodist and the rest of us were grubby politicians. I felt so let down in the end. I realised that everyone is, in fact, fallible.

'David didn't make it easy for himself with some of us. At one stage there was a no-confidence vote in David and I got him some votes. I told him he had my support but not my respect.

'Now I blame myself for spending so much time away as overseas trade minister. David needed friends but he also needed to say: "I accept you as a friend." He was actually a lonely guy.

'I never had an explicit conversation with David and asked to help him. I should have. Looking back, I should have spent time with him. I should have forced my way in, dominated the situation and asked him if I could help.

'One or two approached me saying we needed to move Lange on. I said: "No, no, I'm with David." People voted for David to be PM and Roger to be minister of finance. The people were right.

'Before the vote for the leadership Geoffrey came to see me. He said: "People think I'm a gentleman but I'm not. People don't think you're a gentleman, but you are. Tomorrow I shall be prime minister." I said: "That may be true, Geoffrey, but in just over 12 months I'll be leader of the Opposition."

'People like Bob Tizard were standing down and wanted to keep their cars and ministerial houses, even though they were retiring, in exchange for their votes for the leadership. I said, "No way."

'I also didn't work the Cabinet or caucus well. Many of the critical people in Cabinet lived in Auckland and I lived in Christchurch so because of the travel thing I didn't spend much time with them.

'I'm quite a private person and can be a bit of a loner. You can be a public recluse, you know. You can be public in your job and then go home and close your door.

'I didn't feel inferior, but I wasn't like many of them. I was from Northland. I didn't go to a flash school.

'My response was often to go to a meeting and try to control it and get things done quickly. I think I was too transactional as a politician. I couldn't be bothered with long-winded processes. Then I'd go home and shut everything off. I compartmentalised things. That's just how I operated.

'Probably why I go so hard is I feel mortal. You only have a short period of time — you have to go for it. When you've had cancer it just hangs over you the whole time. It's a disease that just keeps coming after you until you give up.

'I think I have good antennae for people and reading situations. I understood the public more than many of my colleagues. I was more like the public than they were. I'm basically very ordinary. My tastes are pretty ordinary. I like ordinary things. I like ordinary people. Maybe that's why some in the party didn't like me.'

****

Muldoon's National Government was having another horror month in June 1984 trying to keep its one-vote majority. The economy spluttered along and there was front-page news that the price of a loaf of bread was about to go up 10 cents.

Auckland Central MP Richard Prebble's Nuclear Free New Zealand Bill to ban nuclear ships from the country looked like it might get introduced to Parliament, with National MPs Marilyn Waring and Mike Minogue possibly crossing the floor to vote with Labour.

On 13 June the government narrowly defeated the Bill 40 votes to 39. While Waring and Minogue did indeed cross the floor, two former Labour MPs who were now independents, Brian MacDonell from Dunedin Central and John Kirk from Sydenham, voted with the government.

While Waring had promised her vote to National on confidence and supply and would only vote against it on disarmament and rape legislation, some felt that Muldoon was about to lose grip of the government.

Governor General Sir David Beattie was hosting a function at Government House in Wellington the next night, 14 June, for news media executives and some MPs. Moore had the opportunity to attend as well and while it was a cold but fine night and much as he enjoyed the company of Beattie — a Dilworth boy who had battled his way up through the law — paperwork kept him in his parliamentary office.

Labour MPs started hearing in the House at about 10 pm that National was having a special caucus after Parliament rose at 10.30 pm. Word quickly went out to the Labour MPs not to go home after the bells went but to head up to Lange's office.

Lange had popped his head into Moore's office to tell him. Moore immediately thought the special caucus was about one of four scenarios — either Muldoon was being rolled as prime minister, a Cabinet reshuffle because of some dissension, a devaluation of the dollar because the economy was further in trouble than people thought, or they were going to call a snap election. Moore yelled and laughed, punching the air.

He reached behind his desk for a special folder he had on his shelf called 'The Madman Fraser' file. It was named after former Australian Prime Minister Malcolm Fraser who called a snap election trying to catch new leader Bob Hawke and the Australian Labor Party off guard in March 1983.

Moore had prepared a snap election campaign playbook in the highly unlikely case Muldoon was stupid enough to copy Fraser's mad idea.

Muldoon had given the country and Labour only four weeks to get ready. But Moore saw this as an advantage. For one thing, it would mean he had an excuse to bypass Labour's bureaucratic approval processes at election time and just get on with campaigning.

Moore was the campaign manager but not in name. Party President Jim Anderton had named Richard Prebble and Sir Wallace Rowling (Bill had been knighted in 1983) to head a campaign team in Parliament. Moore was too busy to be fussed with all the nonsense going on about positions and titles.

Within 24 hours he'd called his old Eden electorate campaigner and friend Mike Rann in Adelaide who was working for South Australian Labor Premier John Bannon as his press secretary and speech writer. Moore had known Bannon well and Rann was given time off to help Moore along with fellow expatriate New Zealander Don Mackay who was also working in the South Australian Government.

The pair were based in Moore's parliamentary office, along with typists on shifts, for the campaign working on strategy, debate briefings, speeches, press releases and direct mail.

Fish-and-chip paper, burger wrappings, soft-drink cans and beer bottles quickly littered the office. But they kept a low profile because there was resentment among some in the caucus about 'Mike Moore's Aussie Mafia'.

The tensions in the campaign came to a head late in the day before Labour's official campaign launch at the Christchurch Town Hall. The event, which would be in front of 3000 supporters, was due to be televised live for half an hour.

Moore was shown a draft of Lange's speech. It was well written and clever but way off strategy. Its recurring theme was that election day was being held on the anniversary of Bastille Day, on 14 July, and talked about a 'revolution' in New Zealand.

Labour's strategy was supposed to be about 'bringing New Zealand together', not a 'revolution'. New Zealanders wanted unity not more divisions after nine years of a polarising Muldoon Government. But there were those in the campaign who didn't want the speech touched.

Moore and Rann took a copy to talk over with Lange, who simply handed it back and told them to rewrite it. He wasn't being decisive; he just wanted to avoid a fight among the team and having to adjudicate.

Rann worked on the speech until the early hours of launch day, adding material from Hawke's unity messages from his 1983 election and from Bannon's 1982 'we want South Australia to win' campaign.

The 'bringing New Zealand together' and 'let's make New Zealand win' messaging fitted in well with Labour's campaign commercial, which had the hit song 'Up Where We Belong' sung by Joe Cocker and Jennifer Warnes and that featured after Lange's speech.

Moore and Rann gave Lange the speech the next morning and he delivered it brilliantly. The news media gushed afterwards that the unity message struck the right note.

Decades later, in 2005, the *New Zealand Herald* described it as 'a piece of political theatre unmatched in New Zealand before or since'. 'His theme — ironically, it would turn out — was about bringing the country together dispelling the nastiness of the Muldoon years and returning to the politics of consensus. It was a message borrowed wholesale from the Australian Labor Party's successful campaign the previous year.'

Instead of dealing to the tensions, the successful campaign speech only added to them. The party had set up a committee to vet all written materials. The committee objected to one of Rann's direct mail-outs from Lange that said 'We want New Zealand to win', saying it should be changed to 'We want Labour to win'. They also objected to phrases like 'young couples seeking home ownership'.

The committee thought they were all strategists and writers and Rann was becoming exasperated. Moore told him to agree with the committee, ignore them and then put the materials out anyway. There was just no time in the campaign for this nonsense.

The use by Labour of targeted issues in focused direct mail was similar to that trialled by Moore in his Eden campaign in 1972. It was sophisticated and ahead of its time and was adopted later by Labor in South Australia in 1985 and by Hawke's 1987 campaign where it was decisive in winning marginal seats.

Labour won 56 of the 95 seats with almost 43 per cent of the vote, while National lost 10 seats to finish on 37 and just under 36 per cent.

Social Credit won two seats again, but Bob Jones's New Zealand Party, which pulled in more than 12 per cent of the vote and what was thought to be many National voters, finished seat-less.

Incredibly, almost 94 per cent of those registered to vote turned out.

Election night was a blur of excitement and emotional intoxication for Moore. He felt a sense of relief that Labour had finally been able to topple not so much National but Muldoon, whose malevolent spirit seemed to have invaded every pore of New Zealand.

It was as though a suffocating blanket had been lifted and Moore's generation could finally gasp a life-saving breath. The comprehensive victory swept Moore, his colleagues, Labour and the country away.

New Zealand felt like a divided country: rural–urban, rich–poor, white collar–blue collar. While Labour's campaign slogan of 'Bringing New Zealand together' correctly captured the sentiment most in the country wanted, the crisis the incoming government was to face would severely test that.

It was the post-party hangover few expected and one that no single pill-like policy would instantly cure.

One week after the stunning 14 July 1984 Labour victory, *The Economist* magazine probably best summed up what the fourth Labour Government had inherited:

'In a country with 3.2 million people and 70 million sheep, [Muldoon's] slogan was "Think Big". Sir Robert preferred to borrow abroad rather than devalue, saddling New Zealand with foreign debts equal to 45 per cent of its GDP, proportionally more than Brazil has.

'Since Sir Robert became prime minister in 1975, New Zealand's GDP has grown by only 0.75 per cent a year, the slowest of the 24 countries belonging to the Organisation for Economic Cooperation and Development (OECD).

'New Zealanders can count themselves lucky they were rich to begin with. If theirs had been a developing country, the Muldoon treatment would have made it one of the world's disasters.

'Like those Third World leaders who have fouled up their economies, Sir Robert was fond of dismissing criticism by claiming he was "on the side of the people". The people have now had their say. Other populists please note.'

Within a generation of enjoying the highest living standards in the world, New Zealand was almost at the bottom of the OECD table. Employers and their employees already knew that, and they had become locked in a death spiral of regularly increasing costs and regularly demanding wage rises. Many of the economic and political arguments of the time fundamentally revolved around this tension.

The principle and idealism of the new government had to be quickly tempered with desperation. The speed and breadth of the changes were staggering; they had to be. No New Zealand government has made as much change since.

The New Zealand dollar was floated, tariffs were removed, subsidies to farmers withdrawn, financial markets were deregulated, the top personal tax rate of 66 cents in the dollar and the top corporate tax rate of nearly 50 cents in the dollar were lowered to 33 cents and a goods and services tax was introduced.

The Reserve Bank of New Zealand was given statutory independence based on a contract with the governor, local bodies were abolished or amalgamated, and the public service was reformed.

The government rapidly paid down New Zealand's debt by privatisations: debt servicing was costing 19 cents in every dollar, more than New Zealand's public investment in education.

New Zealand's highly unionised waterfront was reformed to lift productivity, taking the turnaround of some ships from up to 14 days to around 30 hours.

Like many, Moore was excited to finally be in government. But he was also mindful of Kirk's view of the public service. Some thought they were the permanent government and it was the role of ministers to rubber-stamp their work.

Moore carefully selected his private staff of government department secondees and made it clear he wouldn't allow ministries to swamp him with paper or jargon. He had a giant rubber stamp made for him with the word 'bullshit' on it and he would sometimes use it on papers and send them back to ministries. His attitude annoyed many in the public service.

The success of the government, though, was down to a prime minister and minister of finance who were totally in sync with each other. Douglas and his two associates Richard Prebble and David Caygill also formed a powerful 'troika' presiding over the economy. They and the rest of the government communicated well with New Zealanders about the situation the country was in and what the prescription was.

Radical change in a short space of time is always difficult, but New Zealanders responded well to the government's clear leadership.

The country was, importantly, also enamoured with Lange. He was intelligent, urbane and quick-witted. He engendered a feeling of pride and independence among New Zealanders. At 41 years old he and his relatively young government were the generational and directional change the now maturing post-Second World War New Zealand was looking for.

The government's nuclear-free New Zealand policy and Lange's highly publicised prime-time television Oxford Union debate success in March 1985 'that all nuclear weapons are morally indefensible' filled many with pride.

Standing up to the US in the middle of the Cold War and outdebating the Reverend Jerry Falwell and young upstarts from the motherland on their own turf told the world to take notice of the country. New Zealanders were drunk with pride.

This sense of the country mapping its own course in the world was, by unfortunate circumstances, reinforced in July 1985 when Greenpeace's *Rainbow Warrior* vessel was sunk by French secret agents in Auckland, killing a crew member.

The nation was outraged when two of the agents were caught and New Zealand had to eventually do a deal with France to place them on a French atoll in the Pacific. Lange was again at his best in expressing New Zealand's fury at what it thought was a friend and ally.

Moore started taking trade missions to explore and open up markets in places New Zealand businesses normally didn't think about.

The reality was that with access to Britain diminishing and protective barriers coming off New Zealand industries, to survive many businesses would have to become successful exporters.

The news media seemed to like Moore's trade missions. He would always ensure a series of news events or announcements for them to report on to justify the expense of the trip and they often went to interesting and exotic places off the beaten track of usual ministerial visits.

The government and Moore were quickly garnering the image of being progressive and pro-business.

The Opposition National Party was in disarray. Muldoon's successor, former Attorney General Jim McLay, was continually ankle-tapped by his predecessor. In the House the young and energetic new government almost taunted the Opposition and wave upon wave of changes seemed to overwhelm them.

National struggled to create any space to get any news media attention. They were also divided about what direction to follow — a conservative Muldoon-lite approach or more free market than Labour was being. The traditionalists in their caucus were also still stuck in the pro-nuclear and pro-ANZUS paradigm, even though the electorate had clearly moved on.

Eventually McClay was rolled for the conservative former Muldoon labour minister Jim Bolger in 1986. But he, too, could make little headway.

As minister for overseas trade, Moore met and became friends with a number of New Zealand businesspeople. He admired the entrepreneurial drive of people like Lion Nathan's Douglas Myers, Aoraki Corporation founder Gil Simpson, Alex van Heeren of Huka Lodge fame, property developer Bob Jones, Fay Richwhite's Michael Fay, Ceramco's Tom Clark and Merv Bascik of Bascik Transport.

It was through Clark that Moore, as minister of sport and recreation, discussed with Fay how the government could assist with New Zealand's first America's Cup challenge, in Fremantle in 1986 and 1987.

While much of the news media and public attention was focused on the changes to the economy coming out of Wellington and the other issues that together were, in effect, an expression of nationhood, a group of New Zealanders was being left behind.

The upheaval in many industries, particularly former government agencies like forestry and railways, resulted in thousands of working men and women losing their jobs.

Farmers being weaned off supplementary minimum price subsidies also had a flow-on effect to freezing works and provincial towns. These were working-class Labour people, many of whom had been the hardest workers for and loudest celebrators of the change in government only a few years earlier.

While many in the cities enjoyed the new-found freedoms in the economy and there was an air of optimism and excitement about the direction New Zealand was going, Moore started becoming concerned about the impact of all the changes on Labour people from around 1986.

As overseas trade minister he was often out of the country and he was becoming consumed with the GATT Uruguay trade round and the prospect of gaining better international access for New Zealand agricultural exporters.

But he had an inkling that the transition from the old to the new economy wasn't going as well as everyone had thought. Yvonne would relay stories to him from constituents, friends and family.

The trade union leaders and captains of industry he took with him on his trade missions also told him everything wasn't as rosy at home as the news media, some of his ministerial colleagues and popular culture was making out.

Nevertheless, Labour was riding high in the polls. A New Zealand Herald-NRB poll in June 1987, just after the Budget, had Labour at a record high of 57 per cent and National at 39 per cent.

Focus group research by Labour was also saying their popularity was almost unassailable and that they could become the natural party of government. Not since Michael Joseph Savage, some 50 years earlier, had Labour been in such a position. For Moore the thought was intoxicating.

Labour's 1987 election campaign was a slick series of photo opportunities that Lange handled well and seemed to enjoy. Bolger was completely out of his depth in dealing with the prime minister and had formulaic rallies reminiscent of a Broadway show including Lockwood Smith singing.

The shadow of cancer was always close to Moore's life and touched the couple again earlier that year. On a trade mission to South America he and Yvonne had to rush home early because brother Kerry's oldest son, their nephew, 21-year-old Christopher, had a turn for the worse in his year-long battle with cancer which had spread to his lymphatic system.

Moore had spent many hours talking with the young man since he was diagnosed with testicular cancer. He tried to give him strength and take away any fears he might have. It was the same cancer as Moore's and if he could beat it, so could a younger and stronger Christopher.

As well as being able to spend the final hours with Christopher,

Moore's abiding memory of that time was breaking the news late in the evening to the trade mission members and accompanying Māori cultural group in Venezuela. The couple and the mission members parted ways with most in tears to the sound of the group singing a Māori hymn.

The couple were deeply hurt to read about Christopher's cancer in the newspapers upon their arrival back in New Zealand, as they thought there was an agreement with the trade mission that everyone would keep the matter private.

While Labour was cruising through the 1987 election, Moore and Yvonne were blindsided locally by some nastiness that hurt them deeply.

At one of his street-corner meetings in Christchurch North a man started abusing the couple. Moore had dealt with many hecklers in the past and it was never an issue for him. Usually a quick comeback line or humour defused a situation or sent the perpetrator scurrying. The heckler accused Moore of being gay, saying his marriage was a sham and it was evidenced by the fact the two didn't have children.

Moore's infertility caused by his cancer treatment had never been a political issue for the couple. His opponents had never used it as a weapon. The two had thought it was obvious why they were childless. But the incident did bring back some regrets they had at the time of his second bout of cancer about not having children shortly after they were married in 1975.

But back then, like now, their lives were hectic. He was a new MP trying to be re-elected and very shortly afterwards was unemployed and she was in teachers training college and young. Being a Cabinet minister and having a media career made their lives even more hectic now so, while a nice thought, adoption was also out of the question.

It was a strange election in Christchurch with Moore and Yvonne also involved in a scuffle with two men delivering leaflets in the electorate that claimed he was 'a communist and a Trotskyite'. Phoney Labour leaflets were also delivered in Geoffrey Palmer's electorate.

Moore easily won Christchurch North again in 1987. While his majority had dropped about 1000 votes from 1984 to around 4700, his percentage of the votes cast went up 3 per cent to almost 60 per cent.

Moore scoured the Sunday papers after the general election. There were photos of Lange and Douglas arm in arm celebrating at the historic Metro Theatre in Mangere. While many around Moore and in the government were ecstatic at the scale of the victory — it was, after all, the first time since 1938 that Labour had been re-elected to a second term — a few local results and numbers stood out for him and caused concern.

While Labour had retained its 17-seat majority over National it wasn't as popular as it thought. Labour's vote had gone up by 5 per cent to 48 per cent in 1987, while National's had gone up 8.5 per cent to 44 per cent. The Democrats, the remnants of the Social Credit Party, got more than 5.7 per cent and came second in five electorates (including the two seats they lost to National).

Interestingly for Moore, Labour almost won the blue-ribbon Auckland seat of Remuera. Incumbent Doug Graham beat Labour's Judith Tizard, who had Roger Douglas campaigning with her, only by about 400 votes. Similarly, in the National stronghold of Fendalton in Christchurch, Philip Burdon only beat Labour's Neil Cherry by some 310 votes.

More of a surprise was that in Manawatu left-wing Labour candidate David Robinson managed to unseat three-term incumbent National MP Michael Cox by just over 130 votes.

While Labour had increased its vote in the marginals, it had lost votes in its traditionally safe seats. Labour voters had stayed home.

The party had selected a number of trade union candidates for the 1987 election — Sonja Davies in Pencarrow, Graham Kelly in Porirua, Liz Tennet in Island Bay, Larry Sutherland in Avon and Ross Robertson in Papatoetoe — in the hope of swaying the government to deliver social policies as a pay-off for the economic sacrifices of many of its supporters in the first term. Moore agreed with their view.

The warning signs were there that a clash was looming, but most were enthralled by Labour's re-election.

But bigger forces were to intervene. In a little more than nine weeks all governments around the world were to be sideswiped by the 1987 sharemarket crash. By the end of February 1988 New Zealand's market had fallen almost 60 per cent from its peak, wiping billions of dollars in savings and plunging the economy into recession. So deep was the impact that it took until 2018 for the New Zealand sharemarket to return to its 1987 highs.

Moore and many others in Cabinet immediately understood that the second term of the government was going to be about carefully managing the country's books in the hope of having any chance at the 1990 election. They were unlikely to get away with more major reform.

Yet within weeks, on 4 December, Douglas and his officials had a memo go to Cabinet proposing not a battening down of the hatches but even more change, a radical levelling of the tax playing field. Douglas had been talking about flat taxes earlier in the year.

'There is a growing sense of malaise that we have lost our way, and are not committed to continuing structural economic reform,' the memo said.

'Anyone in regular contact with businesspeople will corroborate that. But the quid pro quo for both our re-election and for current economic policy is that we must keep going forward.

'The electorate has accepted that stopping the process now is equivalent to going back. We risk never seeing the full benefits of change if we do so.'

Moore was sceptical. He'd read Douglas's book *Towards Prosperity* which had come out just before the election and which challenged the welfare state Labour had created some 50 years earlier.

He also always hated papers coming from the bureaucracy at the last minute that appeared to be rushing him into a decision.

Post-election Moore was more interested in pushing for even stronger CER with Australia. He thought it had a lot more merit than Cabinet was giving it and could help counter the negative sentiment after the crash.

By extending the 1983 CER agreement New Zealand businesses would have access to Australia's 15 million consumers as though they were a domestic market. He thought being more exposed to the Australian economy would make New Zealand businesses sturdier which would grow them for even tougher markets overseas.

On 14 December Cabinet agreed to support a flat rate of income tax and to create a Guaranteed Minimum Family Income (GMFI) via tax credits to encourage the working poor to stay employed rather than opt for unemployment benefits.

Lange and Minister of Social Welfare Michael Cullen weren't convinced and questioned it. Moore had earlier expressed unease about the flat taxes at a Cabinet committee because he believed that flattening of the tax structure benefitted those on higher incomes who could afford to pay more.

Dangerously, he thought, it could lead to a lower overall tax take which would put pressure on publicly funded services like health and education. That, in turn, could undermine social provision and lead to the privatisation of services Labour always saw as critical to an egalitarian New Zealand. User charges would eventually be introduced.

Moore — and some others in the Cabinet — saw the flat tax as possibly a first and very dangerous step away from government provision of health and education.

But Moore found himself in a bind. He strongly believed in Cabinet collective responsibility and while there hadn't been a vote, most seemed to agree to the package, which was to be announced three days later as a statement of principle without specifics while the detail was still being worked on by officials.

He was comforted by the fact that he thought it didn't lock the government into having such an initiative — more work was needed before a final decision was made. It was a complicated package that few ministers or officials were across and wanted teased out further by Cabinet's finance committee.

The flat tax and GMFI were to be part of a series of other major announcements including a phased removal of tariffs, deregulation of telecommunications and local government amalgamations. The fourth Labour Government was still in a reformist mood. While generally supportive, Moore was nervous about the extent of it.

The unity of decision-making message was reinforced by Lange at the Labour caucus briefing less than two hours before the package was publicly announced on 17 December. He reminded MPs that this announcement was a collective decision that bound them all. Moore strongly agreed with that.

On stage in the Beehive Theatrette, where post-Cabinet prime ministerial press conferences and other major announcements are made, were Lange and the ministers with responsibilities for parts of the overall reform package: Palmer, Douglas, Caygill, Prebble, Bassett and Cullen.

Not surprisingly — because of the lack of specifics at the

announcement — flat tax rate numbers started appearing in the news media in the following days.

Moore thought these were being deliberately leaked to try to lock Lange and other doubters into the package. He'd also seen this playbook — don't waste a good crisis — before and understood what was happening.

It was clear to Moore that in the days and weeks after the announcement that Lange was becoming increasingly uncomfortable with the flat tax and GMFI package. This was confirmed the following week when Lange sent all Cabinet ministers a note saying the announcement was an in-principle announcement from the government that could be later changed.

Moore's alarm bells went off. Moore had sympathy for Lange's position but sending notes to colleagues rather than talking face to face signalled a serious deterioration in relationships.

Lange and Douglas were now starting to send letters to one another, each one widening the rift between them.

At the end of January 1988 Cabinet had its first meeting of the year and ministers raised the issue of the package and how work was still being done on the details. Douglas was overseas and couldn't make Cabinet. If Lange had pushed the point in the meeting, Moore and possibly most of Cabinet would likely have quashed the initiative then and there.

But Moore sensed Lange was uncomfortable with being confrontational about the issue. The matter ended, Moore thought, with everyone agreeing not to say anything publicly about the package until discussions could be held with Douglas on his return.

Two days after Cabinet the Labour caucus had its first meeting of the year and no discussion was held on the package. Moore was left to chair the caucus as Lange departed the meeting early to host a press conference in the Beehive Theatrette. There Lange announced that the flat tax proposal might not come into effect in October.

It took Moore and the rest of Cabinet by surprise. The news media and the Opposition National Party saw it for what it was — not a crack, but a fissure, in what had previously been an impenetrable government. Moore immediately knew that this could be the beginning of the end of the fourth Labour Government.

The following week's Cabinet on 1 February was awkward. Few knew what to say initially. The tension in the room reminded Moore of the relationship his mother had with his stepfather. Everyone was trying to be amicable, but barely beneath the surface there was distrust and unhappiness.

In the end a joint press statement from Lange and Douglas was put out that committed the government to the 17 December package but that created some wriggle room for further changes to be made to it if needed.

After Cabinet, Moore and Bassett went to see Lange. The pair probably knew Lange and Douglas best out of all those in the caucus. They fully understood the implications of Lange and Douglas being at war with each other.

They wanted to make sure that Lange was happy with the Cabinet decision and that the government would have a unified front. Moore and Bassett came away from the meeting happy that Lange was fully on board.

The experienced political operators had completely misjudged the situation.

It was the beginning of open warfare and caucus members willingly or unwittingly started taking sides. It was too simplistic to say it was a battle about the ideology of the party. Personal rivalries, ambitions and, sometimes, differences about the direction of Labour played a part.

But even on the question of the direction of Labour, Moore still thought the caucus had more in common than it collectively realised. There was unity about the kind of country Labour was — is always — trying to create.

Moore blames himself for not trying harder to understand Lange and what he was going through in his personal life and for not being better positioned to help heal the wounds between the prime minister and finance minister.

By March 1988 the sharemarket crash and the divisions in the government meant Labour had dramatically dropped in popularity, down to 38 per cent compared with National on 54 per cent according to a New Zealand Herald-NRB poll.

Moore and key members of the government had always understood the importance of the fourth estate in getting messages out to the public.

The fourth Labour Government had ramped up its public relations power by contracting many journalists to be highly paid press secretaries in the offices of Cabinet ministers. They had previously been mostly public servants employed via the Department of Internal Affairs and other government departments.

This increased an understanding in the Beehive of what made for stories, how deadlines worked and who were the key contacts across the industry. This was a powerful weapon for the government. Few realised that it would eventually turn its guns off the Opposition and onto itself.

The ongoing war between the Lange and the Douglas and Prebble camps after the flat tax reversal got so bad that their offices were soon giving 'off-the-record' briefings against each other — not the Opposition — to members of the Press Gallery.

At the height of the tensions between Douglas and Prebble with Lange, Moore would always try to scan Wellington's *Dominion* newspaper first thing on Mondays to read Political Editor Richard Long's columns. Likewise, the Christchurch *Press*'s Political Editor Oliver Riddell always seemed to have some inside news.

Relationships got so bad in the Cabinet and the caucus that reading Long and Riddell was often the best way to find out what was going on.

The offices of Douglas and Prebble were much better, though, at playing the briefing game than Lange and his allies. Moore would take that into account when he tried to read between the lines about what was really happening. Lange was being positioned as unilaterally going against Cabinet's wishes and Douglas as being critical to the well-being of the economy.

The goings-on saddened Moore and he didn't need polls to tell him disunity wasn't an attractive trait for political parties to have.

In August 1988, in between his overseas travel, Moore brought US economist and writer Lester Thurow to New Zealand to try to encourage debate among his colleagues about another economic path for the government.

Thurow talked about savings, research and worker involvement in business decisions with less of an obsession, as Douglas and his followers seemed to have, on keeping inflation low.

Moore was on his old hobby horse of a negotiated economy again.

But it was also a move to counter the 'there is no alternative' mantra and to position himself as different.

The following month Lange reshuffled Cabinet and Moore became deputy finance minister and minister of a restructured Ministry of External Relations and Trade. Moore learned about the changes through the news media.

He tried to call Lange and Douglas about the changes, but without a reply he told everyone his finance portfolio included work on a 'compact' with the trade union movement as a possible way to create jobs but keep wage growth contained.

He was conscious that such a compact would annoy Douglas and labour minister Stan Rodger who would see this as Moore meddling in economic policy and the upcoming wage round, both in their patches. But he didn't care.

The compact seemed to mean different things to different people.

CTU President Ken Douglas had called for more union involvement in government policy development and management of change at Labour's annual conference in September 1988.

Moore's long-held belief about the role of trade unions in economic management matched Douglas's belief that they had to be about more than wages and conditions.

The CTU then did much of the running on the compact idea, producing a series of discussion documents. Moore then ran off the back of the CTU's thinking. He made a keynote speech at the Canterbury Chamber of Commerce in November 1988 where he described the compact as 'a ripple of hope' for future management of the economy.

The speech created a ripple, indeed, in the news media and with his colleagues.

The *Manawatu Evening Standard* editorial on 26 November 1988 said: 'As usual, while all around him appear in some danger of losing their heads, the peripatetic Mike Moore stands out in the storm and talks sense . . .'

The Press editorial on 28 November 1988 said Moore 'has lost none of his crusading zeal'. It said the compact 'offers the chance to break the mould of old, confrontational industrial relationships and to create a partnership that will provide opportunities for investment and for jobs'.

Moore and Ken Douglas saw the compact encompassing trade

union and employer involvement in economic and industry planning in return for wage restraint and productivity increases, similar to what the Australian Labor Government had implemented with its 'accord'. It would mean trade union sacrifices in wage round negotiations today in exchange for a promise in the future of gains for their members. It would mean trade union leaders like Douglas spending a lot of their political capital backing Moore and the compact idea.

The old friends were buoyed by a Heylen poll commissioned by the Treasury in November and released in January 1989 that showed 80 per cent of New Zealanders supported a compact.

This flurry of interest led to Moore becoming Chair of the Cabinet Economic Development and Employment Committee to oversee policy development around the compact which would eventually lead to the idea of a 'Compact Council' comprising government, union and enterprise representatives.

To keep up momentum Moore got a group of businesspeople, including Hugh Fletcher and Sir Jim Graham, and trade unionists to write a report into New Zealand's international competitiveness. While the report, which came out later in the year, didn't go anywhere it recommended the government have less of a focus on inflation targeting, that the dollar should fall and that a 'compact' be used to keep a lid on wage inflation.

Throughout this period other events were taking Moore's attention.

His popularity continued to rise. In a poll of several thousand readers in December 1988, *Sunday News* had Moore as its preferred prime minister, just ahead of Lange and then a big gap back to Anderton, Douglas, Palmer and Prebble.

While it was good news for him, Moore was worried that the government was seemingly spinning out of control. Lange had sacked Prebble from Cabinet and a New Zealand Herald-NRB poll in December 1988 put Labour at 40 per cent support and National at 53 per cent.

This was followed by Douglas resigning as finance minister a few weeks later and there being a leadership vote between him and Lange on 21 December, which the prime minister won 38 to 15.

Moore briefly considered putting his name in the ring but quickly realised it would only make the situation worse. Moore ended up voting for Lange because he believed in his brilliance and secretly hoped he and Douglas could still stitch up their torn relationship.

While Lange and others tried to put the government back together after the Christmas break, 1989 didn't bring much respite for Labour. Moore knew the situation couldn't continue much longer and realised there might be another leadership contest in 1989. If there was going to be one, he determined he would be a part of it.

The mood got steadily worse in the Cabinet and caucus throughout 1989. For Moore the last straw was Lange's speech at Yale University on Anzac Day where he surprised his colleagues by describing the ANZUS alliance as 'a dead letter'.

Lange had promised Cabinet colleagues before leaving New Zealand that he wouldn't discuss ANZUS and the Americans had been shown a version of the speech that had no mention of it.

Moore was furious because he had been working hard behind the scenes to repair the relationship between the countries and officials were in the middle of trade negotiations with the US. Moore was conscious that the speech would also annoy the Australians who had been quietly supportive of New Zealand's delicate situation.

Within days rumours started to swirl about a leadership change. There was talk of a Palmer and Douglas ticket, a Douglas and Palmer ticket, a Moore and Douglas ticket, a Douglas and Moore ticket, and a Palmer and Clark ticket.

The situation was compounded by terrible polls. A New Zealand Herald-NRB poll in May had Labour down to 30 per cent and National at a record high of 63 per cent.

Colleagues were furiously doing numbers of various combinations. Bill Jeffries and Phil Goff were watching out for Moore and subtly promoting him. Lange survived a caucus no-confidence ballot at the end of June with Moore being a reluctant supporter who had also influenced others.

To try to make the peace, Moore told Lange and caucus colleagues that Douglas should be back in Cabinet.

On 3 August caucus voted on two Cabinet vacancies. Moore voted for Douglas and Annette King. Douglas was elected, along with Annette King in a second-round ballot. Moore was pleased King, who he had mentored in the marginal seat of Horowhenua, had won.

That weekend Lange called Moore to say he would be resigning on the Monday. He took the caucus's vote for Douglas as a vote of no confidence in him. The prime minister sounded a beaten man with few friends and nowhere to turn. He seemed a lonely soul.

Going into the Cabinet room on the Monday there was a strange mood. Everyone knew what was about to happen. Moore still hoped it wouldn't. After the announcement, Moore felt a sense of relief and sadness. The most gifted politician he'd ever seen had self-destructed. After his brief statement to Cabinet, several of Lange's friends and foes spoke before they all stood and clapped as he left the room.

Moore was also pleased, however, that there was now a chance to cauterise the government's problems and start afresh.

In Yvonne's mind it was a straightforward equation. Moore was the most qualified in the caucus and the most dedicated to the party — he'd done his time and deserved to be the leader.

Palmer was clearly going to be his opponent, but Moore knew he was a better campaigner, communicator and leader. It was hard to see New Zealanders responding to a lawyer and an academic and he believed the caucus would choose him easily over Palmer.

Some MPs were suggesting that Caygill should be the next prime minister. Moore saw Caygill as one of the driving forces behind the fourth Labour Government and admired him greatly. After himself, Caygill would be his second choice if he ever put his hand up.

A Palmer and Clark ticket was starting to form that evening. Those who didn't want Palmer as prime minister flirted with the idea of Douglas being leader with either Palmer or Moore as deputy.

Moore wouldn't countenance going into any ticket unless he was the leader.

Jeffries did Moore's numbers and to his surprise was finding resistance. The night before the caucus vote Jeffries and first-term Avon MP Larry Sutherland were the only ones in Moore's office; there were no signs of celebration or last-minute desperate horse trading.

Palmer, who was widely seen as the model deputy since getting the role in 1983 and the steady and methodical intellectual in caucus, easily won the leadership vote 41 to 13. Clark beat Douglas for the deputy leadership in a much tighter contest, 29 to 25.

Moore believed Douglas's lobbying for the leadership damaged his chances with caucus.

Some say Moore was just too flamboyant to have as leader after the Lange years and that the calm and predictable hand of Palmer was seen as more attractive.

Others cite an incident some months earlier at a caucus conference in Vogel House in Lower Hutt that turned a number of MPs off him. During one of the breaks a group were sitting around and someone asked Moore what he'd do differently to get the government out of its doldrums. Moore launched into a tirade about how few colleagues ever listened to him but always came to him in times of trouble for advice and help.

Still others say Clark's supporters stuck with Palmer because he was an easier stepping stone for her in future.

Labour immediately got a bounce in the polls. The New Zealand Herald-NRB poll had Labour back up to 48 per cent and National down to 46 per cent. Palmer also shot up in the popularity stakes to 23 per cent from only 3 per cent in April. The closest politician to him was Winston Peters on 14 per cent and Bolger on 6 per cent. Lange and Moore were only on 5 per cent and 4 per cent respectively.

But it wasn't long before the government appeared to have lost its momentum again. Moore believed Palmer, Clark and Party President Ruth Dyson — who he and many Cabinet ministers had funded delegates to travel to Dunedin the year before to vote for ahead of Anderton — were misreading the mood of the country. They were mistaking New Zealanders' dislike of the government's in-fighting for a desire to do nothing.

This error had been compounded by the initial bump in the polls after the change in leadership. Moore believed the spike in popularity for Labour was a sense of relief that the 'white noise' had stopped.

Within four months their popularity had reverted, with National on 55 per cent support in a Heylen Eyewitness poll, and Labour on 38 per cent. By March 1990 this had gone out to 58 per cent to 34 per cent.

The government had a financial package in March, then an employment package promising full employment by 1995 and then the July Budget. But none were circuit breakers for Palmer and the government.

As *Dominion* political journalist Tim Grafton would later write, Palmer was 'happiest in the engine-room of government' and 'uncomfortable on the bridge'.

'His lecturing, pedantic style lacked the common touch and for a prime minister he displayed a disarming naivety when it came to the darker machinations of politics.'

Moore knew he had to cut another path away from the flailing Palmer. He also figured that the ambitious Clark could end up as an unlikely ally.

7

'And he's the man who fights the bull'

'We got that meeting with James Baker because of a lot of hard work by a lot of friends of New Zealand's in America. The rumour was that Brent Scowcroft also fell asleep at the crucial meeting in the White House so the president signed it off. Who knows?

'Our anti-nuclear policy was the right thing to do, but I was always worried that it would be misheard by some in Washington DC. So right from the beginning I and some others tried to keep dialogue going with US officials.

'David and some others were the ones who ended up choosing the elderly destroyer USS *Buchanan* for a visit because it was obviously neither nuclear powered nor armed and so the Americans didn't need to confirm or deny it had weapons on board. But someone leaked the idea while David was overseas and Geoffrey had to deny its entry.

'I was trying to juggle so much at home and abroad. The GATT Uruguay round, the relationship with the US, no one seemed interested in a negotiated economy approach, of changing direction, and Geoffrey Palmer wasn't getting any traction. The longer it went on the worse things seemed to get.

'But when things started to get really bad all those who hadn't supported me came around. "You've got to do something about Geoffrey," they said. "He's in trouble." Sadly for Geoffrey, the media would set him up, have some fun, and he didn't see it coming.

'Within three or four months of Geoffrey becoming prime minister people would come to see me and I'd say: "Get out, you weren't interested in me a few months ago, were you?"

'Jonathan Hunt eventually came to see me. And I poked him in the belly and said: "A year ago it was the marginal seats in trouble, now you're in trouble. Didn't care much about your colleagues, did you?"

'I was pissed off with them, I thought they were cowards. I ignored them at first and took comfort in my work, particularly trying to fix the relationship with the US. Then people like Helen would come and I thought shit it's getting serious.

'So a group of us started to do some thinking and planning about how to manage such a desperate change. A poll was done that showed a lot of Cabinet seats in trouble and that's when it all started to happen. I thought bugger it, we've got to give it a go. I'd rather be shot storming up the hill than lying in the ditch.

'The counter to doing nothing was waiting for what, to become leader of fewer than 20 seats? Jim Anderton's NewLabour would probably have held three or four seats and then he would have called for a unity conference to merge the two parties with him as leader. I wasn't going to let that happen.

'Managing the changeover with Geoffrey had to be done well, otherwise everything would fall over. We'd have a lose–lose. If he hadn't resigned, he would have gone into the election as PM — I wasn't going to force a vote in caucus.

'Helen was an important part of the change. I wanted Helen to be deputy. She was very good. Auckland, a woman and could open a vein of support I couldn't. But I had no illusions. Why wouldn't she want to be leader? I knew that maybe one day she'd have a go for the leadership — nothing wrong with that.

'For a moment I thought about Annette King being my deputy but didn't do any serious work on it. Maybe I should have.

'Maybe I also shouldn't have moved on Geoffrey. I might have been stronger afterwards — if I'd won my seat.

'I knew we'd lose the election. I was just trying to save some of the furniture, some of the seats, so we could have a decent go in 1993.

'A lot of smart thinking went into the campaign, but it was pretty hard trying to turn back the tide. We threw everything at it, though.

'We tried to get up the compact between the employers, unions and government like the Australians had done with their accord. With the highly unionised workforce and centralised bargaining we had it would have worked in time.

'The night before the election Yvonne's mum, Yvonne and I stayed up making sandwiches and things for the election-night function. It was pretty depressing.

'But you find out who your real friends are in moments of adversity. Off-duty diplomatic protection squad members and public servants came and helped us — they could have got into a lot of trouble if discovered.

'Jim Bolger had chartered a Fokker Friendship plane for his campaign and our DPS guys plastered it with "I Like Mike" stickers so things like that did break up the seriousness of the situation.

'I remember on the night of the election one of the media guys grabbed a sandwich, looked at it and dropped it on the floor. That just seemed to sum up a lot of things.

'It's easier being a Nat. Labour is held to a higher standard by New Zealanders and we should be. We fix stuff up and when that's done the Nats come back. It's not so obvious these days but they're still the ruling class and when we're in government it's a bit of a surprise to everyone.'

****

Moore knew he couldn't become entangled in the day to day of the Palmer administration. He had to elevate himself above the narrative of bumbling and incompetence that was quickly emerging.

So Moore turned to the international stage.

He went to Washington DC in March 1990 hoping for a thaw in the relationship between New Zealand and the US.

In retaliation for not allowing the destroyer USS *Buchanan* into New Zealand in 1985, there were severe limitations on the level of access New Zealand officials could have with their US counterparts. There was also a significant scaling back of defence cooperation, especially concerning intelligence sharing. New Zealand was expected to remove its intelligence officials stationed in US facilities globally.

Lange and US Secretary of State George Shultz had met in Manila in July 1986 and agreed the countries would part as 'friends, not allies'.

There had been no high-level meetings between the two nations since, but with President Ronald Reagan and Lange having moved on there was hope for a breakthrough.

Moore and friends of New Zealand's in the Washington DC establishment had been working on repairing the relationship for some time. The fear had always been that hard-line US politicians would use New Zealand's anti-nuclear differences to deny the country access to its lucrative markets. The sooner the relationship was seen to be repaired — with the anti-nuclear issue parked to one side — the less likely there would be any kind of trade retaliation.

Moore understood that there might be an early window of opportunity to improve the relationship with the US with the election of George H.W. Bush as President in November 1988. He'd also discovered that no New Zealand intelligence officials had ended up leaving the US and so there had been little interruption of defence-related intelligence being exchanged between the countries.

A few months into his presidency Bush nominated Florida businessman and prominent Jewish Republican Party fundraiser Melvin Sembler as the US Ambassador to Australia.

Moore discovered that Sembler had served on the National Steering Committee and the National Finance Committee for Bush's campaign and was good friends with James Baker, who was going to be the next secretary of state.

Sembler had also lost a son to drugs and become evangelical about the issue, influencing First Lady Nancy Reagan's 'say no' to drugs campaign that rallied the Republican Party.

On a visit to Australia, Moore went out of his way to meet with Sembler and he struck up a friendship with the ambassador and his wife Betty. Moore explained the long-standing relationship between New Zealand and the US and how damaging the impasse was, and Sembler seemed authentic and genuinely interested in helping.

Moore encouraged Sembler to convey to Baker that while New Zealand would never change its anti-nuclear stance, the two countries could still have a cooperative relationship and pursue common international, political, economic, trade and security goals.

He pointed out the sanctions put on New Zealand by the Reagan administration were being inequitably applied by the State Department, Defense Department, National Security Council and others in the administration anyway. There were many contacts, including intelligence flows, just not a relationship at a political level. Everyone else seemed to be talking with each other, so Moore argued that Baker should be allowed to as well.

Moore kept fanning that idea every opportunity he got with Sembler. He didn't trust the US Embassy officials in Wellington or many of his External Relations and Trade officials to do the task.

The scene was further set with Moore being made the Minister of External Relations and Trade in Palmer's reshuffle of Cabinet in early 1990. Moore could now wear a trade and a foreign affairs hat on the international stage.

Moore then socialised the idea with Sembler that perhaps there was an elegant way high-level political relations could resume between the countries. Moore had had responsibilities for trade much longer than foreign affairs so many would see a possible meeting between him and Baker at that level.

Baker had agreed with Sembler that New Zealand was being treated inequitably across the administration and warmed to the idea of how a meeting with Moore could be constructed. Moore was likely to be in Washington DC in March 1990, so that would be the opportunity.

Meanwhile, the Washington DC bureaucracy didn't like the idea of ending the high-level restrictions and a series of interagency discussions were held to discuss the possible meeting. Agreement on a position couldn't be reached so it was then elevated to a meeting of the deputy secretary of state, the deputy secretary of defense, the deputy secretary of Treasury, the deputy CIA director and the deputy national security adviser.

As there was also disagreement at the deputy level, the matter went to the Oval Office for a decision between Bush, Baker and National Security Adviser Brent Scowcroft who was opposed to New Zealand's stance on nuclear issues.

Baker successfully made the case to Bush, who was fond of New Zealand because of his Second World War service in the Pacific with Kiwis, that there was no sense in continuing the ban on high-level diplomatic contact while military-related cooperation continued uninterrupted.

The bureaucracy didn't like the decision and the meeting was still in doubt up until late the day before. The New Zealand Embassy in Washington DC remained unaware of even the possibility of the meeting until Moore's receipt of the invitation.

In the end Moore got a 30-minute meeting with Baker at the State

Department and they discussed cooperation in combating the drug trade and the GATT Uruguay round of trade negotiations.

Both countries' separate stances on nuclear policy stayed, but everything else would return to the highest level of cooperation.

Attuned to the politics of the moment, Moore refused to give interviews on his return until he was back in Christchurch North with his electorate caravan as his backdrop. One moment he could be with the US Secretary of State in the State Department in Washington DC and the next working with constituents. They were strong images he wanted New Zealanders to see.

Newspaper reports heralded the meeting as a new era in the relationship between the two countries and it was, at the time, Moore's crowning success as a politician.

Not only was it a turning point in re-normalising the relationship between the two countries but it had a profound impact on domestic politics. Opposition Leader Jim Bolger had been watching the situation closely and after the Moore–Baker meeting told his caucus that National had to change its anti-nuclear policy.

National had gone into the 1987 election campaign promising to overturn Labour's anti-nuclear legislation to enable relations to resume with the US. But in the face of the Moore–Baker meeting Bolger only saw political downside for National to go into the 1990 election campaign opposing Labour's anti-nuclear policy and so embraced it.

The White House's Dr Karl Jackson and Dr Peter Watson of the National Security Council's Asia Directorate were assigned to try to persuade Bolger to the contrary, saying he didn't need to change the policy because he was likely to win the election anyway. But Bolger was viscerally unwilling to do anything that might endanger National winning, with his caucus quickly supporting the change in policy.

Moore's continuing efforts from 1985 to protect the New Zealand–US relationship and the Moore–Baker meeting five years later, in effect, helped create an enduring political consensus in New Zealand being anti-nuclear. His work also earned him lifelong friends in the US political establishment that would come in useful later in his career.

What few knew was that Moore was also on another mission when he was in Washington DC. He was talking to Democratic Party political consultants to see if Labour could turn around its likely upcoming disaster in the general election later in the year.

Moore was introduced by his old friend and later South Australian Premier Mike Rann and Australian Labor Party pollster John Utting to Craig James, a young strategist from Squier-Eskew Communications.

Squier-Eskew was founded by Bob Squier, who had worked on presidential campaigns for Hubert J. Humphrey and Jimmy Carter, and he would later be involved with Bill Clinton and Al Gore.

James had an affinity with New Zealand having spent three months in Auckland in 1987 in the company of Labour activists and he and Moore struck up an almost instant friendship. James shared Moore's politics, loved his sense of humour and admired his commitment.

James was surprised about how open Moore was being with him, having only just met. Labour was in serious trouble and unlikely to be re-elected later that year, Palmer wasn't a good campaigner and there was real concern that the swing against the party might be so severe that it would take another generation before it was back in government.

Moore was already in the early stages of his 'Think It Through' campaign, an aggressive approach that was comparative and designed to put pressure on National and make the public hesitate instead of automatically voting for change.

Moore already had envisaged a four-year plan and was thinking ahead to what would be required to pick up the pieces after the election. But he also wondered out aloud with James whether a leadership change before the polls might have an impact.

Moore was worried that Labour might win fewer than 20 seats and that NewLabour might pick up a handful. Then, post-election there would be a 'unity conference' between the parties and a potentially leaderless Labour — without Palmer, Clark and possibly Moore — would do a deal with NewLabour and install Anderton as leader of the Opposition.

After an afternoon of open and frank conversation between the two, James agreed to come to New Zealand to assess the situation and provide an outsider's independent opinion.

Before jumping on the plane, he sent Moore a personal and confidential memo giving his assessment on Labour's current polling and election plans.

James told Moore the government was 'terminal' because voters clearly wanted change and the question wasn't whether Labour could hang on but whether it could 'avoid Armageddon'.

He was concerned that Labour might follow the British Labour Party which had been out of office since 1979. What had compounded Labour's misery was its 1983 election loss under the leadership of Michael Foot where the party had less than 28 per cent of the vote, its worst performance since 1918.

James was blunt. 'To win, all National has to do is run a minimally effective campaign. But if National runs a solid campaign they could deal Labour a defeat of such devastating proportions that 20 years could pass before Labour is in a position to win again. The stakes are indeed very high.'

Given the desperation of the situation, James thought Moore's 'Think It Through' campaign strategy was the best option to salvage anything. At every opportunity, in every communication, at every level, Labour would need to draw sharp comparative distinctions between itself and National.

The memo suggested creating criteria on which voters could make their choice between Labour and National.

'On what criteria do you want people to base their electoral choice? Is it experience? Is it compassion, or something else? It has to be something that Labour is and National is not. Once the criteria-of-choice is established then a strategy to make that criteria paramount in voters' minds must be put in place.'

After six years and so much change, people had forgotten National's disastrous 'Think Big' policies. Labour wasn't so lucky, as voters would easily remember the pain of the last six years.

'Labour could spend millions to convince voters that they were doing a good job and that things would get better, but it would be a waste of time and money. Voters don't want to hear it. Every iota of polling data indicates that people are fed up. They want the government that's been causing them all this pain to feel a little pain themselves on election day.

'So, instead of trying to convince voters that Labour is so good, why not convince them that National would even be worse?

'To achieve this, Labour must take the offensive and define National before it defines itself. By being aggressive, by being comparative and by providing the information and evidence to prod voters into "Thinking It Through", Labour can make National an unacceptable alternative.'

Part of the strategy was to do 'projective' polling that compared the leaders of Labour and National and tested what were the best messages to use against Bolger.

It was an approach James and his firm were using that year to support a young and little-known Democratic candidate, David Worley, in a congressional contest in Georgia against incumbent and rising Republican star Newt Gingrich.

Congressman Gingrich was well in front, 55 per cent to 16 per cent in head-to-head polling. But the polling showed it was possible to create messages that brought the candidates level. In November that year Worley came within 974 votes of pulling off a stunning upset.

Moore was counselled to start carefully positioning himself for Opposition. He needed to ensure he was re-elected in Christchurch North, had a chance to deliver nationwide messages during the campaign, and was able to define what a party under his leadership would look like that avoided 'the taint of a Labour defeat and the ugly recriminations that will surely follow'.

James had genuine concerns about Moore's re-election in his seat because of the massive swing coming against Labour and reminded him of the need to stay local in his messaging in Christchurch North.

Moore understood this advice well. But he was more interested in James's thinking about his leadership positioning.

Moore's goal should be to have voters say to themselves on election day: 'Why isn't Mike Moore the PM?' or 'Why isn't Mike Moore leading Labour?' But to do this he had to create some room between himself and the rest of Labour's leadership not to be impacted upon by the upcoming defeat.

'I am not suggesting that he undermine the leadership in any way. But I think he may need to take steps to avoid being labelled a "loser" or a "failed leader".' To do this James suggested Moore continue to deliver Labour's messages for the campaign but at the same time tell his personal story that was 'courageous and inspiring and one to which people can relate'.

Moore's life set him apart from others in Labour and should be his positioning. James summed up Moore's narrative succinctly:

'Mike Moore is a common man who has become an uncommon leader. He has dealt with political victory and defeat with equal ease.

'He has confronted and conquered the most feared disease of our generation — and through the experience, gained a deeper appreciation of what is truly important in life. He has proven he can communicate with a hard-working New Zealander or the United States Secretary of State with equal ease.

'And he has always made decisions based on principle and led by example — while never forgetting where he came from or who he is.'

James visited Christchurch and Wellington for six days in early August 1990, with Moore picking up his expenses, and met MPs, party officials, government staffers and business leaders.

While there he helped prepare projective polling to test messaging for the election campaign, what the public thought of Opposition Leader Jim Bolger and, critically, what the result would be under a Palmer versus Moore prime ministership.

Some of the polling was done by Labour's pollsters and others paid for by Moore's business supporters.

James's post-trip report was bleaker than expected.

'Most likely, Labour will lose in the October 27 election regardless of who is leading the party. This is a harsh but realistic assessment,' the report stated.

'Voters have been worn down by the demands placed upon them by the radical economic restructuring — and they are tired of waiting for the promised pay-off. In fact, voters are so disgusted by the Labour Party that they are prepared to make Jim Bolger, a man they clearly don't like, the prime minister.

'The Labour Party, regardless of who is leader, has to fight monumental forces in the next election. The push of history and the deep discontent with the Labour Government are more powerful opponents than National and Jim Bolger will ever be.'

The election wasn't about who would run the country but whether Labour would survive as a political entity in the 1990s and into the next century. The stakes were that high.

Party head-to-head polling, adjusted for undecideds voting, showed what many other polls at the time were saying: National 56 per cent and Labour 34 per cent. That meant if the swing against the government was uniform across the country the election result would come close to wiping out Labour with even its safest seats in jeopardy.

But the results were interesting when respondents were asked if they thought Labour's Geoffrey Palmer or National's Jim Bolger or 'someone else' was best as prime minister. 'Someone else' on 46 per cent beat Palmer (28 per cent) and Bolger (12 per cent) combined.

'Clearly, National's appeal is not driving this swing. Bolger is barely tolerated by the electorate. National has not proposed any popular policies that have caught voters' imaginations.

'The only reasonable explanation for the move to National is that they are not the government. Voters seem to want to cause some pain in the lives of the people who have been causing them pain for the past six years. National appears about to become government by default.'

The polling then tested Moore's appeal. Many people didn't know much about him but when they heard his story, 50 per cent found him 'very appealing' and another 33 per cent 'somewhat appealing'.

Those who were positive thought he was in touch and understood the needs of working people and was himself hard-working, experienced and an effective representative of New Zealand.

Importantly, people thought Moore understood Kiwis and their needs.

'Mr Palmer — like Mr Lange before him — is many things, but empathetic he is not. Based on the strong positive response to Mike Moore's story, there seems to be an excellent chance for him to make an emotional connection with New Zealand voters.'

Recent Moore public statements about fighting against paid medical care, everyone sharing in the benefits of the economic reforms, returning to traditional Labour values and fighting wage cuts were all positively received in the research.

James believed Moore was already well-liked, people related to him and he had tapped into the important underlying themes in the electorate about fairness and compassion. The bonus was they had also discovered two possible comparative issues around health care and wage cuts to use in the campaign.

With this messaging they polled again to test responses between Palmer and Bolger and then Moore and Bolger. Again, the results surprised.

Before arguments: Palmer vs Bolger

Labour	30%
National	49%
Undecided	13%
Other parties	8%

After arguments: Palmer vs Bolger

Labour	36%
National	47%
Undecided	11%
Other parties	6%

After arguments: Moore vs Bolger

Labour	49%
National	39%
Undecided	9%
Other parties	3%

Normally in polling, undecideds are redistributed among the contestants in the same proportion as committed voters.

But for this poll the undecideds were redistributed to National because a fair assumption was that if they had been unmoved by the positive arguments they'd heard, they were unlikely to vote for Labour anyway.

This showed a stark contrast between Palmer and Moore.

Palmer vs Bolger

Labour	36%
National	58%

Moore v Bolger

Labour	49%
National	48%

James thought carefully before typing the following paragraphs in his report because he understood the limitations of polling — they are based on a best-case scenario tested in a vacuum, uninfluenced by the distractions of a normal election campaign. He also understood the possible consequences of what he was saying.

'Do these results mean that if Mike Moore were prime minister that the Labour Party would win the election? No, they do not. Do they mean that with Mike Moore as prime minister, the Labour Party would perform better in the election? Yes, the results strongly indicate that.

'And do the results mean that the Labour Party should consider changing leaders before the election? The results suggest that the Labour Party should carefully consider this option — because the party's survival may be at stake.'

Moore immediately thought that the government should change its election goal to the survival of Labour because the chances of Palmer keeping the party alive were nil. But a best-case scenario would see Labour retain enough seats to have a viable Opposition after October.

Changing leaders this close to an election was unprecedented. The only similar case was Bob Hawke taking over the Australian Labor Party in February 1983 and defeating Prime Minister Malcolm Fraser just over a month later. The major difference was, though, that Hawke and Labor weren't the disliked incumbents.

But it was clear voters were still warm to Labour if it was seen to be traditional, fair and compassionate rather than the heartless image the government had. This didn't mean abandoning or radically altering economic policy. It meant having a government that was more caring, and the public thought Moore could bring that back because of his back story.

Moore was much more of a vivid contrast to Bolger than Palmer. If he could position himself as leading a more traditional and compassionate Labour, he could almost be seen as running against the government.

'Changing leaders would allow Moore to renounce the attitude — not necessarily the policies — of the current Labour Government and say that he intends to take the party and the country back to its traditional values — fairness, equality, tolerance and respect.

'When Bolger attacks on specific Labour Government policies, Moore would simply have to say: "That's what they did — I'm going to do things differently. This is how I'm going to do things . . ."'

Strategically, Moore would have to position himself much as an

Opposition leader does. He would not have time to submit a budget or make policy — he would only have time to set broad goals. This would be a huge advantage in a short campaign.

That way the electorate could, if done well, have a choice between a Moore without any Labour baggage against Bolger.

'Each leader would explain his visions for New Zealand's future to the voters, and then let the people decide. If the election were contested on this level, Labour would at least have a chance of winning.'

Moore was concerned that as a senior member of the Cabinet it would be difficult to separate himself from the government. But, he thought, it might be achievable because he had previously expressed reservations about the direction of the government and had stood unsuccessfully for the prime ministership when Lange resigned.

It was one thing to test the notion of a leadership change with the public, and how a Moore campaign would run, it was another to go through the practicalities of removing a prime minister so close to an election.

Moore showed the research and suggestions to his closest allies in Cabinet, transport minister Bill Jeffries, revenue minister Peter Nielson, education minister Phil Goff, agriculture minister Jim Sutton and energy minister David Butcher, and they agreed a change was needed. In fact, some colleagues had been on at Moore for some time to roll Palmer. As the days ticked away in August, there was also a fear that any window for change was rapidly closing.

Moore was also nervous about the idea. He always wanted to be prime minister but doing it now looked incredibly desperate and opportunistic. The easiest option would be to wait until after Labour's defeat in October when Palmer would fall on his sword and take over in Opposition.

But, as some colleagues kept reminding him, even if he were re-elected in Christchurch North there might not be much of a Labour Party to inherit post-election — possibly fewer than 20 seats — and his dream of being prime minister would be over anyway.

MPs pulled on his heart strings. Everything Moore had in his life was because of Labour so he owed the party. If Labour could return to Parliament with maybe as many as 30 seats, it might have a chance of beating National in 1993 and certainly in 1996.

Moore and Yvonne talked a lot about the situation. As always, she was concerned that others in the party were thinking of themselves first and not him.

People were once again trying to take advantage of Moore for their own career prospects, including a number who had voted for Palmer ahead of him for the deputy leader's role back in 1983 and for prime minister little more than 12 months earlier in 1989.

Moore even got advice by long-distance phone call from one of his oldest and dearest friends, Singaporean Loo Chong Yong. They had both been to International Union of Socialist Youth meetings in Asia and Europe together in the late 1960s and early 1970s. Loo, who became friends with a generation of Labour MPs, would later become a Member of Parliament in Singapore and a well-respected and successful businessman in Asia.

Like Yvonne, Loo was cautious and warned about the self-interest of Moore's backers. He thought the better approach would be to wait and inherit the leadership.

He ominously warned Moore that if he took the leadership now and polled poorly against the new government in the 1990 to 1993 period that he would open himself up to being deposed by someone like Helen Clark who it was presumed would remain deputy.

Even if he stayed high in the polls, losing the 1993 general election would surely see him having to bow out after two losses too.

Loo advised him that the better approach was to be patient and go hard after 1990 with whatever remnants of the party he had to work with.

Moore and his backers worked through the scenarios. If a change was to occur, there needed to be unanimous or near unanimous support otherwise Labour would once again look divided.

There were also indications that Palmer wouldn't willingly stand aside and finance minister David Caygill, who had done a good job calming the markets and giving credibility to the government after Douglas left, wouldn't stay in the role if there was change.

There were two scenarios, in particular, that he feared. They were labelled 'disaster number one' and 'disaster number two'.

Under the first Palmer would be rolled, then Caygill would quit and other ministers would follow in protest. This would be positioned in the news media as Labour melting down and Moore's election campaign could never get off the ground.

The second one had Moore narrowly beating Palmer in a caucus vote. Then the rest of the election campaign would be consumed by the Moore and Palmer/Caygill factions fighting each other publicly.

He determined that the only way a change in prime minister should be considered was under four critical conditions.

The first was Moore being guaranteed a near unanimous vote in caucus. The second was that no more than two top ministers quit in protest but that they were able to be quickly muzzled. The third was that all MPs — those for and against Moore — were willing to get behind him in a show of unity. And, finally, that Moore be given a reasonably free hand to define the campaign message and reduce it to a choice between himself and Bolger.

Unless these conditions were met, it wouldn't be worth it for Labour or Moore to attempt a challenge. In fact, an unsuccessful challenge could do unnecessary damage and cost the government more seats than it was already destined to lose.

'It would be like a ship getting battered against the rocks on the way out of the harbour,' James told Moore.

At the 27 August Cabinet meeting, Labour pollster John Utting didn't show ministers leadership numbers but gave them a blunt general briefing on the electorate's mood. Utting told them that at this stage only 18 seats out of a caucus of 57 were winnable with little prospect for improvement.

At the caucus meeting the next day polling numbers were discussed and it was a difficult conversation.

Panic set in with some MPs in that last week of August. Delegations and memos headed Moore's way. He agreed with a small group of supporters that Palmer had to go and that they should try to see if he'd fall on his sword at the following week's Cabinet and caucus meetings.

He cancelled his planned trip to Brussels the following week for a GATT meeting and when that got out it fuelled speculation.

Clark had also been asked by her Cabinet colleagues to discuss the leadership issue with Palmer.

Clark was asked later on TVNZ's *Frontline* story 'A very New Zealand coup' by journalist Linda Clark if she considered she'd been a loyal deputy in what had transpired.

'I do. But I'm also a loyal deputy prime minister to the government and for the party and in the end, I cannot suspend judgement about what is happening,' Helen Clark said.

'I think prime ministers who have a bit of spark, character, a lot of ideas — some may be good, some may be bad. But there is a life and energy about Mike Moore that is very appealing.'

Speculation was rife all weekend that there was a possibility of a leadership change. It wasn't helped by the fact that Palmer's Resource Management Bill failed to pass under urgency in Parliament on the Saturday. Some thought it made him look weak.

The prime minister had also issued a media statement on the Friday night saying he would take New Zealand's speaking slot at the United Nations General Assembly general debate scheduled for early October, less than four weeks from the general election. As Minister of External Relations and Trade, Moore was expecting to speak and had planned to focus on world trade issues. Some news media interpreted this as Palmer pushing back against Moore.

A variety of polling data was being quoted in the news media all weekend, some of it emanating from Moore's office.

But on the morning of Cabinet, on Monday, 3 September, Palmer seemed resolute and had no intention of giving up the prime ministership. Speaking to news media before the meeting he said: 'I want to make it absolutely clear to every New Zealander that I am not quitting,' he said. 'I am staying where I am. I am going to fight the election.'

Labour's official pollsters, who were managed out of Deputy Prime Minister Helen Clark's office, were due to update Cabinet that morning. The numbers were dire.

The Cabinet was shown a slide presentation of how badly Labour was trailing National and how far behind Palmer was from Bolger. The numbers confirmed what many had known for a long time.

Then they were shown data that startled all of them. It became the final straw.

It was a slide that translated the swing against Labour into a pendulum graph that had all the seats in Parliament named on it. Its swing was so extreme that had an election been held that day, most of those sitting around the Cabinet table would no longer be there, including Moore and Clark. It left only 16 or 17 seats, including the four Māori ones.

It wasn't news to Moore. He'd commissioned a poll of his Christchurch North seat in August that had him only 1 per cent ahead of National.

The pollsters then left the Cabinet room. Palmer asked his ministers for their opinions. The conversation around the Cabinet table was restrained and reflective in tone.

Despite his best efforts, Palmer wasn't getting cut-through with blue-collar New Zealanders, some said.

So depleted of seats would they be — anywhere between 10 and the low twenties — it was unlikely Labour could become the government again possibly for a generation.

Some thought it was unfair to put the blame on Palmer, while others said it was unfair on Labour people not to give them the best fighting chance against National.

Moore and Clark said little during the discussion, but it was clear that if Palmer was to go, the pair would be the new leadership team.

There was no threat during the meeting of having a leadership spill at the following day's caucus and no ultimatum. Some ministers walked out of the Cabinet discussion thinking Palmer was staying on.

Later that day Moore tried to force Palmer into fronting the news media to talk about the leadership by hosting his own press conference that afternoon, making sure the Press Gallery and most others in the Beehive knew well ahead of time that it was happening.

Palmer's office postponed his usual Monday-afternoon post-Cabinet press conference until after Tuesday's caucus meeting. Instead, he gave a lunchtime speech at the Wellington Rotary Club where he avoided the ongoing rumours and spoke about international relations before heading back to the Beehive without taking questions.

Palmer also didn't respond with his own press conference. So Moore, who chaired the Cabinet Drugs Committee, had to go ahead with his. He held a bizarre press conference with a visiting US Drug Enforcement Agency official. Moore made the news media contingent listen to the official and then refused to discuss the leadership.

Palmer appeared to be hanging on. Moore wanted to avoid a head-to-head vote with Palmer at caucus the following day. News media speculation continued, with the afternoon newspapers saying the prime minister's resignation was as a fait accompli.

Moore thought the numbers would be tight if there was a vote, but a ballot was not the strategy. They also didn't want to force Caygill, who a month earlier said he would resign if the prime minister was ousted, into the Palmer camp out of loyalty. The better solution was to have him stay on as finance minister. Neilson was Moore's standby finance minister if Caygill resigned.

If there had been a showdown in caucus between Moore and Palmer, the prime minister may well have squeaked home. But a caucus vote, even if Palmer had won it, would have severely wounded him and would have made his election chances even worse than they already were. Conversely, if Moore had won such a battle, the stench of the contest would have handicapped his election campaign from the start.

If Palmer hadn't stepped down, Moore wouldn't have challenged him in caucus regardless of the numbers. The mere discussion in Cabinet that morning appeared to have made the leadership change possible.

While the leadership was the prerogative of the caucus meeting the next day, Palmer had made his mind up to leave that evening. This was unknown to Moore.

Driving out to Miramar that evening, Moore mused to TVNZ journalist Linda Clark, who was accompanying him with a film crew: 'Those who love me say don't do it. This will be interpreted as the most ambitious and reckless thing I have done in my life. It is not in my interests.'

In Neilson's Miramar electorate Moore gave a tub-thumping speech — ostensibly to open his friend's election campaign — to a crowd of about 120, including some NewLabour hecklers. He was already trying to define the campaign as 'a choice between Mike and Jim' and positioning himself already as the prime minister.

'Leadership is the issue because of the media,' he said. 'You don't put Jim Bolger on television enough. Put him on more, get him up, we want people to see the stark contrast between the Labour Party, which some say has too many leaders, and the National Party, which has none.'

In the lead-up to a possible change Moore had also been thinking about his deputy. He and many others in the caucus rated new Cabinet minister Annette King. He'd even jokingly suggested to her when they were on a flight together from Hamilton a few months earlier that she should be deputy to him.

Moore had plenty of time for King. The former dental nurse had won the marginal seat of Horowhenua in 1984. Annette Faye King — or 'Faye-King' as Moore jokingly called her — learned many of her campaigning skills from him.

He willingly passed on all his tips from his Eden campaign and tried to divert government initiatives — roading and tourism funding — to favour hers and other marginal Labour electorates.

King was more like him than Helen Clark, had great empathy with ordinary New Zealanders and their struggles, was liked by the news media and he could trust her.

But he reluctantly concluded King would struggle to hold her seat and unless he kept Clark as his deputy, moving Palmer would be impossible. Any kind of caucus unity wouldn't hold. Besides, Clark also tapped into a vein of voters he admitted he struggled to reach — mostly urban middle-class educated professionals.

For some caucus members the goings-on were unacceptable and they were happy to try to break the façade of unity. Eden MP Richard Northey made a brief statement of anger and stood against Moore on 4 September in protest. It's thought by some that the caucus vote was Moore 42 and Northey 12.

Northey broke with the unity theme afterwards, saying: 'I thought that somebody who would be a better leader of Labour than Mike Moore should stand.' The party's paid Auckland regional organiser Andrew Beyer was reported echoing similar disapproving sentiments to the *New Zealand Herald*. Former Prime Minister David Lange also objected to the change, describing those behind it as 'poll-driven fruit cakes'.

Moore wouldn't forget those comments or those who voted for Northey.

Before heading to Government House to be sworn in as New Zealand's thirty-fourth prime minister, Moore told a press conference that he was driven to ensure everyone shared in the rewards of the new economy.

'It's no secret that I've wanted to lead the Labour Party,' he said. 'I'm humbled, therefore, by the trust, the responsibility that I now feel for the people of New Zealand. I have no mandate from the people.

'Over the next eight weeks I will put to New Zealand a stark and clear choice between what Labour can give and what National can take. I promise to give this country all the hard work, compassion I can muster.'

Only minutes earlier Palmer played his part in the transition. He was magnanimous in his remarks about what had gone on.

'I think the question really is who is best able to conduct this campaign in the coming eight weeks in a general election which is of critical importance to New Zealand,' Palmer told media.

Moore was relieved. On becoming prime minister, he kept the celebrations muted. The country was in shock at the change in leadership, there were upset members of caucus and there was an election to win. At 41 years old Moore was now one of New Zealand's youngest ever prime ministers.

His first test was to face the Opposition in Parliament that afternoon for the last week of the House before the election in eight weeks' time. No sooner had the Speaker read the prayer than Moore was on his feet to read a ministerial statement to Parliament about the change in prime minister.

National MPs were raucous and beside themselves with joy.

'I believe history will judge Palmer very well,' Moore shouted at the Opposition benches.

'I know history will judge him very well because I intend to write that history — when I get the time, which I expect will be in the late 1990s.'

They openly laughed at him, but he seemed oblivious to it and kept going. While Yvonne, who had hurriedly flown from Christchurch to Wellington that morning, sat watching in the public gallery on the floor at the back of the House, Labour MPs sat awkwardly in their seats throughout, some forlornly throwing interjections back. They seemed to bounce off an invisible force field in front of the Opposition benches.

While some of his colleagues just seemed to stare into the distance, Moore kept going, quoting a poem by Domingo Ortega that was said to have been in the wallet of former US President John F. Kennedy and read during the Cuban missile crisis. Ortega was a Spanish matador from a poor rural upbringing who went on to fame.

Ortega's poem summed up the challenge and the loneliness of political leadership. It was the same for Moore, although the subtlety of the message was lost on the occasion and most in the House that afternoon.

'Bullfight critics ranked in rows,
'Crowd the enormous plaza full;
'But he's the only one who knows—
'And he's the man who fights the bull.'

Moore was fighting the National Party bull all on his own, while his critics watched on.

When Lange resigned a year earlier and was replaced by Palmer, Bolger's speech immediately afterwards to the House was seen as highly partisan. This time, in reply, Bolger paid tribute to Palmer and his wife, saying the former prime minister had left in a dignified manner. They were hardly armour-piercing words, but they ate away at the wounds on the government benches.

At the end of the week — having spent most of Friday moving his office from the seventh floor in the Beehive to the ninth-floor Prime Minister's Office — Moore headed for Christchurch and the comfort and soft shoulders of his local party members and patrons of the local workingmen's club in the electorate.

Dinner and drinks on Friday night with ordinary New Zealanders. No agendas, no coded messages, no feinting praise or nasty comments. Just simple, plain, filling and tasty New Zealand. It was one of the few times he and Yvonne were able to relax in the following eight weeks.

The next day when the prime minister's car turned up at his home to take him to an official engagement, Moore looked at the driver and asked him what it was like to drive one of the ministerial limousines. Although he hadn't driven one before, he told the driver he should sit in the back while he tried. So, for the prime minister's first official engagement, Moore drove the driver.

Soon after becoming prime minister he was briefed on the Bank of New Zealand, which in 1990 catered to many of the country's homeowners, small businesses and charities, being in financial trouble.

Moore Family Collection

Moore Family Collection

Above: One of the few photos of baby Mike and brother Kerry with their dad, Allan.

Left: Young Mike as his boyhood hero, British racing car driver Stirling Moss, wearing gear borrowed from the local garage that stirred his young imagination.

New Zealand Herald Archive

Victory celebrations on election night 1972 with the Eden campaign team: a 23-year-old Mike embarks on his political journey.

Moore Family Collection

Mike and mother Audrey with Eden party supporters and their chartered bus greeted by Prime Minister Norm Kirk and Party President Charles Bennett the day of his maiden speech to the thirty-ninth Parliament of New Zealand.

Moore Family Collection

The wedding of the year in 1975: Mike and his bride Yvonne Dereany.

John M. Miller

Jubilation as Mike is elected the first Labour Party junior vice president at the 1975 party conference, with Yvonne and mother Audrey.

John M. Miller

Northern Māori MP Matiu Rata inspired Mike into politics and was his lifelong mentor.

John M. Miller

Mike addressing the 1975 Labour Party annual conference in Wellington.

Moore Family Collection

Mike's 1972 Eden campaign vehicle, the iconic New Zealand-designed Trekka.

New Zealand Herald Archive

The 'fish-and-chip brigade' after the failed coup to replace party leader Bill Rowling with David Lange in December 1980.

John Nicholson, *Dominion Post*, EP/1984/4893/27-F, Alexander Turnbull Library Wellington, New Zealand

Happier times in late 1984: Mike and Prime Minister David Lange sample lamb kebabs at a regional promotion at Parliament.

Moore Family Collection

Mike and Yvonne are introduced to one of his heroes, Nelson Mandela.

Stuff

One of the many trade missions Mike took around the world, this one selling Chinese gooseberries to China.

New Zealand Herald Archive

A lifelong dream come true, becoming Prime Minister of New Zealand in September 1990.

New Zealand Listener

Facing the inevitable defeat: election night 1990 at Mike's Christchurch campaign headquarters.

New Zealand Herald Archive

Full circle: Mike returns to his alma mater, Dilworth School, in 1991.

NZME

Outside APEC meetings in Auckland in 1999, Mike hears out lone protester and old union mate Jim Butterworth.

Mike Moore, third Director General of the World Trade Organization, in Geneva.

AFP

Chinese Trade Minister Shi Guangsheng and Qatari Minister Yousef Kamal celebrate the accession of China to the World Trade Organization in 2001, an achievement Mike considered the greatest in his life.

World Trade Organization

The launch of the WTO's Doha Development Round in 2001, which Mike hoped would uplift the Third World.

Moore Family Collection

Mike presents his credentials as New Zealand Ambassador to the United States of America to President Barack Obama, with Yvonne and First Lady Michelle Obama, in August 2010.

NZDF

Mike with Prime Minister John Key and Department of the Prime Minister and Cabinet head Maarten Wevers in conversation with US Secretary of State John Kerry and US Senator John McCain in Washington DC, 2011.

NZTE — photo by Dana Ann Photography

The military history between New Zealand and the US often moved Mike: at a commemoration outside Chicago's Soldier Field in October 2014, the day before the All Blacks played the USA Eagles.

NZTE – photo by Dana Ann Photography

Mike with All Blacks legend Eric Rush and his Chief of Staff Matt Hawkins, sharing a lighter moment at the Field Museum in Chicago in October 2014.

University of Canterbury | Te Whare Wānanga o Waitaha

From one pass in School Cert to being conferred an Honorary Doctor of Commerce: Mike with University of Canterbury Chancellor Dr Robin Mann (left) and university academic Dr John Vargo in 2007.

Moore Family Collection

The true believers gathered to celebrate Mike's seventieth birthday on the deck of his beach home overlooking Matauri Bay in Northland in February 2019.

Moore and finance minister David Caygill came up with the three options for its future: nationalise, do nothing and let it fail, or refinance.

Moore was impressed by the analytical skills and rigour of Caygill who was across the details and grasped the issues better than many of the officials.

They agreed to refinancing, which would mean more than $600 million in taxpayers' money being lent to the bank on commercial interest-bearing terms. But in doing so, they made the political decision to keep it quiet until after the election. Being transparent so close to the election, he concluded, would give Bolger licence to mischaracterise what had gone on at the BNZ and the commercial loan arrangement reached.

As prime minister, Moore hoped to finally get some traction on the idea of a 'compact' between the government, business and trade unions. The idea was to try to control wage growth in exchange for other social gains for workers that could be delivered by the government. This would provide economic stability and help lift the nation's productivity, Moore believed.

Called the 'Agreement for Growth', the 17 September announcement was Moore's big election gamble. He needed to demonstrate that his government would be different in substance, as well as tone, from the Labour administration to date.

Under the agreement unions would limit wage rises to 2 per cent unless justified by higher productivity. The government also promised to cut its spending forecasts in the next financial year to try to control the predicted deficit blowout of $2.2 billion and deal with the drastic drop in economic growth from 2.4 to 1 per cent.

If all that held, the Reserve Bank was expected to cut interest rates, which many businesses were citing as the main reason why they were holding back on investing and creating jobs.

After the election an ongoing 'domestic summit' between the government, unions and business would meet to share information and give macroeconomic policy advice. The government would also crack down on tax avoidance, benefit abuse and expose wasteful spending in the public sector.

Moore was worried that the sacrifices of working people over the past six years hadn't been translated into gains and he was hopeful the 'growth agreement' would do that. He was concerned, though, that in the government's actions to get control of the deficit blowout those same working people would be hurt. So, he also gave a commitment that those on lower incomes would be protected.

The agreement had been hurriedly hammered out between Moore, associate finance minister Peter Neilson and CTU President Ken Douglas, Secretary Angela Foulkes and economist Peter Harris. It hadn't gone as far as earlier discussions.

The eventual 'growth agreement' was an informal one after a hastily called CTU national executive meeting — which not all members could attend — but was strongly backed by the powerful Engineers Union, which was led by former Party President Rex Jones and affiliated to Labour, and the Service Workers Federation led by party executive member Rick Barker.

The agreement sounded good in theory, but trade unionists were nervous they might be giving away too much for their upcoming wage rounds for no guaranteed returns for their members.

Moore needed time to work with the trade union movement on the agreement, but he didn't have it. His best hope was that his strong relationships with Ken Douglas and some of the key players, and trade unions' fears of National's industrial relations agenda, would keep the agreement together at least until the election.

Moore wrote a five-page letter to 50 CTU-affiliated trade unions on 21 September, saying that 'unless people with jobs bear some of the burden jobs will be lost'. NewLabour Leader Jim Anderton told trade unionists to 'revolt' against the agreement.

A few days later the Employers Federation, which wasn't part of it and had been working with National on its industrial relations policy including an Employment Contracts Bill, said the agreement was no more than a non-binding suggestion and that employers should continue to bargain with unions based on their individual circumstances.

Moore's only regret was that he wasn't able to convince his Cabinet colleagues months earlier about such an approach to economic management.

The CTU, with the assistance of former Labour President Margaret Wilson who had become an adviser in the Prime Minister's Office, had been quietly meeting the Palmer Government regularly for about 12 months trying to convince it to adopt a different policy agenda.

Palmer had also supported a Moore Cabinet paper, which he couldn't present because he was overseas at the time, pushing for more work on a compact-style approach to economic management. The proposal was defeated after Douglas, who had been resurrected in the Palmer Cabinet as police and immigration minister, spoke against it.

While the agreement was consistent with what he'd been advocating for most of his political career it was, nevertheless, a desperate ploy; but he had few other cards to play.

Commentators were sceptical, but they gave Moore credit for changing the election agenda in his first two weeks in charge and trying to shake voters out of their inclination to vote National.

The *Auckland Star*'s editorial on 20 September 1990 gave him some credit: 'Consensus is that Mike Moore is ahead on points after the opening rounds. But he needs a knock-out punch. Still there is little doubt he has livened up what was shaping as one of the most tedious election campaigns, had Geoffrey Palmer remained in charge of the apparently doomed Labour Government.'

Labour's television campaign broadcast caught many by surprise too. Instead of glossy pictures of New Zealand and people it was a half-hour talk-show format with well-known entertainer Gary McCormick chatting with Moore and Yvonne in front of a studio audience.

It was a mixture of what a different Moore Labour Government would look like and folksy anecdotes about his upbringing and personality. It was deliberately light on policy, which they knew would annoy political critics, with the format created to try to keep an audience that would otherwise have switched channels. It was risky but different.

In interviews afterwards, Moore stuck to the core messages of returning the country to the values New Zealanders remembered.

National's broadcast had beautiful vistas of the country and New Zealanders interspersed with Bolger speaking at a 1000-strong rally at Wellington's Michael Fowler Centre.

Labour's official campaign launch was in West Auckland on 30 September and Moore and Yvonne spent the day at the Avondale flea market — where they bought snapper and pūhā — visiting radio stations and going to the Sunset Rest Home in Mt Roskill.

Eating cream-filled sponge cake, he was in familiar territory talking to the pensioners: 'You looked after us. Now it is our responsibility to look after you,' he told them.

Labour's 1990 campaign was, for the most part, disorganised. To try to increase their coverage in a short space of time, Yvonne was called in to the campaign and went off separately at times around the country on an electioneering programme.

The 35-year-old was considered one of the hits of the campaign by some news media and travelled with her own press secretary.

There were few resources and even less enthusiasm from activists nationwide. The party was waiting for the inevitable.

On his first full day of campaigning, the Unemployed Workers Union picketed a rally Moore had with King, who was minister for employment, in Palmerston North. At the picket was a sign: 'Final words from a dying government'.

At the rally a person cried out 'triple-figure unemployment' to which Moore argued that everyone should be angry about it because he was.

But the answer, he told them, was not to protect railway or waterfront jobs by making taxpayers or exporters pay for them. The answer was to create an internationally competitive economy that created genuine jobs.

There was a glimmer of hope for Labour. A Dominion/TV3/Gallup poll in early October had Labour jumping 7 per cent to 32 per cent and National falling 2 per cent to 42 per cent.

When assessing the leaders' characteristics, the polling had Moore ahead of Bolger who scored very low on strength and communicative ability and exceedingly high on weakness and being uninspiring and fairly high on indecision. He only beat Moore on honesty and stability. A Heylen poll for TVNZ's *Holmes* programme was similarly harsh on Bolger.

Writing in the *Auckland Star* on 5 October, political journalist Colin James said: 'Bolger appears to be, in the voters' minds, almost the leader you have when you are not having a leader.' James also said Yvonne was proving to be one of the stars of the campaign.

A New Zealand Herald-NRB poll during the campaign had Moore

well ahead of Bolger with males, females, 18–24s, 25–34s, 35–44s and 45–54s. Only in the 55-plus group was Bolger competitive with Moore. The numbers were similar for who had conducted the best campaign.

Moore was relieved that he didn't need to worry about his home base of Christchurch North while he campaigned around the country. He knew he could rely on his locals.

Every now and then Moore would make diversions back to his seat — it was, after all, still vulnerable — for events.

One almost resulted in disaster. His local team arranged for Moore to go on a pub crawl in the electorate. The driver was a Mormon party member who never drank, which would enable Moore, Yvonne and others to have a glass with patrons in each establishment.

Moore went to all the pubs and had no qualms about jugs of Canterbury Draught in the roughest of pubs. At the Papanui Tavern, which had a reputation for local gang members, tensions arose when a customer recognised one of Moore's Diplomatic Protection Squad members as the police officer who helped convict him some years earlier.

Moore had to intervene to keep both men apart.

But there were lighter moments, too, like when on a visit to the Harewood Pub Yvonne was press-ganged into writing notes on beer coasters for the men drinking there to take home to their wives and girlfriends saying they were late because they'd been talking with the prime minister.

Back in Wellington, Moore's office was trying everything to grab media attention and position his Labour Government as different from the past.

A Cabinet paper was developed and the details of it found its way into the news media that Labour was considering slowing down the tariff reductions on imported tyres. Upper Hutt and Christchurch had tyre factories — Dunlop and Firestone — and hundreds of jobs on the line.

He would constantly tell any news media outlet that would listen that he'd like voters to pause for a moment at the ballot box before making their vote and think of the New Zealand they wanted — one that had more heart under him or one that was harder nosed under Bolger.

National countered that with newspaper advertisements nationwide that linked Moore with the Labour Government of the last six years, saying he'd been number three in the Cabinet.

'Mike Moore has played a key role in every disastrous decision the Labour Government has taken,' the advertisements said. 'When you're thinking of the future . . . remember the last six years.'

Moore desperately tried everything. They revealed that the Clyde Dam, which had been initiated by the former National Government, needed $800 million worth of stabilisation works, as an example of how Bolger couldn't be trusted.

Moore unveiled a scheme to create 40,000 jobs by paying the country's 100 biggest companies a subsidy equivalent to the dole for each extra worker they took on, and a national identity card linked to the Inland Revenue Department and Social Welfare to stop benefit fraud.

The announcements were mostly hurried and, as a result, often lacked much detail. But it was an attempt to get the headlines and present, as per the strategy, a different-looking government under Moore.

He was throwing everything he could to make his Labour look different and it was getting some traction, but it was clear to many in the campaign that it was too much to ask. In the middle of the campaign an editorial in the *Evening Post* of 2 October summed it up well.

It said he was a down-to-earth and compassionate man, but his appeal wouldn't overcome some of National's irresponsible promises. Despite National's cliché-ridden campaign, Bolger had every reason to be confident.

'The electorate is in a vengeful mood,' the editorial said. 'The government lost its way with the Lange–Douglas split and the conviction of a grand economic plan is gone. Realistically, all Mike Moore can do is limit the damage and put enough pressure on National to test its leadership and its policies.'

Two weeks out from the election, news that Bolger described as 'the final nail in the Labour coffin' broke.

Some 7.9 per cent of the workforce, or 199,300 people, were unemployed at the end of August — the highest levels of unemployment since the Depression in the 1930s. It had gone up 11,300 from the previous month.

All Moore and King could do was repeat that Labour had a 20-point plan that would see the country back in full employment by 1995.

Near the end of the campaign, desperate to get a positive headline, the government announced it would review the multi-billion-dollar Anzac frigates project that only in November 1989 it had formally agreed with the Australian Government to proceed with.

The deal, which was to buy two frigates for the Royal New Zealand Navy with the option of two more, was important to the relationship with Australia and the defence force's capabilities. But strong lobbying by the peace movement and public concerns about the costs at a time of high unemployment made it unpopular.

Moore thought the project was important for New Zealand's presence in the region and for keeping Australia onside in a post-ANZUS world but knew he had to politically sacrifice it. But he couldn't bring himself to squash the project altogether and instead said it would be reviewed, diluting the announcement's impact.

It made no difference anyway. But for a few minor mistakes — Bolger saying a protester hadn't been raised properly by his mother and saying CTU President Ken Douglas had passed information on to the Soviet Union — National ran a safe and steady campaign. Its well-funded campaign could afford to charter a Friendship aircraft to take Bolger and the news media efficiently around New Zealand.

Moore was also distracted by the crucial upcoming GATT Uruguay round of agricultural trade talks scheduled for Brussels in December. He'd been working on them for the past four years and was instrumental in the establishment of the Eminent Persons Group that was preparing to lobby in Europe ahead of the summit. It meant Moore, himself, was often on late-night and early-morning calls on non-election related business.

The *Auckland Star*'s editorial the night before the elections at least gave Moore some credit.

'Moore has fought a good fight,' it said. 'There is no doubt that he succeeded in at least steering Labour back into a race Geoffrey Palmer had all but given up on before it even started.

'In the end Mr Moore just didn't have enough time — and when it comes to the crunch, he is still the purveyor of the same goods Labour has been peddling for six years. It's Mr Moore's bad luck that the electorate at large has remained in an unforgiving mood.'

It also warned him that he 'may one day end up keeping an eye on Helen Clark et al with some justifiable apprehension.'

On election day Moore voted early, visited each of the polling booths in his electorate and went to two fairs. People were polite towards Moore and Yvonne, but the couple could tell many had not voted for Labour as many of their eyes avoided contact.

The Bishopdale Community Centre was the venue for Moore's election-night gathering and the crowd was small. It was clear from early on that Labour would be thrashed. Many of the faithful had worked until the polls closed at 7 pm, had gone home to tidy up and have some dinner then saw the early results and stayed away.

Many of Moore's local team who turned up were upset. Moore, his mother-in-law Rosie and Yvonne drove in their own car to the community centre within an hour of the polls closing at 7 pm. They wanted to be with the team.

In his early interviews to news media at the community centre he refused to give up. 'I'm an incurable optimist,' he said while also trying to smile. But he was also preparing for the worst, saying: 'We know New Zealand is far healthier and stronger than in 1984.'

Before long Labour seats started falling. Trevor Mallard, from bellwether seat Hamilton West, had an 8 per cent swing against him and was on television conceding early. It was the first in a long night of bad results.

Moore praised Mallard as a good MP who had a long future ahead of him in the party.

The evening almost became farcical when the team was trying to prepare for the concession phone call to Bolger in Te Kuiti. The phone at the community centre had a toll bar on it and when the operator was called and asked for assistance, she said a form had to be filled out and sent in the following week to get it taken off.

When it was explained to the operator that the phone was needed for the prime minister to concede the election to the leader of the Opposition and how this was all being broadcast live, she replied that she knew because the call centre was watching the television coverage.

The operator was politely told that she would be on live television shortly telling the prime minister that he couldn't concede the election because his phone had a toll bar. The operator then said she'd make an exception this time and take the toll bar off.

After all that drama, when the staff called Bolger's line there was no answer the first time. Eventually, the leaders spoke and Moore congratulated Bolger on a good campaign and how someone in his team was in charge of the transition and would be in touch with his people to make the arrangements.

It was a stilted conversation. Moore asked Bolger how his wife Joan was and Bolger inquired after Yvonne. Moore said they were both lucky men. Bolger agreed.

Bolger told supporters at the Waitomo Cultural and Arts Centre that with his victory 'the politics of inclusion begins'. The National Government would 'go down a different path'.

Moore was shattered but knew he had to address his team in the community centre. He told them that unlike Muldoon he would ensure a smooth transition for the incoming government.

Holding red roses and hugging Yvonne in front of a New Zealand flag, he told the faithful not to give up and that the country would once again turn to the Labour Party.

'Every day is a privilege, every hour is an honour. I'll just quote someone far better than me: Martin Luther King — keep hope alive, keep hope alive.'

It would be '36 months, less one half-day' until Labour came back, he told them.

The following week a local businessman and supporter sent Moore 36 and a half bottles of champagne.

8

Young horses

'Jim Bolger, he had some abilities. He would always stick to his notes. I could hit him with a concrete block and he'd stick to his message all the time. We went after him over his broken promises and he'd just say over and over: "The BNZ, the BNZ." I may have thought he was useless, but he still beat us.

'I knew they'd come after me after the election. The only way to keep them at bay was to have the opinion polls — the people — with me. And we worked our guts out.

'Before the 1990 election defeat we mapped out a strategy to get back in 1993. We created a Labour Listens campaign to go around the country and re-engage with our people and let them vent. We got this smart young MP Steve Maharey, who I thought could be a possible future leader, to front it.

'We also got researchers to work out all the promises made by National Party candidates in their local newspapers.

'I was always worried that Bolger would call a special conference of the National Party to say he couldn't keep his promises. That would have stuffed us. He might have lost some seats, but he would have been fine. But he didn't have the nerve or the skill to do it.

'So, every day we would hang him on his broken promises.

'In the first few months we got the inexperienced ministers to say things which we hoped would hang them later on.

'I also got around the country and did a ton of radio shows each week, not just National Radio interviews, but all the music and light-hearted stuff. No one did that in those days.

'I didn't feel any animosity towards the fourth Labour Government, not me anyway. The animosity came from some party members. Labour rewards those who scab to the left but never forgets those who scab to the right.

'They labelled me a right winger — what does that mean? Everything I've ever written, spoken about and fought for has been about the poor and those without.

'I'm not prepared to say even now that what the fourth Labour Government did was wrong. We shouldn't expunge that from our history.

'We held caucuses outside of Wellington which was new back then. At regional conferences we'd try to do canvassing in the morning and then have our meetings in the afternoon. We had to get out and be seen, to hold our heads high.

'In the House it was like the Greeks against the Persian hordes. You can only fight one at a time as they come through the pass so we weren't worried that we were heavily outnumbered.

'For three years we were heads down and arses up. We had a great team. Helen wanted Trevor Mallard in the office and Heather Simpson came across too. They were good.

'Some of the new MPs were very talented and because we were such a small caucus they got elevated quickly. Some of them had a great sense of humour which helped relieve the pressure on a small Opposition.

'I came to like George Hawkins — he'd been around the party in South Auckland when I was, which wasn't good for his standing with some in the party. He had a stroke during the term so I and a few colleagues ran his electorate clinics for him while he recovered. He was very sick, pipes in and out of him.

'One morning he whispered that the party were going to open nominations early for his Manurewa seat and he became very agitated and the doctor was worried. I kissed him on the head and said: "Don't worry mate, I'll speak to the selection committee." George gasped and said: "That's no bloody good — you lost two seats in South Auckland already."

'You have to love a guy whose first political act when a schoolboy was to put a dog turd in the letter-box of a Tory MP — his tactics went downhill from there. Once Winston Peters was having a rally in his electorate on a Sunday afternoon, so George had a car go around the area with a microphone explaining the meeting had been cancelled.

'A bill got introduced to Parliament, once, and Paul Swain said to me: "What's our line on the bill?" I said: "I don't know. I haven't spoken yet.' We laughed and laughed.

'Another time in the House Bruce Gregory fell asleep while I was speaking. All the Nats just started laughing. I couldn't do anything but join them. We put a press statement out later with the first paragraph: "Zzzzzzzzzz."

'But there was always tension in the caucus because there were still divisions from the fourth Labour Government. People like Richard Prebble saw themselves as the carrier of the torch for Roger Douglas, while others wanted to reunite with Jim Anderton.

'Some didn't want the defeated MPs back. But the party needed people like Phil Goff, Annette King, Trevor Mallard and Jim Sutton. I kept in touch with them after the loss. I remembered what it was like losing in Eden and the phone not ringing.

'Bill Jeffries was keen to run again in Heretaunga but because he had a private law practice and still needed to earn a living, he couldn't declare too early. When some in the party found this out, they brought forward the selection and Bill couldn't go for the seat. Everyone knew he was close to me. He was very well known; he probably would have won the seat.

'The selections were difficult. The party hierarchy were deliberately looking for people they thought wouldn't vote for me in a leadership contest.

'Nominees would ring and tell me they had been asked outright by head office. It was a purge and involved paid members of the party. I know I shouldn't have been surprised — head office disliked me my whole career.

'Someone said to me once it was because I was a better organiser and fundraiser than many of them, the jobs party members paid them to do.

'So whenever I did fundraising I knew that all I was doing was helping pay for my assassins.

'The Alliance was proving to be a threat, too, but it was clear some in the Labour hierarchy wanted to be friends again with their disloyal scabbing mates.

'But Clark was like me — she saw the threat of the Alliance and we were united that we couldn't let them split our vote like Social Credit did in the late seventies and early eighties. And I knew she could fight them better than me because she knew Anderton well and how he thought.

'I thought we could reunite the party around a different approach to the economy, similar to the compact idea Ken Douglas and I had been working on in 1989 and 1990. Luckily it had suddenly become a thing internationally and progressive thinkers were calling it 'third way' economics.

'It was also an interesting period of change in the news media. I always saw the media as a mix between those who went to posh schools and working-class kids trying to break out.

'The media was becoming more personality driven and with a bigger focus on Auckland. Socially I enjoyed the company of many of them. I always liked the old guard like Oliver Riddell and Ian Templeton. They were straight and only interested in the story. I loved Tom Scott; he was so talented as a writer and cartoonist, often at my expense. People like Paul Holmes and Barry Soper I couldn't help but like because they're rogues and have a sense of humour.

'My office worked so hard and they should be applauded for getting Labour back into the ring again. We just walked over the white-anters in the end. We were in a hurry and impatient and that increased the animosity between some in the party and me and my office.

'But we had a credible Labour brand that could challenge the Nats after only three years.'

****

Election night 1990 was a disaster — Labour's worst in history — but not as awful as Moore had expected. He'd set his bar a lot lower. But the message was clear — they hadn't been voted out of office so much as they had been voted into Opposition.

There had been many close races, though. Out of the 97 seats in Parliament 21 were either won or lost by Labour with a majority of less than 1000 votes.

On election night National's Pauline Gardiner had even won Wellington Central only to have it overturned later after special votes were counted. In some electorates as much as 20 per cent of the vote went to Green candidates, splitting the vote to enable National to win.

Instead of the remaining 29 seats, Moore expected closer to 20. With 29 he knew he could create a sometimes effective — certainly noisy — Opposition that could hold Bolger and his new government to account.

But to do so he knew he had to rely on a core group of MPs and have an office that could, in effect, replicate the party structures that had been disseminated nationwide.

Among the 28 MPs who lost their seats were highly experienced and capable parliamentarians like Trevor Mallard, David Butcher, Bill

Sutton, Bill Jeffries, Annette King, Margaret Shields, Peter Neilson, Phil Goff, Ken Shirley, Ralph Maxwell, Jim Sutton, Kerry Burke and John Terris.

Almost a quarter of Moore's new Opposition were new MPs who would have to learn quickly or sink quickly.

There was no shortage of former Labour MPs and staffers who came asking Moore for jobs. Some near begged him, while others tearfully were concerned about how they were going to take care of their families.

Only two were employed — losing Hamilton West MP Trevor Mallard, who was keen to run in 1993 for a likely vacant Wellington seat, and defeated Miramar MP and revenue minister Peter Neilson.

Despite his youth, Mallard was a seasoned political operative used to running a marginal seats campaign that Moore knew he would have to run in key seats in 1993. Mallard was always keen and hungry, and Moore saw a bit of himself in him. Clark was also keen to see him given a job in the office.

Neilson was a very different personality. Quiet and studious, he had been a strong supporter and helped Moore with his numbers during the leadership bid. The state-house boy and former public service economist would also be an important cog in the office to help combat National's new Minister of Finance Ruth Richardson.

More important to Moore, though, was the staff he surrounded himself with. He kept a core group who were with him when he was a minister and then prime minister.

Then he recruited people with media, writing, data analytics, party political and grass-roots campaigning skills. Most of the men and women were professionals, not party members, and all had one trait in common — they were young, in their twenties and thirties.

Moore always liked what he called 'young horses' that could run and run. They would start early and finish late and were in most weekends. Like him, they worked 24/7.

Party General Secretary Tony Timms initially called them Moore's 'Praetorian Guard', after the elite Imperial Roman unit that guarded emperors. Timms later labelled them Moore's 'Beagle Boys', a name he'd remembered the team having called other young campaign organisers from the 1992 Tamaki by-election.

The Beagle Boys were a Walt Disney cartoon gang who eagerly and continually tried to rob Scrooge McDuck. Some in the caucus and party used it as a name of derision, but it was a title the team adopted with pride.

Moore's office quickly gathered a reputation for being tight-knit, brash, loyal and hard-working. Depending on your faction, they were either a confident or arrogant group.

With Labour in debt after the 1990 general election and its organisational structure in disarray in most parts of the country, the Office of the Leader of the Opposition and its resources and activity took on a critical role.

Moore knew early on that he wouldn't be able to rely or trust some members of the party hierarchy to deliver anything. He believed that many of the party's salaried staff were incompetent, poorly led or secretly working for a rapprochement with their friends in the Alliance. In the electorally important city of Auckland, Moore was constantly exasperated by the party's organisation.

If there was to be any kind of comeback, it would have to be led by Moore and his office. For Moore's political enemies within the party, this made him even more sinister and less trustworthy.

But Moore and his team didn't bother to smooth over ruffled feathers. Three years was little time to turn the worst defeat in history into anything close to a victory in 1993. Moore and his team constantly pushed and upset the party hierarchy and sometimes members of caucus.

While he did care about the reputation he was creating, Moore pushed on. His career in the party had taught him that was the only way.

Deep down he didn't think Labour could turn it around in one term but kept it to himself. He also knew that if he didn't win, Clark would probably replace him.

Moore was happy for Clark to retain her confidante from her ministerial office, Heather Simpson, and to allocate her a researcher from the Opposition Research Unit and a media person.

Among Labour's seven new MPs was some promising talent Moore initially thought: Palmerston North's Steve Maharey, a Massey University lecturer and Palmerston North City Councillor, long-serving Papakura Mayor George Hawkins, Eastern Hutt Council of Trade Unions research officer Paul Swain, Dunedin North veterinarian Pete Hodgson and Christchurch Central lawyer and trade union secretary Lianne Dalziel.

Moore became good friends with Hawkins, who originally stood against him for the Papatoetoe selection, and liked him for his old-fashioned campaigning skills.

Hawkins had a stroke during the term and, like Moore was with his cancer, became paranoid about it being widely known because his opponents in the party would use it to try to select someone else for his Manurewa seat. Moore immediately understood this and visited him regularly during his convalescence and arranged a roster of MPs to do his electorate work.

The first caucus after the election — on Thursday, 1 November, dubbed 'Remembrance Day' — saw many farewell speeches for outgoing MPs and muted congratulations for the newcomers. With all the formalities over and with the outgoing MPs out of the caucus room, Moore told the remainder to spread out, have a seat either side of them and to slouch. He was bringing in the television cameras and he wanted Labour to look like more than 29 MPs.

It was a long way back and he needed everyone — MPs, staff, the party and the public — to know he had no doubts it was possible. He could never admit, no matter how privately or in a low moment, that victory in 1993 was unlikely otherwise people would give up before trying. They might even think about the leadership then.

Moore quickly gave many of the new MPs meaty responsibilities. He was trying to balance enthusiasm and energy with experience and egos. He also knew he'd have to rely on key MPs over the next three years to help carry key areas of work and help run the party and the politics.

In addition Moore asked Maharey, a self-confessed policy wonk and former member of the party's policy council, to run a 'Labour Listens' campaign nationwide as a kind of healing process for the public and party.

In a policy sense, it was also creating a framework for 'third way' politics that took advantage of the market where possible and government intervention where necessary.

More importantly for Moore, it was a chance for MPs to get out and meet people again and allow them to vent whatever anger they hadn't used up in the general election. It was an attempt to draw a line under Labour's past so the fourth Labour Government wouldn't be an issue in the 1993 general election.

Moore wanted to rebuild the party and understood it had to be done from the grass roots in a way that reaffirmed its purpose and values.

Maharey and many of the other new MPs accompanied Party President Ruth Dyson around the country, staying at camping grounds and being billeted in party members' homes as cash was so short.

The caucus was in a mixed mood. Those who had survived the 1990 onslaught were relieved but also pleased they had a chance to press the reset button on Labour. Some of the new intake saw it as an opportunity to quickly leap ahead, given the constrained talent pool.

But all the carrying on only partially masked a bigger ideological issue the party had to face. Moore's old friend Ken Douglas, who was now the president of the Council of Trade Unions, was quick to lay down the challenge.

Barely a week after the first caucus, on 9 November 1990, Douglas told the party conference that it wasn't disunity that lost Labour the election but the policies of deregulation and the politics of arrogance that saw working people desert them. He reminded them that government wasn't about power but involvement.

'The warning is that you must avoid the trap of finding excuses for why you lost the election: that it was all because of disunity, or you weren't understood or you weren't appreciated. If you do that you will find yourselves marginalised in the debate on New Zealand's future.'

Finance minister Ruth Richardson's first Budget handed Labour a great start. It saw radical change and a huge reduction in government spending, particularly in social areas. The unemployment, sickness and families benefits were cut, charges were introduced for public hospitals and the apprenticeship system was abolished. It caught much of the public by surprise and was not the 'decent society' Bolger had promised in his election campaign.

In her excitement, Richardson had described it in a television programme as being 'the mother of all Budgets', mimicking Saddam Hussein's pre-first Gulf War promise of 'the mother of all battles' a few months earlier.

Moore and his team had been discussing for weeks a label for the event that would brand the Bolger Government much like Labour finance minister Arnold Nordmeyer's 1958 'Black Budget'. They latched on to Richardson's own title.

The turmoil of the 'Mother of all Budgets' and other goings-on in the Bolger caucus obscured a debate Labour was also having about its identity, one Moore was carefully trying to manage. It surfaced in May 1991 not via left-leaning MPs, as Moore thought it might, but through Ohariu MP Peter Dunne, who was seen as an ally of Roger Douglas.

Dunne was critical of the 'Labour Listens' campaign, saying it was hardly the basis of a sustainable programme of political recovery and, instead, needed to focus on what kind of policies a modern social democratic party would need. He said Labour had to forget about its usual prescription of higher taxes and more social spending and accept the thrust of policies like the Employment Contracts Act.

Moore knew he had to put a lid on the debate otherwise it could spiral out of control if left-leaning MPs publicly countered Dunne or if some in the party demanded some kind of retribution.

Dunne had raised some points worthy of debate, but his timing and the way he did it were awful. The government was struggling and the new Labour Opposition was just starting to gain some credibility and look united, all within about six months of its greatest ever defeat.

Moore remembered all too well that the first party conference after an election defeat was always important. It was about showing the public, the news media and party members themselves that Labour had learned its lesson and was still a force to be reckoned with.

He was pleased Maharey would be presenting on the 'Labour Listens' campaign and 11 policy papers would be debated in breakout groups rather than having endless potentially inflammatory remits considered by the conference. He thought Maharey was one of the brightest in the new intake and a potential future leader.

He wanted MPs and party members to draw a line under the 1990 defeat and the divisions caused by it and refocus on winning in 1993. That's why New South Wales Labor Leader Bob Carr, who had seen his party thrashed in 1988 and come within one seat of winning three years later, was guest speaker.

Carr hit the right tone, telling delegates to avoid recriminations and 'a psychology of failure', to not think because Labour was leading in the polls that it would easily win in 1993 and to not be afraid of rethinking policies.

'In light of the electorate's rejection of some of those policies, in light of the deep anxiety many of your traditional supporters felt, in light of the excesses of the eighties, you will now rediscover and reassert traditional Labour values,' Carr said.

Moore knew his keynote speech to the conference, the seventy-fifth in its history, in Palmerston North's Centennial Convention Centre on the afternoon of Sunday, 1 September, would be critical.

It would be all too easy to tell delegates that everything the fourth Labour Government did was wrong and disown its actions. Many politicians would have pretended they had nothing to do with it. It would have been easier for him to decry Rogernomics and use it as a stepping stone to resurrect his 'growth agreement'.

The trick with his speech was to say the early parts of the fourth Labour Government's agenda were correct, but that it wasn't the whole answer. A more negotiated style of economy, as he'd promoted with the 'growth agreement' just before the general election, was now called for. Labour needed to reject the view that the state should dominate and that the market should rule alone — there had to be a third way.

The original draft of the speech Moore had signed off on the Friday talked about farewelling Rogernomics.

On reading it again on the Sunday morning he wasn't sure it hit the right tone and hours were spent in his hotel room with staffers and a laptop trying to craft the right words for a couple of paragraphs. It was finally agreed about 60 minutes before it was meant to be delivered.

'Rogernomics has had its day and though its day was important and historically necessary, it's now a new day, a new dawn, and New Zealand must move on,' Moore said to almost instant applause from the 400 in the hall.

It was just what the party members wanted to hear and it grabbed the headlines and editorials for the next 24 hours, including a powerful Tom Scott cartoon of a Roger Douglas statue being pulled down by hordes, similar to scenes when dictators are overthrown.

The conference didn't paper over differences in the party, though.

Party President Ruth Dyson said Labour couldn't present voters with a manifesto so broad and unspecific that it covered just about every possibility. But Ohariu MP Peter Dunne warned against detailed policy that locked in future Labour governments, saying the party needed broad consensus on what it stood for and what its priorities were.

The Engineers Union and the United Food and Chemical Workers Union also argued for industry supports and protections against cheap imports, while former commerce minister David Butcher and finance spokesperson David Caygill argued against them.

The conference had proved difficult on other fronts that the news media didn't pick up on. A number of defeated MPs, including Roskill's Phil Goff and Horowhenua's Annette King, turned up.

Moore liked their energy and company and was welcoming of their attendance. He was keen for them to be selected and re-elected in 1993, although they were weighing up their options. Goff and King had been strong local MPs, were good thinkers, in touch with ordinary New Zealanders and would be loyal to him.

Some others at the conference, including a small group in the caucus, openly shunned them. The wounds of the fourth Labour Government's internecine warfare were still raw.

But after the turmoil of some party gatherings in the 1980s, the relative public calm of this conference made it seem like a success.

Part of moving on from the past was Moore also sorting out his finance spokesperson. Caygill had thankfully stayed on as minister of finance when Moore became prime minister, despite his reluctance. But it was now time for a new look.

In Moore's mind it was a choice of St Kilda MP and former social welfare minister Michael Cullen, Dunedin West MP Clive Matthewson or Dunne.

He'd carefully watched the three since the general election and given them tasks, as tests.

Moore had been leaning to giving it to Matthewson, a civil engineer who was telegenic, approachable and intelligent. While he'd only been an MP two terms, he had the solid look of someone you wanted looking after your family's savings. But Matthewson seemed lost in the headlights of Opposition and seemed to be struggling to adjust. Moore couldn't wait for him to get ready.

Dunne, on the other hand, seemed to have checked out. He was clearly frustrated with the push-back from the left in the party against Douglas and his policies. His Wellington seat of Ohariu was middle class and prone to boundary changes, so old Labour policies were unlikely to get him re-elected.

For Moore, Cullen was a pleasant surprise. He hadn't got to know the Otago University academic that well in the previous term. Cullen, a working-class boy originally from London who won a scholarship to Christ's College in Christchurch, had played the important role of senior whip in the first three years of the fourth Labour Government, rallying sometimes reluctant MPs for the many important bits of legislation that were passed.

In Cabinet he did interesting work around superannuation as social welfare minister and had been used by Lange as an associate finance minister to help counter the influence of Douglas.

Moore had wrongly boxed Cullen in as one of the party's academic elites because of his doctorate in social and economic history.

Cullen seemed to relish the opportunities of being in a small caucus and in Opposition. He was intelligent and quick-witted — perhaps a little nerdy — but he could more than hold his own with anyone in the House. Importantly, he was courageous and would stand up to anyone in the government or the party.

To Moore he seemed a good mix of old-fashioned Labour parliamentarian with a strong work ethic and understanding of the importance of the news media in modern politics. His wife, former East Cape MP Anne Collins, was also down-to-earth and good company.

One of the first duties for Moore and Cullen was a mini-tour with their wives of provincial New Zealand. It was a dry campaign run, a chance to see how the pair resonated with ordinary Kiwis in factory smoko rooms, schools and in editorial meetings with provincial newspapers.

Moore came away from the week-long tour reinvigorated. He joked that Cullen liked Wattie's tomato sauce on everything, just like him. It was like he'd made a new best friend.

He also learned another important lesson: bypassing the Parliamentary Press Gallery and going directly to regional newspapers and radio stations. While the Gallery was important for caucus morale and getting to opinion leaders, Moore increasingly believed that New Zealanders didn't read the political columns in the major newspapers.

The regional news media were also on the lookout for local stories, so he fashioned national issues with provincial angles. A cut in a national roading budget would mean a local highway in Hawke's Bay, for example, wouldn't be built.

Moore got his office to readjust its media strategy to be 'more retail and less wholesale' and the Official Information Act was regularly used for fishing expeditions to gather localised material.

Mallard's understanding of ministries and government departments and where to look for interesting information within them became invaluable for finding story ideas for the team.

Regular weekly slots were also organised for him on regional radio where he'd have non-political discussions with local announcers about ordinary issues like the weekend's rugby and the latest television programmes, while slipping in a joke berating the local National MP. It was light and entertaining and a long way from the seriousness of Wellington.

But there was one exception to his team's focus on regional news media rather than the Parliamentary Press Gallery and that was television news. No sooner had the TVNZ and TV3 Press Gallery teams finished their morning conference calls with their news bosses in Auckland than the office was trying to find out what the stories of the day were.

That would then determine the focus of Moore's office and its resources that day. Everything would be done to try to get Moore and the Opposition into the main TV stories of the day — from the types of questions asked in the House, to changing any likely speeches that day by MPs, to digging up research for the journalist working on the assignment.

The competitiveness between TVNZ and the relatively new TV3 gallery teams meant intense interest for exclusive stories.

A few seconds on the 6 pm news that evening was better than anything else the whole Opposition could do that day to slip up the government.

Members of Moore's team would gather with him in his office after the late television news to review the daily media coverage and then quickly refocus on opportunities for the following day.

Ideas were regularly thrown around, Moore often making the most contributions. His staff would regularly challenge them which led him to often bemoan how 'other politicians are surrounded by yes men and I'm surrounded by no men'. Sometimes the standing joke was said with more seriousness than others.

Moore often encountered resistance about his daily tactics from senior MPs at the daily 'procedures' meetings. Some were locked into the parliamentary rituals of asking questions that could potentially embarrass the prime minister and his ministers, thinking a victory in the House was important.

But it didn't match Moore's hunger to get on TV or his impatience for action.

This strategy also included their approach to the monthly television polls. Moore's office kept detailed records of the frequency of the polls and what weekends the pollsters were likely to be in the field.

They'd keep interesting stories in their back pocket and give them exclusively to the applicable television news team to coincide with when that channel was likely to be in the field polling New Zealanders.

When people were polled about their preferred prime minister and preferred party, they were more likely to be favourable to Moore and Labour if they'd just seen them on the evening news holding Jim Bolger and National to account.

Moore's media strategy was rounded off with a strong focus on talkback radio which was gaining traction, particularly in Auckland with Radio Pacific.

'Talkback teams' around the country would be regularly faxed key messages on issues of the day to call Radio Pacific to discuss. In the lead-up to major events there would be a concerted push that would often result in whole debates being swayed Moore and Labour's way.

Talkback radio, Moore figured, was popular with working men and women in factories, in shops, in lunchrooms, on construction sites and while driving their cars. So important to him was it that Moore eventually had a regular Sunday-afternoon show on Radio Pacific that he broadcast out of his front room in Dormer Street, Christchurch.

He and the team had modelled the swing voter they had to get. He was probably a tradesman or perhaps in a lower middle management white-collar job. She was probably working part-time to bring in some extra money. They had a couple of kids and would probably go to a campground by a beach each year for their holidays.

They didn't mind paying their taxes so long as everyone else did and it went to funding hospitals, schools and the police, and helped people who fell on hard times. Their basic plan for retirement was to sell their mortgage-free home, downsize and live off the rest and their pensions. They didn't ask for much in life, just a fair go. Moore called them Ken and Marion.

Moore and Labour did the unheard of and consistently outpolled Bolger and his government from 1991 to 1993.

Moore knew from previous campaigns that if he could create an inevitability of Labour becoming the government, or at least being in the race, for 1993 and being seen as the natural party of government then it would likely become self-fulfilling.

While he was wary of her, Moore went out of his way to spend time with Clark to discuss issues.

They were both concerned about the state of the party, particularly its finances and organisational presence in greater Auckland where there were 26 seats. They knew it made Labour vulnerable to the emergence of a third party. Both had seen it before with Social Credit splitting Labour's vote in 1978 and 1981, allowing National to win.

While Labour was navel-gazing, Jim Anderton, who had won the Labour seat of Sydenham, was transforming his NewLabour Party into a coalition of parties.

NewLabour, the Democratic Party (formerly Social Credit), Mana Motuhake and the Greens formally merged to form the Alliance in December 1991.

It wasn't long before the Alliance had its first run at an elected office, standing former communist and republican Bruce Jesson in an Auckland Regional Council by-election in a working-class ward in Panmure and Glen Innes.

Labour picked former deputy prime minister and Cabinet minister Bob Tizard, who had represented much of the area for the past 34 years and whose daughter Judith was now the local MP.

Moore thought Tizard was the wrong choice. He had lost his youthful vigour and, as a retiree, was more interested in golf than politics. Labour needed a young person with energy and who could do the door-to-door retail politics needed to win such a contest.

Reports to Moore confirmed his suspicions that Tizard was likely to lose the postal ballot. So Moore sent two of his team from Wellington into the ward to help out. Hardly anyone from the Auckland party turned up to assist as the two went out door-knocking desperately trying to gather votes for Tizard while he, sure enough, appeared to spend much of his time on the golf course.

Jesson won handsomely and it gave the Alliance a strong platform, particularly in Auckland, to attack Labour. Radio Pacific's talkback, which was popular in Auckland, lapped it up. Moore and Clark's fears were being realised.

It got worse within months when Muldoon retired from Parliament in December 1991, causing a by-election in his National stronghold Tamaki in February 1992. While the news media focused on whether former World Cup-winning All Blacks captain and Bolger pick David Kirk or local and Muldoon friend Clem Simich would win the National nomination, Labour was again in disarray.

The by-election would consume resources the party didn't have and the fight would be for second place against the Alliance's Chris Leitch.

The Alliance wanted to convince heartland Labour voters, through the nationwide news media coverage the by-election would get, that it was the true Opposition.

Moore again pulled together a team from his office, while Clark found a credible candidate in public servant Verna Smith, and some presentable nominees for a fake selection process.

Labour's campaign was a total mess. A house in the electorate was hired as a campaign headquarters and became a bizarre focal point for discontent.

Young party members from Dunedin and Christchurch willingly gave their time to travel to Auckland to campaign and did more than any of the on-the-ground local organisation.

When some former MPs like Phil Goff turned up to go canvassing, they were given the cold shoulder. More stupidly, when the son of former Cabinet minister Michael Bassett volunteered his time many wouldn't talk to him.

Moore did a number of pub visits and street-corner meetings in the electorate, particularly around the few state-house and working-class areas in the electorate. When he did one outside party headquarters for the local neighbourhood, some paid officials and Auckland party officials refused to go outside to show their support.

As expected, Simich won but with a severely reduced majority of just over 1200 votes. Frighteningly, Labour picked up just over 2100 votes — less than half its total in 1990 — and came third to the Alliance on more than 6600 votes.

But it was an important and early lesson for Moore and his team about the state of the party and the attitude of some paid and unpaid officials. It convinced him even more that he needed to go it alone and create alternative structures if he was to stand any chance in 1993.

He continued to worry about the vote-splitting abilities of the Alliance and Labour's lack of presence in Auckland. Few donations were coming in and party membership was low.

His concerns were compounded by what he was hearing from the business community. Many executives who had grown up in Labour households were sympathetic to Labour but were reluctant to make donations. If they knew that Moore had some say over how it was used, they felt more comfortable.

So Moore came up with the idea to establish the Mike Moore Supporters Club (MMSC) to channel donations that otherwise would not have come to the party and create a membership that was willing to support Labour but not become members yet.

Moore also hoped to eventually have MMSC affiliated to the party, like some trade unions were, so that it could have formal influence within Labour.

During Moore's term as leader of the Opposition, MMSC raised about $250,000. Party General Secretary Tony Timms had reported to the 1991 conference that Labour had a debt of $375,000.

MMSC provided electorates that wanted it a computerised — hardware and software — version of Moore's election-day 'get out the vote' management system.

But MMSC further antagonised some in the caucus and those in the party who didn't like Moore. It was another example, for them, of Moore being 'presidential' as in the 1990 general election when he and Yvonne campaigned together rather than Moore and key ministers.

But Moore ignored them. They complained that it was another example of him trying to take charge, like when he forced through changes to the party logo.

The logo had been three square blocks in an 'L' shape with the word 'Labour' underneath. Moore wanted to modernise it and make it more middle New Zealand in its appeal. While some agreed with the need for change, they variously wanted a red rose like the British Labour Party or a logo that incorporated a Māori or Pasifika theme.

Moore pushed through a change that had New Zealand on top in smaller font and a waving New Zealand flag on the left of the word 'Labour'.

An early test of Labour's readiness came when Wellington Central MP Fran Wilde ran for the capital's mayoralty in 1992, forcing a by-election for her seat in December that year.

Moore had tried to convince Wilde to be the mayor and local MP, perhaps donating one of her salaries to charity. Moore didn't want Labour losing its own seat in a by-election less than 12 months out from the general election. But Wilde would have none of it and resigned.

Fortunately, former All Black, High Commissioner to Zimbabwe and Race Relations Conciliator Chris Laidlaw had expressed an interest in running for Labour. National's 1990 candidate Pauline Gardiner was more hopeful this time and the Alliance chose 1978 Values candidate and high-profile journalist Denis Welch.

Unlike Tamaki, this was more of a three-way race with the real possibility that the Alliance would split Labour's vote, allowing National to win.

Labour's local organisation was better in Wellington than in Auckland with Labour MPs, Moore's office and Labour headquarters able to divert resources to the campaign. Laidlaw's campaign manager, local party activist Brenda Pilott, was also experienced and able to navigate Moore's office and the Labour hierarchy well.

There was still some tension, though, between Moore's team and some party officials, who clearly didn't like the leader's involvement, and this spilled over to heated words and almost fisticuffs at Laidlaw's victory party on the night.

Laidlaw won by 855 votes, with almost 39 per cent of the vote which was down about 2.5 per cent from 1990. Gardiner got almost 33.4 per cent of the vote which was down almost 7 per cent on 1990. While it came third this time, the Alliance still pulled in almost 22 per cent of the vote.

Interestingly, as in Tamaki the Alliance seemed to be pulling across more swing National voters disgruntled with the Bolger Government rather than further eroding Labour's base. While Moore was pleased that Labour's base was reasonably firm, he knew he had to attract back those swing National voters if he was to have any chance in 1993.

Election year was going to be one media opportunity after another for Moore. He had a week-to-week plan right through to a likely election in November.

It started with the launch of his book *Fighting for New Zealand: New Zealand in the 21st Century*, on New Year's Day at Piha beach in West Auckland. He knew the news media would be light on news that day and the backdrop would be ordinary New Zealanders enjoying a day out.

Published by MMSC, it sold about 1500 copies in its first week, making it one of the top-selling books in the country.

The book continued Moore's thinking on a partnership between government, workers and businesses to promote economic growth and what New Zealand needed to do to prosper in the global economy. He also advanced the idea of moving from social welfare to social security.

But the book also had a practical purpose. Tens of thousands were delivered to letterboxes in marginal seats and enclosed a postcard bookmark that encouraged readers to send to Moore in Parliament requesting to be a supporter.

He followed this up by organising a seminar of local and international speakers to follow Labour's economic policy launch in March 1993.

The 'Waipuna Seminar', named after the Auckland conference centre where it was held, discussed a policy framework that moved on from free-market orthodoxy. It was a continuation of his attempts to move the party on from the closed economy versus Rogernomics debate some in the news media and party were still locked into having.

The seminar involved bringing to New Zealand in person or via video conference the Dean of the Sloan School of Management at the Massachusetts Institute of Technology, economics author and adviser to President Bill Clinton Robert Kuttner, Princeton University academic Robert Wade, Chairman of Europe's Business Council for Sustainable Development Stephan Schmidheiny and locals like Deputy Leader Helen Clark, CTU President Ken Douglas, Auckland University economist Susan St John and the Greens' first publicly elected official, Wellington City Councillor Stephen Rainbow.

In his introduction Moore framed what had happened in the Bolger Government as being the result of a poverty of intellectual ideas in New Zealand that had given free rein to the extreme monetarist doctrines of finance minister Ruth Richardson.

'We are in the 1990s, not the 1980s. Reaganomics and Thatcherism are dead,' he said. Unfortunately, much of the economic debate in New Zealand was still locked into last decade's sterile rhetoric. 'It's time for the monetarists to be challenged head on at the highest possible level,' he said.

The seminar also followed his strongly held conviction that it was the role of a political party in a democratic society 'to show the future to the present generation'. A political party like Labour had to be a focal point for debating ideas and establishing public policy.

The gathering explored 'third way' partnership politics between industry, workers and unions, and sustainable development as an alternative economic path, something Moore had tried in vain in government with his 'compact'.

The class struggle rhetoric of seminar participant Robert Kuttner also appealed to Moore. His book *The End of Laissez-Faire* was recited to the seminar: 'The oldest chestnut in the conservative mythology is the claim that greater equity unfortunately comes at the expense of efficiency and growth and that if we truly wish to help the poor the best strategy is to stop hobbling the rich, for they are the source of society's wealth and growth.

'This view, that has timeless appeal for people of financial means, is contradicted by history. At many times and in many places, economies have grown faster by diffusing their wealth more broadly, and in this enterprise government is an essential factor.'

The 'Waipuna Seminar' was Moore's attempt to demonstrate to the news media and the intellectual left that his government wouldn't abandon the gains of an open economy but would be different from the Bolger administration and the fourth Labour Government.

Moore spent much of 1993 away from Wellington on mini-tours of the provinces. He was at his best and happiest out campaigning, not having to deal with some of his troublesome colleagues. It brought back memories of when he'd been elected to the party's national executive in the early 1970s and spent weeks on the road around the country.

He spent time in marginal seats and ones the polling told him were potential wins. West Auckland, the East Coast, Hawke's Bay, Waikato, the central North Island, the west coast of the North Island and the South Island saw him multiple times — 'the further south you go, the bigger the sausage rolls,' he used to enthuse.

Moore discovered that many local candidates and party organisations weren't ready for the general election and were unlikely to ever be. They were either naïve, overly optimistic, didn't know what they were doing or lied about their campaigns.

While annoyed, he was pleased he'd seen this first-hand so that he could divert some resources from his office and from MMSC. But he was angry with Labour Party headquarters for either at best being out of touch with what was going on nationwide or at worst keeping him in the dark about the real situation.

His tours again confirmed for him the need to run his own show and not rely on the party, via head office, for any advice, resources or organisation.

National was having its own problems with Tauranga MP Winston Peters being sacked from Cabinet in late 1991, eventually leading to him resigning from Parliament in early 1993 and forcing a by-election which he easily won as an independent with the major parties not standing.

This led Peters to form the New Zealand First party which Moore believed in the short term would be good for Labour because it would divide National. Longer term he was concerned that Peters might turn New Zealand First into a more nationalistic party that might attract older more conservative Labour voters too.

Moore and Peters had always got on, as they were both from poor rural Northland backgrounds and had both been treated with disdain by the hierarchies of their respective parties.

In preparation for the election campaign, Moore invited his old friend Craig James out from Washington DC in June 1993 to give his assessment of their chances.

Moore didn't admit it to anyone except Yvonne, but he thought Labour would fall short of winning back government at the end of the year. The caucus and party were still fractured from the Lange–Douglas split, Labour was struggling to attract donations and members, and the Alliance was running interference.

James, who met with MPs, party officials, Leader's Office staff and businesspeople in Auckland and Wellington, had a different view. With focused use of resources and a disciplined campaign and messaging, it was winnable.

His assessment was that 50,000 to 75,000 voters across key electorates would determine the election. Moore's office had already been narrowing down who they were and where they lived and once that was done the campaign had to continually communicate to them.

James warned Moore that given Labour's extremely limited resources — dollars and people — the campaign would need to be better planned than anything he'd done before in his career. He was already concerned by what he was seeing: everyone working hard but both on things that mattered a lot and things that didn't matter much.

With less than six months until a likely election, he was concerned that there was no agreed campaign strategy with established priorities. He urged Moore to do three key initiatives in the following two weeks: take an inventory of all resources and budget accordingly, establish a clear, functioning and responsible chain of command, and establish a campaign timeline and stick to it.

Money, time and people, he said, would determine the framework of the campaign but few seemed to appreciate this. 'Once priorities are clearly established then any day-to-day decision can be made with them in mind. Your actions will become focused; your movements will have purpose,' James said in his memo to Moore.

James was also worried that beyond Moore there were no clear lines of authority. People felt that unless an order came from Moore it didn't have to be obeyed and this was a situation that would be untenable during a campaign. He said Moore had to stop being the campaign manager and the candidate at the same time.

A campaign director, an implementer, was desperately needed. 'This person would take orders from Moore — who remains the party's best strategist — and the campaign committee and would see to it that they are carried out. To be effective, this person has to clearly have the authority of the leader and the campaign committee,' James said.

James even recommended to Moore a campaign structure with names of people attached to key roles and personnel who would target Labour's 10 to 15 seats needed to take back government.

'If you set up your organisation like this and give people the proper authority, then this should take pressure off the leader so he can spend more time being the candidate in this election instead of the campaign manager,' James urged.

While a detailed timeline leading up to a likely election date had been developed, James suggested rethinking its activities by determining the most important ones at the end and working backwards. That would enable better focus on priority seats and initiatives and prevent last-minute changes on a whim.

Moore was particularly keen to hear James's views on messaging because everyone seemed to have a view on this. Labour had for some time hammered Bolger on 'broken promises' and this had helped successfully undermine the government.

Right from going back on their word about getting rid of the surtax on pensions, Moore and the team had labelled them as a government that broke promises. Labour went out of its way to find anything that could resemble not fulfilling a commitment and made sure the news media carried this narrative.

But James urged Moore not to use this in the campaign. The focus groups he'd sat in on thought that Labour had previously broken promises, too, so it was 'a pox on both your houses'. They viewed people using this line as hypocrites.

Instead, Moore needed to prosecute National on what it had done to the country by making the case for the government's policies destroying the values that made New Zealand unique. The campaign would need to find personal stories about the ordinary tragedies occurring every day in New Zealand and, most importantly, present these arguments in a real and as non-political way as possible.

'As individuals, members should try to avoid letting the debate slip to the level of political bickering. Remember, people are hurting — they want empathy, understanding and help. The sight of a bunch of politicians arguing does little for them. You want to take the position of the person who stops the school yard bully from picking on the other kids.'

James told Moore all the polling suggested 'heart' was a key phrase to tap into as it signified compassion and caring but also courage and conviction. He recommended that the campaign slogan be something like: 'Put the heart back in New Zealand'.

Importantly, it had to be backed up with three to five fundamental rights that Labour would restore — such as free universal health care — that demonstrated how Moore would 'put the heart back'.

Those three to five core policies would be all that the campaign was about and secondary policies shouldn't even be on the radar.

He said National wanted to base the campaign around the recovery of the economy — Bolger had been doing 'heartland' tours of the provinces — and Moore needed to avoid that as the battleground.

The narrative, therefore, needed to be that there might be a recovery for National and its rich patrons, but for millions of Kiwis who had to work for a living there was none. They had to pray each day that they didn't get sick, they had to worry about whether they still had a job tomorrow, and they had to ask themselves if their children were able to afford an education to succeed in future.

'The point is, don't argue university economics with National — argue pocketbook economics.'

The news media strategy had to also show discipline with everyone staying on the message of the day. Less was also more, and the quality of the media hit was more important than the quantity. The campaign, therefore, should limit itself to two media opportunities a day: one for the national news and one for the local media of the place they were visiting.

'The idea isn't to dominate every news cycle in a day, but rather to dominate the day's news. There is a big difference.'

James's memo gave specific recommendations around research, direct mail, radio and TV advertising, and media training for Moore, Clark and Cullen.

For the advertising he strongly recommended that Moore not front them but instead use real people to tell their real stories about what National had done to them. As for the political broadcast each party had at the beginning of the campaign, Labour should invite 50 undecided voters into a studio to ask Moore, Clark and Cullen about anything they liked — even hostile questions.

'Again, the feel should be real. It will give the opportunity to empathise with the people's anger and address their pain. An opening like this will stand in stark contrast to the National opening.'

Moore had instead gone with 'Jobs, Growth, Health' as the campaign slogan. All the polling had shown they were the issues New Zealanders were worried about. They wondered if they would still have a job tomorrow, if the economy was growing and the health system seemed to be falling apart. They were also supposed to be the main topics talked about by Labour during the campaign.

Labour's campaign ended up a combination of what James recommended and what other polling and Moore's instinct told him.

The print advertisements had a three-quarter-page colour photo of Moore and Yvonne walking arm in arm through a leafy park with the headline: 'Only by listening can you hear a country's heartbeat'.

There were multiple versions with different copy. They had Moore recounting stories such as the 18-year-old unable to get a job and the mother worried about her children's education and briefly discussing Labour's answers.

Three-minute-long radio advertisements, featuring speeches Bolger made during the 1990 campaign where he made promises that he later broke, mixed with a catchy hillbilly-style song, were also played around the country.

In their rush to set the political agenda the campaign almost got off to a disastrous start.

Six weeks before the election Peter Dunne came up with a policy about the car assembly industry that was important to Wellington with its Ford and Mitsubishi plants.

The industry was doomed with tariffs coming off and then second-hand late-model imports flooding in from Japan. But unemployment was a major issue and Labour needed the Wellington seats.

Dunne's idea was to ban all Japanese imports unless they were older than 10 years. That way people could still buy cheap old cars, but late-model cars assembled locally would get an advantage.

The announcement was timed as an exclusive for Wellington's

afternoon newspaper the *Evening Post* and given to them under embargo late the day before.

On the morning of the announcement Moore asked his team to kill the announcement because Caygill had warned him it would anger the Japanese car importers so much they would make huge election donations to National. Moore's team spent the morning successfully persuading the *Evening Post* that there were still issues to be ironed out with the policy and that it would be announced another time.

Moore officially launched Labour's campaign in front of 700 people in Christchurch, saying Labour would remind New Zealanders of the promises the government made during the 1990 campaign. 'We will punish them with their own words, with their own promises,' he said.

He also made a strong pitch for middle New Zealand, saying they were under financial pressure because they weren't rich enough to be able to afford all of the government's user-pays charges and they weren't poor enough to get benefits from the state.

He said New Zealand needed to 'march forward as a caring society that embraces individual opportunity, underpinned by social security and social opportunity.'

But Moore did create a problem for himself by straying off script and extending Labour's policy of not paying the dole to people under 20 to those under 30 by 1996 and to everybody in 1999.

National's launch, in New Plymouth, tried to define the election as a choice between the government's economic recovery and consistency versus Labour's likely higher taxes.

'Don't let Labour put your money where their mouth is,' Bolger said. He also said many of the Labour MPs in 1990 were the same in 1993.

But some of the coverage of Bolger's launch also seemed off message. He spent time having to counter Labour claims that the Queen's chain, the public access to the coast, rivers and lakes, could be privatised under proposed government legislation.

The bigger concern for Labour was there was no proper campaign director. Moore couldn't find a suitable candidate for the role so a number of people controlled the budgets and organised the diaries and schedules. 'I need another me to be campaign director,' he complained. Pete Hodgson was, however, made 'campaign spokesperson.'

But focusing efforts around the key targeted seats to optimise scarce resources was being followed.

The only possible flaw in that strategy was it relied on accurate polling and local insights to determine which seats got assistance and — as Moore found out after the election — some electorates deliberately deceived they were so desperate for resources.

Television New Zealand held 'hometown debates' with Bolger and Moore hosted by Paul Holmes, and the campaign team saw them as critical to the election. They would have huge television audiences and given Labour's depleted resources were the best way to get Moore to New Zealanders.

The first was in Bolger's King Country electorate in Te Kuiti on 21 October. Labour Party people were bussed down from Hamilton to attend and Moore's team got to the venue early to give handwritten questions to a group of them to submit from the audience.

Some of the questions were deliberately provocative — not patsies — to elicit a response from Moore on a topic Labour had strong messages about. Out of the 10 questions planted about six ended up being asked of Moore.

The team also asked where they could sit and were told anywhere, so they positioned themselves opposite Moore.

In his two-minute opening statement Moore went hard on one of Labour's campaign themes, jobs.

'Tonight is not about Mr Bolger, it's not about me. It's about New Zealand and the kind of country we can become, what kind of country we are now. I think New Zealand deserves better.

'Te Kuiti is a good place. But there's a sad side to Te Kuiti. And, unfortunately, there are too many sad sides to our towns and cities at the moment.

'Three years ago, Mr Bolger did stand in this hall and he did tell you that 25 per cent unemployment in Te Kuiti was a crime and was outrageous. And Mr Bolger was correct when he said 25 per cent unemployment in Te Kuiti was bad.

'He promised you to halve it. It's gone up by about 20 per cent. One in four teenagers are standing around with nothing to do but to get into trouble at night.'

He finished by talking about another theme, health, and how he'd visited a hospital earlier in the day.

'I met with the nurses and they're angry they were employing more bureaucrats. Nurses ought to be about sick people and doctors and not about charging people to go to their own hospitals. I think it's outrageous.

'I can never tolerate or accept the situation in my area, for example, when somebody with money can jump to the head of a queue. Not because they're the sickest, not because they're in the most pain, not because a doctor says you ought to go first, but you've got some money so you can jump the queue.'

Bolger started the debate with a statement about the targets the government had set itself and how they hadn't met all of them. It quickly became a rowdy meeting with many in the audience booing Bolger and cheering Moore.

Host Paul Holmes' first question to Bolger was about his broken promise to abolish the superannuation surtax. While he countered by saying the bailout of the BNZ after the election meant many promises couldn't be kept, he struggled for the rest of the debate.

It was generally thought that Moore, who came across as calm and in control, won the debate and National people were heard later complaining to Holmes about the evening. News media commentary afterwards was not so much about the debate but how some thought Holmes had made the programme about him.

The second debate was a week later at St Bede's in Christchurch. But this time Bolger's people demanded a pre-debate meeting at the venue with Moore's team and TVNZ to discuss the rules for the evening. Cosgrove, as Moore's local campaign manager and electorate secretary, attended.

Bolger's team were fuming. From the airport all the way to St Bede's Moore supporters had plastered posters saying 'Come and mash the Spud at St Bede's tonight'. 'Spud One' was the nickname the media gave Bolger's chartered plane in the 1990 election and he subsequently picked up the label.

That evening a group of young supporters, headed by a future brother-in-law of a National Cabinet minister, approached the campaign asking how they could assist Moore on the night. They were given a stack of bright fluorescent stickers the size of saucers that had emblazoned 'I like Mike' on them. This group then stuck them to their foreheads and sat in the audience opposite Bolger during the debate.

National was better prepared for the St Bede's encounter, bringing many of its own supporters. Moore used similar messages to the first debate, interspersed with stories of people he'd met on the campaign trail.

'Real leadership is based on credibility and some moral authority. Real leadership can offer some vision and direction and some hope,' he said. 'And people will respond if you don't say one thing and do the other.

'Employment is the greatest issue facing our country and we ought to focus on what the people want to hear, policies. One person has become unemployed every day since he took over.'

Some thought Moore won that debate as well.

All the indications were that Labour would win back the West Coast. Its candidate Damien O'Connor was a Westport boy and his father was a well-respected local farmer. O'Connor had set up and run a tourism company, Buller Adventure Tours.

Moore was fixated on winning back the West Coast, considered the home of New Zealand's labour movement and a seat it had lost for the first time in 1990. He called it the party's 'Jerusalem' and he saw it as his duty to win it back.

What had particularly galled him was how Bolger campaigned on the West Coast leading up to Labour Weekend — a time to celebrate the 40-hour week that unions had fought hard for — during the 1990 election campaign. Moore took it as a direct insult to working-class New Zealanders and hadn't forgotten it.

He told his office to put particular effort into the visit. Moore's advance team of Clayton Cosgrove and former Electrical Workers Union official and Cullen ministerial adviser Barry Ebert discovered O'Connor had a strong and loyal local party but there weren't many of them in it. There was real concern that Moore would go to a series of events that had few people in attendance. So the day before, all the party faithful, their families, their friends and anyone else they could find were encouraged to turn up to a briefing.

They were divided into three groups of about 30 people, given placards and rotated around the various events. When Moore flew in to Hokitika airport he was greeted by an enthusiastic crowd who when he moved on went to another pre-assigned event.

One of the funnier moments came when the campaign wandered past the local theatre which was showing a staged production of *Peter Pan*. Two of the characters, Captain Hook and Tinker Bell, were outside having a cigarette and Moore posed with them for a photograph.

The deception of the trip almost came unstuck in the last event in a local pub when a journalist mused how some of the people looked familiar to her, before laughingly saying everyone on the West Coast was probably related.

With the tight schedule of the campaign and the need to get to provincial seats Moore and the team often used helicopters, the cost being covered by donors. The helicopters saved on car travel, waiting around at airports and created a buzz in smaller towns, particularly if you landed at a school. Despite all the advantages, Moore hated helicopters. They were often jerky in motion and, unlike with an aircraft, he thought it was unsafe if anything went wrong.

All his worst fears came to fruition on a quick trip to the Wairarapa from Wellington. Flying over the Rimutakas on the way home, low cloud obscured the capital. The pilot told everyone he'd have to head south and hug the coastline to find his way back.

A few moments later he mentioned that everyone should keep an eye out for an Ansett aircraft that was also in the area. For a brief moment there was a break in the clouds and one of the team saw the aircraft off in the distance.

Moore's confidence in helicopters wasn't helped when upon landing back in Wellington the pilot got out and kissed the ground.

A month out from the elections Labour had pulled level with the government on 37 per cent in a One Network News-Heylen poll. Moore was also ahead on the preferred prime minister stakes with 20 per cent support, compared with Peters on 17 per cent and Bolger on 12 per cent.

Moore was concerned about the party's Auckland operations and where the Alliance was strong, so he spent a lot of time there during the campaign. For about nine months before the campaign he'd try to spend every Friday there.

But there was another threat from the Alliance that everyone missed in the excitement of campaigning. In a little-reported speech on 30 September in Kapiti, Alliance Leader Jim Anderton said his party would refuse to form a coalition with either Labour or National if it held the balance of power after the elections. The Alliance would support the government of the day on confidence but would vote against policies it disagreed with.

Moore had enough of his own problems during the campaign.

At his local campaign launch on 16 October, less than a month from election day, Lange talked about the need for Labour to have a progressive tax policy. This was seized upon by National that Labour had a plan all along to raise taxes. The tax and spend slogan was a common accusation National threw at Labour early in the campaign and Lange's comments confirmed it in some minds.

It was a punch to Moore's solar plexus. It was a deliberate act of sabotage, Moore thought. Moore was dismissive in his public comments about his old friend, further alienating the two.

Then a few days later Caygill and Laidlaw were quoted as telling the business community that the Employment Contracts Act hadn't turned out as bad as people had thought and that Labour would only make cosmetic changes to it, even though it was policy to repeal the legislation. Caygill and Laidlaw later claimed they had been partly misinterpreted and partly misreported.

The caucus had mostly shown discipline throughout the campaign, but all this did was confirm for some voters what they'd always suspected about Labour — they were a party that hadn't quite worked out yet what it stood for after the fourth Labour Government.

There was tension, too, among some of Moore's office. Some agreed with Moore that the news media had been overly critical, while others thought he was being overly sensitive.

Communications Director Geoff Mein had been asked, during a critical period in the lead-up to the campaign, to do a major research project on the balance of the news coverage of Television New Zealand and its political editor Richard Harman in particular. Mein had become distracted from other important planning and the exercise only added to the workload of key staff and fuelled their paranoia and irritability.

Moore had earlier in the year fallen out with one of his political advisers, Trevor Mallard, who in 1993 was starting to focus on running in the Pencarrow seat.

There was also disagreement around critical polling work, with

Labour's usual pollsters UMR Insights being asked by Moore to work with his old friend Paul Heylen and his research company.

Despite the problems, Moore was feeling good about the campaign. The debates against Bolger seemed to go in his favour, he'd had strong rallies nationwide and some polling had indicated, particularly in key parts of the country he'd been targeting, that voters were coming across to Labour.

The day before the 6 November election the *New Zealand Herald* had a front-page story that said National were 'odds on' to win the election by between five and 13 seats and some in the party were even predicting by as many as 20.

9

Chardonnay socialists or dry reds

'Elections are about finding your pockets of support, putting your resources there and getting them out to vote. I'd run marginal seats campaigns most of my life and just extended it across the country in 1993. It was about putting limited resources into places that made a difference. The key is having the right people and we had a great team. They were smart and worked so damn hard for the cause.

'Every now and again you'd get excited, but it was always going to be hard to win in 1993. I had the view that if I couldn't come within five or six seats of the Nats in 1993 then I should give it away. But I thought I'd come close enough to keep the detractors away.

'We got so much closer than anyone thought we would. If we'd only won those seats we should have. Even so, we had Bolger on the ropes and he would have had to throw in the towel in a few months and we would have collapsed the Alliance vote and won the new election.

'I knew some MPs were meeting behind my back — very small numbers. And some in the party were deliberately selecting candidates who wouldn't vote for me.

'But I was too busy trying to win. Besides I'm good at conflict avoidance. I'm good at denial. I didn't want to know about it. It was painful and I couldn't stay awake worrying about this kind of shit.

'Prebble warned me — he was the only one who did in the three years — that I needed to be careful about what I said. I thought I'm not going to start doctoring my speeches to make some in caucus happy. It wouldn't have made any difference anyway. Those people always disliked me and I disliked them.

'They didn't move against me until that final seat in Waitaki was lost. I'd been talking to some of the Nats. I'd been speaking to the Speaker before the election and said: "No commitments but if it's close, we might approach you."

'I'd also been speaking to Michael Laws and Peter McCardle about what could possibly be done.

'I knew I was always vulnerable to Helen. Steve Maharey was also figuring it out. I could possibly have played them off against each other, I suppose, but I couldn't be bothered. I was just so exhausted all the time.

'The thing that hurt her was she never fronted at all, never said: "Hey Mike, this is it", not once. After all these years we still haven't talked about it.

'The public and rank-and-file party members were great to me at the time. I was flooded with letters of support. People stopped me in the street they were so outraged.

'Martin Luther King said that in the end we will remember not the words of our enemies but the silence of our friends. I felt a bit like that at the end.

'A number of those who voted against me later apologised, looking for me to give them absolution. There were various excuses. A number of them have kept in close contact over the years and become good friends. I haven't forgotten but I have forgiven.

'The problem with politics is it becomes so personal for some of us on the left. I've had many disappointments in my life but losing the leadership like that after all I'd done hurt me the most.

'It took me a long while, but I do admire Helen as a politician. She's the toughest politician I've worked with, against or for. Not anyone gets to be prime minister and she went on to do it for three terms. I do respect her, yes, it's true.

'As for her henchmen and women, well they thought they were doing the correct thing like the fish-and-chip brigade did with Rowling, I suppose. But with the fish-and-chip brigade we didn't hide who we were. We stabbed Rowling in the belly.'

****

Election day always had its traditions for Moore and Yvonne: vote early and then visit each of the polling booths in the electorate and any school fairs or functions in and around the electorate. While the law prevented any more campaigning, he could still be seen by any wavering voters and everyone could be the deciding person in a close race.

Moore then spent time at local technology company Aoraki Corporation, which was run by old friend and major supporter Gil Simpson and where the election-day system was set up.

Moore's old voter identification system, which had its origins in his 1972 Eden campaign, was now computerised, which meant every electorate in the country that had it could be efficiently turned out.

Just after 1 pm, 3.30 pm and 5.30 pm electorates were told whether their target voters had turned out or not and locals hit the phones — supplemented with more than 30 callers from a phone bank at Aoraki — to encourage them to the booths.

The only limitation of the computerised system was how much of each electorate had been canvassed by local organisations. MMSC had organised the whole system, selling electorates a networked computer for $100 with a monthly running cost of $10.

Some electorates embraced it fully, while others were less enthusiastic because they didn't have the resources or because they didn't like Moore and MMSC.

The system even predicted within a couple of hundred votes who would win each seat. Even though he had the numbers in his head, Moore could hardly believe what he was seeing on the television and was hearing on radio that evening.

A strong swing towards Labour seemed to be in progress in key seats. The only question was would it be big enough to pull back Bolger's majority of 34.

Moore, Yvonne and his media staff made two false starts to head from Dormer Street to the election-night party at a former car sales showroom in Papanui. He wasn't sure whether he should wait for a clear indication of the result or go be with his supporters. Bolger was nowhere to be seen in the news media.

On election night it looked like National had finished with 49 seats, Labour 46, New Zealand First 2 and the Alliance 2. A handful of seats might change after the special votes were counted within the following two weeks.

After the special votes were counted National was still on a knife edge with 50 seats, its vote having collapsed almost 13 percentage points to 35.05 per cent. Labour had picked up 16 seats to have 45, but interestingly lost 0.46 percentage points to sit on 34.68 per cent of the vote.

Labour's vote had hardly moved from 1990, but there had been a dramatic change in the seats — the party's biggest turnaround bar the 1935 election. The marginal seats strategy had been hugely successful.

So close was the election that 17 seats were decided by majorities of less than 1000 votes, of which 12 were by less than 500.

The deciding factor had been the Alliance, which picked up two seats, and took 18.21 per cent of the vote, and New Zealand First, which also won two seats, and took 8.4 per cent of the vote.

While the Labour comeback had shocked many, what was overlooked was the loss of seats that Moore had been expecting to win. Richard Prebble lost Auckland Central to the Alliance's Sandra Lee by almost 1300 votes, Chris Laidlaw lost Wellington-Karori to Pauline Gardiner by 480 votes and Bruce Gregory lost Northern Māori to 32-year-old Tau Henare by 416 votes.

In addition, and despite predictions, Heather Simpson couldn't beat Peter McCardle in Heretaunga, losing by just over 800 votes.

Moore also had outside hopes for Birkenhead, Eastern Bay of Plenty, Kapiti, Rotorua and Western Hutt dashed by National which won by 104, 806, 1038, 429 and 1542 votes respectively.

The Gregory and Simpson losses hurt Moore the most, though.

The Gregory defeat meant Labour's grip on the Māori seats was finally loosening. Moore kicked himself for not paying more attention to them. Gregory's hold on the seat had been slipping for some time, having won it by fewer than 1000 votes in 1990.

Moore had remarked to some MPs a few years earlier that he thought something strange was going on in the Māori seats. But the Māori MPs were confident.

Moore was keen for a good candidate in Heretaunga now that his friend Bill Jeffries couldn't stand.

With the assistance of Barry Ebert from his office, who was involved with the local party and was on Labour's ruling council, he helped Simpson get the selection ahead of strong union candidate Rick Barker and high-profile local body politician Nicola Meek. Moore even met with her in the electorate in the lead-up to the election to see how she was going and was sure she'd win easily.

Moore, Yvonne and his staff finally headed across to election headquarters a few hours after the polls closed. They were greeted by a mob of local party faithful, beside themselves in the thought Labour might be pulling off a miraculous victory. In the flurry getting out of the car and into the venue Yvonne was accidentally knocked over by news media jostling for better positions.

Moore was almost overcome by the raucous reception, the handshakes and hugs as he and Yvonne struggled their way to the stage, which had a giant New Zealand flag hanging behind it.

He was determined to thank party members in the room and nationwide who had kept the faith in Labour and turned out to work for its return to power. These were the people, Moore thought, who had shown courage in the face of others in the party who had given up the fight or really wanted to join their friends in the Alliance.

With the way the seats appeared to have fallen, he was hopeful of possibly picking up an electorate through special votes or doing a deal with New Zealand First which had two seats. He wasn't sure what the Alliance would do given Anderton's public animosity towards him, Clark and Labour.

Moore wanted to quickly thank the crowd and make a bigger speech later in the evening when there was a clearer picture of where all the seats had fallen. At that stage in the evening only about 60 per cent of the votes had been counted and television had yet to make a call on the result.

Television covered all 1 minute and 45 seconds of that off-the-cuff speech live. It was a speech some of his critics in the caucus would later use against him.

'Right, I just want to be here to thank the people in this party, in this region and this city who have looked after Yvonne and me.

'You looked after us when we first came down and we were lonely. You looked after me when I was sick. And you are the true believers. And I want to applaud you.

'Tonight will be a long night. It will be a long night for Mr Bolger and Miss Richardson. But it won't be as long and cold a night as it has been for all the young people in this country since they were elected.

'It will be a long and cold night for Mr Bolger, but not as cold and lonely as it has been for one in four teenagers who have been out of work.

'It will be a long and cold night for Miss Richardson and Mr Bolger, but not as long and cold as it has been for the pensioners.

'It will be a long and cold night for Mr Bolger and Miss Richardson, but not as long and as cold a night as it has been for the 400,000 people out of work, for those people who are sick and waiting to get into their own hospitals who have been told for the first time in New Zealand history they will have to pay to go to their hospitals.

'And for those young people who were told they'd never have to pay a student fee again, I tell you this: hold on, help is on the way. It will be a long night.'

Bolger wouldn't speak for many hours to come and when he did at the Waitomo Cultural and Arts Centre in Te Kuiti television had called the result a hung Parliament. When he did, Bolger's more than 14-minute speech talked about how New Zealand would not be plunged into a constitutional crisis and how he was open to working with the other parties in Parliament.

Bolger's pitch was the opposite of Moore's. He talked about stability and wanting to work with the other parties. He cleverly used the fact that the country had also that day voted for a mixed member proportional (MMP) electoral system.

'There will need to be a much greater working together,' he said. The four leaders had a responsibility to 'make the election work for New Zealand' and he cited the superannuation accord the parties had signed as an example of how they could all work together in a multi-party way.

TVNZ couldn't get Moore on to respond to Bolger but found Helen Clark in her electorate instead. Asked if she agreed with Moore's view that National didn't have moral authority to govern, Clark said Labour could potentially form a coalition government with the Alliance and New Zealand First on the current vote count.

'I don't think everyone voted for a return of Jim Bolger,' Clark said.

Jim Anderton quickly poured cold water on a coalition when TVNZ crossed to him. 'While the people did not vote for a National Government, they did not vote for a Labour Government.'

Moore finally came back on, but instead of a set-piece speech he had an interview. He said the public service would have already drafted a contingency paper about how to deal with a hung Parliament and that should be sent as soon as possible by Bolger to all the party leaders.

The responsibility for dealing with the situation was now with Bolger who was still the prime minister. Everyone now needed to wait the 10 days for the special votes to be counted.

Moore thought he had never been more powerful in the caucus because he might just be able to cobble together a coalition government or force Bolger to go to the country again.

The day after the election Clark and Cullen flew to Christchurch to discuss the situation with him. They were photographed smiling together in suits looking over papers like a government in waiting.

They pulled together a five-point plan of compatible policies that they put to the Alliance and New Zealand First to possibly be the basis of a coalition agreement.

The plan called for the MMP electoral system to be brought forward for an election as early as the end of 1994. This would ensure the Alliance and New Zealand First wouldn't have to face the possibility of electoral oblivion under a first past the post early election because MMP was expected to take two years to implement.

There was also the repeal of the Employment Contracts Act, the scrapping of hospital charges, the removal of plans to privatise accident compensation and the removal of the 26-week stand-down period for the dole.

Moore was trying to make the Alliance and New Zealand First an offer they couldn't refuse to entice them into coalition talks. With about 65 per cent of the electorate having voted against National, Moore argued that the public wanted change.

But the Alliance and New Zealand First kept their distance while they waited for the special votes to be counted.

Back in Wellington later that week Moore asked the Reserve Bank Governor and the head of the Bankers Association for meetings. The dollar, interest rates and the sharemarket were in limbo because of the uncertainty about who was going to govern and Bolger's refusal to confirm Ruth Richardson would be his finance minister.

Nothing of substance happened at the meetings. They were only photo opportunities to again make it look like Labour was the government in waiting and to try to create some momentum with the minor parties.

Instead of being a joyous occasion the first caucus, three days after the election on Tuesday, 9 November, saw angry questions directed at Moore. It was an unusual meeting for a group of people new or returned to Parliament and who were on the verge of forming the next government.

Even Moore's Chief Press Secretary Paul Jackman, who had gone in to brief the MPs on what to expect with the news media, was given a difficult time by some of the caucus. The mood was as though they had been soundly beaten rather than being the government in waiting.

Before the caucus MPs had been discussing the leadership. Clark had even been canvassing people's moods, although she was careful not to raise Moore's name directly.

A group of MPs including Lianne Dalziel, Ruth Dyson, Pete Hodgson, Steve Maharey and Judith Tizard had been discussing rolling Moore for Clark.

The fact that Labour got within one seat of winning back power and that Bolger might be forced to go back to the country within months only hastened their resolve.

At that first caucus Moore's opponents were all prearranged to make speeches about the need for him to stand down. In the end only Lianne Dalziel and Steve Maharey spoke against his continued leadership.

After caucus Moore asked to see Maharey in his office where he and Yvonne, chain smoking, confronted the Palmerston North MP. Moore asked Maharey what had happened. Maharey told him that people had previously indicated they were keen to discuss the leadership, but it appeared they'd now changed their minds.

Both men left the meeting annoyed — Moore because his leadership had been questioned and Maharey because it appeared his colleagues had left him and Dalziel out on a limb.

Despite the obvious problems, Moore was sure nothing would happen because Bolger was going to struggle to hold a government together. He couldn't believe the disgruntled MPs would go through with it with the prospect of being in government so tantalisingly close.

Bolger had to pick a Cabinet and there were already strong indications that Richardson would be dropped from the finance portfolio. If he did that, would she resign from Parliament?

He was also sure that there were defections to New Zealand First in the wings — Hawke's Bay's Michael Laws and his good friend Peter McCardle from Heretaunga were the obvious contenders — and that Bolger would have to go back to the polls sometime in the next six months.

Moore was sure Anderton knew that too when he quickly pledged the support of the Alliance for National on all matters of parliamentary confidence. Another election would almost certainly have seen third-party votes collapse back to the main parties and possibly see the Alliance lose its two seats.

Moore also had a 'plan B' to force the Alliance to vote against the government in Parliament. He had a private members bill drafted to repeal the Employment Contracts Act. He knew Alliance supporters wouldn't stand by and watch Anderton and new MP Sandra Lee vote with the government to stop a repeal of the legislation all the trade unions hated.

While waiting for the special votes to come in, a strange mood was developing among Labour MPs. Many stayed away from the leaders' floor in Bowen House and started gathering in small groups in offices.

The core plotters met immediately after that first caucus. They felt they had no choice now, with their cover seemingly blown, but to go through with the challenge, having initially stumbled.

Party General Secretary Tony Timms volunteered to talk to Moore.

Moore could no longer be in denial. He knew it would come one day and that it would probably be Clark, but the speed of it just after an election Labour had almost won — could, in effect, still win in the coming months — stunned him.

He was angry given what he'd done in recent weeks, what he'd done since late 1990 to keep Labour a credible party and now that the government looked like it might collapse. He had expected to at least be treated with respect.

In the lead-up to the election campaign, a number of candidates around the country had received direct and less direct and subtle queries on their views of Moore's leadership. While on the surface everyone was committed to trying to win the 1993 election, some MPs and party officials weren't sure if Labour was ready to be in government again.

A group of the younger and newer MPs, while not close to Clark, just didn't warm to Moore and his style.

One of the traditional roles of party whips is to watch the leader's back. But Senior Whip Jonathan Hunt, who had been a long-time Clark supporter, said nothing to him. He never liked Hunt but had known him a long time and nevertheless felt betrayed. It took Junior Whip Liz Tennet, the MP for Island Bay and a former trade union official, to warn Moore of the rumblings.

Moore went public with the challenge on 25 November, 19 days after the general election.

Moore and key staff retreated to Christchurch to deal with the challenge, which looked like it would come to a head at caucus on 1 December.

He tried a number of times to call Clark but could only get her answerphone. He wanted to make her a deal: give him six to 12 months to try to bring the Bolger Government down and if he failed, he would stand aside for her. If he was successful and became prime minister, he would commit to handing over the reins to her after a set period. But she never returned his calls.

Unusually for a leadership challenge, Moore didn't receive a delegation of MPs — other than Maharey's visit — asking him to step aside. That seemed the usual way for Labour to get rid of its leaders.

Instead the dagger was delivered by Labour President Maryan Street. He'd always liked Street and thought she was better than her predecessor Ruth Dyson.

Street had talked to Moore a number of times and eventually asked him to step aside for the sake of the party. Unusually, she had also made her views on the leadership contest public through an interview with the *Evening Post* on 11 November where she said she'd written to Moore saying he should stand down graciously because Clark had the numbers.

Moore asked her to arrange for a 'peace conference' with Clark given she was not returning his calls and to reinforce his offer to her.

When Moore heard nothing back, he decided the best form of defence was attack and spoke to party members via the news media, urging them to make their views known to their local Labour MPs about the coup.

He derided the plotters as 'chardonnay socialists', the dinner-party set who wouldn't know the difference between a handle and a jug of beer. They called him a 'dry red'.

Moore knew he was popular with many party members and the public, particularly after the close-run election, and hoped the pressure might cause some MPs sitting on the fence to go with him.

The common complaint by some opponents of Moore was that he was 'a flake'. The refrain was now being used to rally MPs against him.

It was the sort of thing that the smug middle class used to say of the working class, Moore used to think. It was a throwaway line indicating their intellectual superiority and knowledge. To him it was a badge of honour, a confirmation that they weren't true Labour and another reason to hate them.

The complaints all came out: he really hadn't disowned Rogernomics, he'd upset the trade union movement, his election-night speech was terrible, the title of his recent book *Fighting for New Zealand* was violent, his office was too macho.

It was also put about that the CTU, a trade union body not affiliated to the party, was somehow angry about Moore's reluctance to wholeheartedly condemn the Employment Contracts Act.

The very public fight had unintended consequences when some Moore supporters started plastering posters around the electorates of key Clark supporters. Moore was furious and called his office asking if they'd arranged it, only to be told it had nothing to do with the protests. This was exactly what his opponents wanted to be associated with him, he shouted.

Moore spent some time back at his old haunt, Orana Wildlife Park on the outskirts of Christchurch, trying to think through what to do. Every which way he looked at it, he couldn't quite seem to muster the numbers.

He knew he was going to lose. He vowed not to walk away meekly but to go into caucus and force the vote, to make MPs clearly choose sides.

For the leadership ballot to occur there first needed to be a successful majority motion for an election. Hunt, in what Moore thought was some conscience-salving move, told him before caucus he doubted there was a majority for a 'spill motion'.

Moore had never liked Hunt, who had always boasted about being on the right side of every leadership ballot but who some viewed as switching his vote at the last minute to stay on side with the leader of the time.

Moore's confidant Cullen had similar advice. Some Labour electorate committees, having listened to Moore's public description of the plotters as backstabbers, had given their MPs strict instructions to vote against a spill motion, even though they might have supported Clark longer term. Some MPs told him that.

Cullen's counsel was that Moore might survive such a motion. He could then use the months that followed to prove himself to the many new MPs who were planning to vote against him before the usual post-election New Year caucus leadership vote.

But Moore thought Cullen was being overly optimistic about the caucus and their willingness to eventually support his leadership. If the caucus wanted a brawl, bugger the consequences. He was going to give them one and would sidestep a spill motion.

In caucus Lange, who had accompanied Clark into the room, moved that there be a leadership vote 'forthwith'. This meant that when some MPs later tried to debate the motion they were told to sit down. Moore expected nothing less these days from his old friend. He thought he'd become erratic in his behaviour since giving up the leadership and his personal and health difficulties made him unpredictable.

Moore knew that all his work for Lange in the 1970s and 1980s and trying to help him patch up his relationship with Roger Douglas and other colleagues, and in recent years being understanding of his health issues, would count for nothing.

Moore seconded Lange's motion because after such a public fight with Clark he didn't want to hang on to the leadership merely because a spill motion had been unsuccessful. He saw Rowling hang on to his leadership by a single vote: his own. Afterwards it had been debilitating for Rowling and Labour.

Moore didn't want to hang on to his leadership because of a technicality. He wanted to be a leader with a mandate from caucus, not because of a procedural issue. He didn't want that. If they were going to stab him in the back, they had to do it at that meeting, effectively, in full view of the public.

It was a miscalculation. A few MPs interpreted this as Moore not willing to fight for the leadership. After a long and exhausting election campaign, he was now giving up, some thought.

On the morning of caucus Maharey, who had a giant piece of paper on his office wall with where the votes were likely to fall, met Clark alone in the Bowen House carpark. He told her she had the numbers.

MPs Harry Duynhoven and Paul Swain, who had indicated from the outset that they were supportive of change, swung back and forth with who they would vote for, but Maharey told Clark it wouldn't make a difference to the outcome.

Candidates for the leadership were asked to stand. Moore and Clark immediately took to their feet. Twenty-five days after leading Labour to a near stunning comeback election victory, Moore was defeated 26 votes to 19.

Clark votes: *Helen Clark, Rick Barker, John Blincoe, Mark Burton, David Caygill, Chris Carter, Lianne Dalziel, Ruth Dyson, Taito Phillip Field, Martin Gallagher, Pete Hodgson, Jonathan Hunt, Graham Kelly, David Lange, Janet Mackey, Steve Maharey, Trevor Mallard, Richard Northey, Mark Peck, Jill Pettis, Suzanne Sinclair, Larry Sutherland, Paul Swain, Judith Tizard, Jill White and Dianne Yates.*

Moore votes: *Mike Moore, Margaret Austin, Geoff Braybrooke, Michael Cullen, Peter Dunne, Harry Duynhoven, Jack Elder, Phil Goff, George Hawkins, Judy Keall, Annette King, Clive Matthewson, Damien O'Connor, Ross Robertson, Jim Sutton, Peter Tapsell, Liz Tennet, Whetu Tirikatene-Sullivan and Koro Wetere.*

Moore walked out of the caucus by himself and across the lobby into his office, where Yvonne was waiting, and closed the door.

He didn't know how to feel. It was like being told again that his father had died. He almost wasn't sure what it meant or how he was now supposed to behave. But he knew everyone would now be looking to him for a reaction — of grief or anger.

All the newly elected first-time MPs, except for the West Coast's Damien O'Connor, and six out of the seven new MPs from 1990 voted for Clark. That hurt Moore, given all he'd done to get them elected. A number would apologise to him years later saying they made the wrong decision and had done it under severe pressure from Clark's people. Moore didn't believe some of them.

Some hoped that Cullen would then become deputy as a peace offering to the Moore camp and beat the economically dry Caygill. But Cullen was beaten for the deputy leadership 23 votes to 21 with one of his supporters, Judy Keall, accidentally spoiling her vote.

The Māori MPs were angry after caucus and came to see Moore, some suggesting they resign in protest. Moore urged them not to. Others steadily came to see Moore and give their condolences, including a few who voted against him.

The bitterness continued the following day when some of Moore's staff came in to the office to be dismissed and hand in their security passes and parliamentary credit cards. A few had been offered roles in Clark's administration, but most were content to leave and few had expectations. They hugged Moore and said their final farewells to colleagues and MPs.

As part of that transition one of the people Clark had brought down from Auckland to assist had been abusive to a number of the outgoing staff, leaving some in tears. A few of Moore's staff had to be restrained from confronting him. Clark later rang at least one of the affected Moore staff to apologise for the behaviour.

Moore and Yvonne were at a loss to know what to do or who to turn to. So they headed to the one place Moore knew he was welcome and where people accepted him for who he was — his childhood home in the Far North. It was like a warm embrace. No one judged him in the north. If anything, he had to leave behind his 'big city ways' and remember he was no better than anyone else.

The couple spent time in Kawakawa and Moerewa, visited his old mentor Mat Rata and Labour Māori Vice President Dover Samuels at Matauri Bay and stayed at a friend's bach in the Opua inlet only accessible at high tide on a rickety dinghy they'd also been lent.

The Far North had always been his healing bandage, the best place to dress his wounds.

10

The Democratic Coalition

'The coup left me bewildered. The treatment of the staff and the damage to everyone's reputations was really sad.

'What depressed me the most was how many MPs wouldn't come near me afterwards. You'd be talking to someone, telling a joke, and someone would come by and it would finish. What was going on? It was politically incorrect to talk with me. It was embarrassing — old friends of mine running for cover.

'Jonathan Hunt had a pattern where he'd come and see me on a Wednesday and say: "Go home Mike, you don't need to be in the House." They had me speaking last on bills really late at night and things like that. They were just trying to get me out of the place not for my own well-being but to avoid causing themselves embarrassment. I'd helped save their seats or got them elected in the past; now they didn't want to be seen with me. What a bunch of cowards some of them were.

'Helen wouldn't talk to me. Maybe I was hard to talk to anyway.

'I'd been on TV with Michael Laws talking about what the new MMP system would mean for New Zealand politics. I was pissed off with Labour and he was pissed off with National and we stayed in touch.

'I was pretty naughty. Laws and I arranged for a public meeting in Napier and it was packed and all the media started speculating about a centre party being started. I have to admit I liked the attention and I enjoyed the angst it caused some of them.

'Then it just started gathering its own steam. More people kept coming along and talking with me or Laws.

'I was never really sure if it would be a goer but kept going along with the idea. Everyone seemed enthusiastic and the polling we did just blew me away. It got quite a bit of steam, but we only seemed to be attracting disappointed politicians and others who just wanted to be in Parliament. Other than being convenient to a bunch of people, we didn't seem to have a base to the party.

'Yvonne was supportive of me, but I knew she didn't like the idea of me leaving Labour — neither did I deep down.

'Laws was getting pissed off with me not committing and he eventually went off to New Zealand First. It was fair enough from his point of view. The idea of the Democratic Coalition then just petered away. I know I let down a lot of people, but I just couldn't do it to Labour.

'Helen was doing really badly in the polls and MPs started coming up to me and whispering that I should make a comeback. But all it did was make me angry. Some of them were the same cowards who rolled me.

'I did think for a while that I could have a comeback if I played it straight and gave Helen a clean run for three years.

'When Phil Goff and the others came to see me about rolling Helen I was really surprised. I said to them: "Tell me you're here because you love me." I told them I wasn't going to do anything. If they wanted it, they had to go get it.

'Yvonne told me not to do it. I went to Helen and said: "The drums are beating." I told her if I had the numbers, I would roll her. I felt that I should say that to her because that's what she didn't do to me.

'At that stage I was still unhappy with everything. If I'd leaked things to the papers to undermine Helen and if I'd built myself up in the polls, I might have been able to be leader again. But at that stage I didn't know if they deserved me, frankly.

'At one stage Michael Cullen was going to see Helen. I said to him: "You're not going to spook her." I said to him in front of the others: "When you go in there David Caygill is going to get rolled and you'll end up deputy."

'And Cullen's response when I challenged him later on it was: "Oh, you can still be leader if we win the election." Technically that was true but if she wins, she deserves to be leader, I said.

'Helen showed great strength and stood up to them and I showed great weakness by standing back.

'The animosity between Helen and me was avoidable if we'd sat down and broken bread together. She had some nutters around her, though. She may have tried, I don't know. I might have said no, too, given the mood I was in. But the longer things went, the harder it became.

'The whole making peace with Helen was staged. The week before the election I met her at a rally. I met her at an election stop and we said nice things about each other.

'The cameras were pointed at us and I put my hand on her shoulder. The body language was more important than what I said. Neither of us really embraced the moment, but it was symbolic and Labour got its photo op. It was the right thing to do to try to get Labour elected.

'I should have handled things better. I should have been more supportive of Helen, but I just couldn't be bothered at the time. The leadership loss still hurt.

'Even so I did try to lever Labour in with Winston Peters after that first MMP election. I had late-night drinking sessions with him, but he was bullshitting me along. I knew Winston had contempt for Bolger, but he was always going to go with him — he understands the dance of MMP better than most.

'In the end Helen got nine years as prime minister and was an impressive leader. She controlled the party and the caucus like few before her. It certainly beat my eight weeks.'

****

People can be cruel.

Those you once shared a drink and plenty of laughs with, helped get elected, can suddenly just know you as a passing colleague — that glance across and the raising of chins, while walking by in the corridor. Even the whispered 'gidday mate' while scanning the surroundings, hoping no one can see. They're all the insults pretending not to be.

In the post-coup Labour caucus, brimming with new, old and retreaded MPs, the atmosphere was uncertain. Would the new leadership disavow all knowledge of the fourth Labour Government, would it strive off in a new interventionist direction for the party to contrast itself to National and bring back the left-wing activists who were now with the Alliance?

How would the Moore and the Clark backers work together after such a divisive leadership battle?

No sooner had Moore vacated the leader's office than Bolger shored up National's position by offering the Speaker's role — and with it later a knighthood — to Labour's Eastern Māori MP Peter Tapsell in place of National's current Speaker Robin Gray. Clark presented the deal to the Labour caucus as a fait accompli and there was little resistance to it from Labour MPs.

National had a little more wriggle room in Parliament now.

Moore hated being in Parliament. He swung from being melancholic to angry. He didn't know whether he should be in Wellington surrounded by the smiling assassins or back in Christchurch with Yvonne who was probably angrier than him.

Labour's Leader of the House Jonathan Hunt would sidle up to Moore in Parliament on a Wednesday and tell him to head home and rest. Initially he took the advice to avoid the stares and the awkwardness. Then he realised what Hunt was possibly doing: trying to avoid the stares and awkwardness for himself.

As in the past, it was all about Hunt, Moore thought. The more Hunt offered a helping hand the more he wanted to push it back into his face.

Moore's only consolation at the time was Labour and Clark's poor poll ratings. The backlash against Clark from the public after the coup was swift, long-lasting and would eventually almost cost her the leadership.

From an election-night result of almost 35 per cent of the vote, the change in the leadership had seen Labour slump in opinion polls to 24 per cent in early 1994 and then to a low of 17 per cent in August. Meantime National had peaked in 1994 on 43 per cent, while the Alliance had been second place most of the year with a high of 35 per cent in August.

The caucus was basically split along voting lines and Moore couldn't be bothered with much despite the efforts of a few MPs including Annette King to try to mend bridges between the sides.

But Labour wasn't alone with its political problems. National had a huge one.

Hawke's Bay MP Michael Laws is described with many adjectives, depending on your political views and your past interactions with him.

Moore had once called Laws the 'Alan B'Stard of Parliament' after the egocentric MP character played by Rik Mayall in the late 1980s and early 1990s British comedy *The New Statesman*. B'Stard was unscrupulous and was funny because he was everything people wanted to believe of politicians.

Moore and Laws had an unusual relationship. Moore liked the fact that Laws was an outcast in his own party — similar to him — and admired his grass-roots campaigning skills and use of the news media.

Moore was, however, weary of Laws' populism and what he thought was a lack of a philosophical base. Laws thought all New Zealand politics was based on relationships people could form with each other and the electorate.

In early 1994, as the country was digesting its decision in the 1993 referendum to have MMP as its electoral system, Moore and Laws appeared together on TVNZ's *Fraser* news and current affairs show.

The producers of the show had been clever — two high-profile disaffected politicians in a room with a camera and a clever journalist who knew when to use leading questions, when not to finish sentences. It had the makings of great television.

While they might have been backbenchers, Moore and Laws weren't naïve. They understood they were being invited to perform — and how they loved to dance.

Laws had been a strong proponent of proportional representation when Moore had opposed it. Moore believed, like Clark and many other senior Labour politicians at the time, that MMP would make it difficult to govern. It might also eventually fracture one of the main parties and he feared it might be Labour.

The *Fraser* debate was about how under MMP a well-organised centre party could be a good go-between for future Labour or National governments. It was clear that National wanted to be a centre-right party, Labour a centre-left one and the Alliance and ACT parties were on the extreme of both. And who knew what Winston Peters and the new New Zealand First stood for? There was room in the centre, was the moot.

That centre party would almost certainly always be in power. Ian Fraser hinted that any centre party needed to have Moore and Laws in it. They both loved the idea and enjoyed the flirting.

Both talked on the show about how a centre party would make sure Labour and National weren't forced to be extreme by the smaller parties on the outside of them. Moore described it as giving the political system 'ballast'.

The Free Democrats in West Germany had commanded the centre and much of the power since the Second World War.

After the show Moore and Laws continued talking and agreed they should catch up again.

Soon after there was a severe hailstorm in Hawke's Bay that devastated many of the orchards in Laws' electorate. Instead of inviting the Minister of Agriculture John Falloon to inspect them, he curiously asked Moore. The pair were photographed by news media touring the damaged orchards.

Moore loyalist Napier MP Geoff Braybrooke had been suggesting to his former leader for some time that he should spend some time with Laws.

Braybrooke was old Labour, working-class Catholic, a former London 'bobby' who — like Moore — distrusted the university-educated middle-class MPs in caucus. Through old-fashioned door-to-door campaigning and running strongly on local issues he had made Napier solid Labour.

Laws wasn't Braybrooke's cup of tea but the two learned to get on with each other, along with Hastings MP Rick Barker — a proud West Coaster who voted for Clark in the leadership spill but later became a good friend of Moore's — as a united Hawke's Bay lobby in Parliament.

Braybrooke also organised a meeting of 'orchardists and anyone else' for Moore and Laws in Napier. This immediately attracted national media attention.

Despite the feints of innocence at the time, this was no accident.

Moore was still in mourning about the leadership and clearly enjoyed the attention and the grief his actions were causing Clark and the Labour hierarchy.

For Laws, Moore was the big fish he needed to reel in if he was to start a centre party. Laws had deliberately targeted him.

Moore had broad electoral appeal, was politically smart, was energetic and National told him they could do a deal with him. The other likely choice for National in the upcoming first MMP election in 1996 was New Zealand First's Winston Peters, and Laws knew there would be friction there.

In their time together in Hawke's Bay, Moore and Laws openly talked about forming a centre party.

The logic of such a party was powerful. A good centre party with good candidates could command potentially 10 per cent of the vote and be in coalition with either Labour or National. It could possibly be in government permanently, they thought.

Laws would talk about the possibilities and Moore would agree and then add his two cents' worth before expressing doubts. Moore was conflicted. He would be abandoning the working-class battlers in Labour. What would 'the ladies with the fat arms and the big urns of tea' say? What would they say about him in the Papanui Working Men's Club?

Laws continued to make the running on the idea of a centre party. A few months later a group of them met with National Party President Geoff Thompson and National activist Michelle Boag to see what the business community and others might think of such a party. Boag was well connected into the boardrooms of New Zealand, particularly in Auckland.

Moore saw them as potential funders.

No commitments were made and, if anything, further doubts were sown when Moore made it clear that any funding couldn't be tied to the centre party committing only to National. Moore knew that Thompson and Boag were keen to ensure that any National funders who helped back the centre party meant their party would end up in the box seat ahead of Labour in any coalition government negotiations. Moore refused.

Moore and Laws continued to meet for friendly backslapping dinners, mostly at the Yangtze Chinese Restaurant in the Robert Jones Building on Lambton Quay in Wellington. Moore often met Sir Robert Jones, someone whose opinions he didn't share but whose company and out-of-the-box ideas he enjoyed, and other business leaders there because it was a restaurant not popular with journalists and the chattering classes so confidential, often boozy, gatherings could be held.

Laws kept pushing Moore to dump Labour and help him set up a centre party. Labour was at such a low ebb. Clark continued to struggle in the polls.

And Moore kept chipping away at the party's hierarchy, about their political correctness and inability to connect with ordinary Kiwis and their life views. He would write op-eds and give speeches that clearly showed there were divisions in the caucus and that the rifts hadn't been healed.

Clark and her people saw it as Moore being disloyal to the leader, while he saw it as trying to keep Labour true to its base.

Moore even sent out a newsletter called *From the Centre* which continued to fuel speculation about an imminent departure.

Moore liked Laws' enthusiasm, his political analysis and his optimism but was always uneasy about leaving Labour. Laws didn't understand his deep ties to the soul of Labour. His connection with Labour was in his blood; it was tribal.

Laws' arguments — strong and convincing as they were — appealed to Moore's brain but not to his heart. This was the party of Moore's heroes: Savage, Fraser, Nash and Kirk. What would his mentor Mat Rata say? What would the likes of Marge McCrenor, the loyal party member from the state house in the Christchurch suburb of Bryndwr, say? What would Mother say?

As 1994 went on Moore continued to toy with the idea of a centre party but not commit to it.

The idea got a huge boost in July and August 1994 from the most unlikely of quarters — the National blue-ribbon seat of Selwyn in Christchurch.

Less than 12 months earlier Labour candidate and Moore ally Ron Mark, a local businessman, had almost pulled off the unthinkable of unseating finance minister Ruth Richardson, who won by just under 900 votes.

The traditional solid-blue seat was being vacated by Richardson after she was dumped as finance minister after the 1993 general election and had languished on the back benches for months.

It was a double-edged sword for National and Labour. National's majority in the House was slender, so a victory was critical for the government. Clark had barely been Labour leader and now her electoral appeal would be on display for the nation to see.

And on the sidelines was Jim Anderton and his Alliance party eager to displace Labour as the real Opposition, and New Zealand First with its high-profile candidate Tim Shadbolt.

Labour's campaign was awful by most measures. The party selected Avonside Girls' High School principal and former Communist Party member Marian Hobbs, who was a kind and gentle soul unprepared for the nationwide glare of an important by-election.

At an early Clark and Hobbs campaign stop in the lunchroom of what would normally have been a Labour-friendly local factory — Belfast's Colyer Watson fellmongery — was a sign 'Bring Back Mike' pinned to the staff notice board. The television news cameras caught the image and the awkwardness of the situation and beamed it into living rooms that evening.

The image conveyed to New Zealand was a Labour uncomfortable in the presence of ordinary working Kiwis and to the news media a poorly organised party.

The showing in Selwyn was having an impact nationally. A One Network News-Heylen poll on 2 August 1994 had Labour slipping to third place for the first time since 1980. National was on 35 per cent, the Alliance 28 per cent and Labour 27 per cent. Moore was also higher than Clark on the preferred prime minister stakes with 10 per cent, compared with her 5 per cent.

National's high-profile David Carter, from an old and successful Canterbury family, eventually won the by-election but only by just over 400 votes from former Social Creditor and now Alliance candidate John Wright.

Hobbs, who would eventually become Wellington Central MP and a Cabinet minister in Clark's fifth Labour Government, came a distant third with just over 2000 votes or just over 10 per cent of the vote.

Labour and Clark's poor showing in the by-election was further evidence for those pushing Moore to create his own party that the time had come.

Laws was becoming increasingly impatient, too, because his own future in the National Party was becoming perilous. Bolger and the leadership had no time for him and many of his caucus colleagues saw him as a troublemaker destined for a bad ending of which they wanted to be well clear.

Meantime Moore continued to meet Laws, and colleagues Braybrooke and Henderson MP Jack Elder were part of the grouping, as was National Heretaunga MP and Laws ally Peter McCardle.

Moore had also gathered around him some local support from Christchurch. Mark and lifelong confidant and later Labour Cabinet minister Clayton Cosgrove were already doing work on the party. Potential candidates were being approached and lined up.

Former Moore campaign organiser Jeff McIntyre, who had helped create MMSC, was doing a lot of work behind the scenes on a possible party. As far back as 1991 McIntyre had spent some time in Germany with the Free Democratic Party to see how smaller parties campaigned under MMP, which Moore thought would win the 1993 electoral referendum.

The Free Democrats had helped form most of the coalition governments since the Second World War, being the junior partner of both left- and right-wing parties in West Germany, and usually polled between about 6 to 11 per cent. Moore wanted to know how third-party 'kingmaker' parties presented themselves to the electorate.

The crucial lesson was that the tail couldn't wag the dog. The smaller party in any coalition had to know its limitations. In campaigning it also needed to know its niche and ruthlessly choose policies and candidates that appealed to those voters.

The Free Democrats pitched themselves as fiscally responsible and targeted businesspeople with a social conscience and those who didn't like the major parties.

Moore was used to running marginal seats campaigns. Under the first past the post system Moore was used to focusing on about 15 to 20 marginal seats. Safe seats were all but forgotten about. Under MMP every vote counted and resources would, for the first time, need to go to target-rich environments instead. His whole campaign mindset had to change.

Moore continued to hint that he had more coming in his political career. In one story with *Sunday News* in January 1995 he was asked about recently turning 46 years old and laughed it off, saying that Muldoon was first elected at that age.

As 1995 came around people's attention was briefly engaged by the formation of United New Zealand, which also aimed to take the centre ground ahead of the first MMP election.

It had four National (Bruce Cliffe, Pauline Gardiner, Peter Hilt and John Robertson) and two Labour (Margaret Austin and Clive Matthewson) MPs, plus former Labour and now Independent Onslow MP Peter Dunne.

It was led by old Moore Papanui rival and later friend Matthewson.

United's launch was a media muddle. They came across as confused and unsure of what they stood for, other than self-interest. They were all good sincere people, but they hardly grabbed the electorate's attention.

Moore saw this and wanted to avoid the same positioning in any centre party he was part of.

Nevertheless, United quickly did a deal to support National and Dunne was made a minister in Cabinet.

Laws kept moving on the centre party. He was the driver of it. Momentum was gathering and meetings continued to be held at the Yangtze. These were social and serious. Moore kept setting the team tasks to do and when completed he would ask for more.

Constitutions, policy, the 500-minimum membership requirement for a party with the Electoral Commission, candidates, party names and logos were discussed.

The name was an issue. Moore believed the word 'coalition' was critical to the name because it indicated it was a party of different people. Labour and National people could vote for it. Laws wanted to call it the 'People's Party'. Moore thought that sounded like a communist party and in the end persuaded everyone that the 'Democratic Coalition' would be the name and its colours would be yellow and black like the Free Democrats.

Everyone was focused on launching for the 1996 general election because if they didn't take the opportunity, they were sure someone else would as politicians started to figure out MMP and how to play its game. It was also clear to everyone that Moore would be the leader.

Noise continued about the possibility of the party. It got so loud that former Social Credit Leader Bruce Beetham resurfaced and offered Moore a coalition with his New Zealand Centre Coalition.

That party was a strange mix of Beetham's old Social Credit Party, the New Zealand Party and a group called United, which was a mix of the Confederation of United Tribes and one-time march organiser Tania Harris and her supporters. Beetham, as he was when he was an MP with 21 per cent of the vote in the early 1980s, was deadly serious. But Moore found the idea laughable.

Laws was also promoting with Moore the idea of joining forces with Winston Peters, his old rival and friend. Moore was sceptical because of Peters' crusade against corporate New Zealand. It wouldn't be conducive to bringing in donations from the business community.

A New Zealand First MP even approached Moore informally — so it could be later denied — and offered him the role as deputy leader to Peters. Tongue in cheek, Moore told the MP he was only interested if it was the leader's role.

Meanwhile, planning for the Democratic Coalition continued with more urgency with weekly breakfast meetings at Laws' Wellington home with Elder, Braybrooke and McCardle.

A major and probably final weekend of planning was arranged for Christchurch in August 1995 at the offices of Aoraki Corporation, the home of Moore's old friend and donor Gil Simpson.

Heated discussions were held on major policy issues. McCardle pushed his pro-Catholic family issues, while people like Laws wanted more individual freedoms and responsibilities.

The contradictions in the positions of the many at the gathering weren't lost on Moore, although he found the free and frank discussions without political repercussions refreshing as it reminded him of Labour Party debates in the 1960s and 1970s.

They agreed that the party would generally be liberal on social issues and conservative on economic ones. Conscience issues would be dealt with by referenda. A Hawke's Bay doctor and friend of Laws, Rosy Fenwicke, was made president of the party. Laws was to finalise the constitution.

One of the tasks Moore was left with was to get some polling done on the party and see how its aims would play with the voters. Moore's old friend Paul Heylen from Heylen Research helped and the research was startling: 8 per cent of those polled said they would support the Democratic Coalition if it was led by Moore, with another 25 per cent saying they would consider voting for the party.

For a party that had only been speculated on by the political media this was an extraordinary result. Instead of being encouraged by it, Moore was a combination of annoyed and concerned. It was like someone had slapped him in the face and woken him from his slumber.

He thought there was no reason the party could not be in front of Labour. He'd hoped the Democratic Coalition could supplant Labour on the centre left of the political spectrum and force Clark to the hard left with Anderton and the Alliance.

He was also fearful. This party could work if he left Labour and led it.

If he was prepared to knife his tribe in the back, he would find himself once again in the political box seat where he would finally be shown some respect.

There was even an outside chance it could collapse Labour's vote into the low 20s and the Democratic Coalition would challenge it as the official Opposition party. This was serious. This was frightening.

Labour was having its own internal issues but managed to keep a lid on dissension. In October 1995, with the Alliance outpolling Labour 23 per cent to 20 per cent, a group of Clark supporters talked to her about her leadership. If she had stood down, Cullen had indicated he wanted the leadership. But Clark successfully batted them away.

All the while the 500 signatures were being gathered to legally register the Democratic Coalition and by the end of 1995 more than 600 people had signed up. On top of that, policy was ready, the constitution was agreed and party functionaries were in place nationwide for a proper party launch. It was a miracle it hadn't been leaked.

They agreed to launch the party in early 1996 and for Moore to launch a referendum in Christchurch in the New Year as a precursor to him announcing his departure.

He had also been working on a book to be published in 1996 called *Children of the Poor* that took its title from one written by Labour's most prominent outcast, John A. Lee, who had been expelled from the party in 1940 and went on to launch the Democratic Labour Party.

It was all coming together well.

To everyone's incredible surprise the *Sunday Star-Times* of 28 January 1996 carried a front-page lead story rounding up what MPs were considering defecting from their parties. Prominent among the likely was Moore who, the story said, was under intense pressure to leave and form a centre party with the likes of Laws and McCardle.

Later that Sunday, Moore put out a press release saying he'd had an exploratory committee look at the idea of a party and had even done some polling on it. 'I still believe Labour is worth fighting for,' his press release said. 'If I thought the fight was impossible then the only honourable course would be to leave.'

This was the turning point for Laws who came to the conclusion

Moore would never leave Labour no matter how badly the party treated him. Moore didn't have the fanatical drive required to set up a new party. Laws believed that all the talk of a centre party was just his elaborate way of dealing with the grief of losing the Labour leadership.

Moore wasn't convinced such a party would last. It was based too much on big personalities and egos with policies that seemed to contradict each other. For Moore, standing for something mattered.

Soon afterwards Laws visited Moore in his parliamentary office for a final decision on the Democratic Coalition. Elder and McCardle joined them.

Laws announced that he was going to take up an offer from Peters and join New Zealand First. He promised to continue to work on the quiet for the Democratic Coalition and after the 1996 election would work hard to get the two parties together.

For Moore there was disbelief and relief. Laws had probably been the most committed to the new party. But the news now meant he was free from any obligations to the others to form the party.

For many of those who had been working on the party, Moore was seen as the horse and Laws the jockey. There couldn't be a successful race without both working together. It was over.

It was to be a tumultuous year for Labour. The party was languishing in the polls with little money, Clark was desperately unpopular, National had rid itself of Richardson and managed to recover from the shock of nearly losing in 1993, and with Laws joining a resurgent New Zealand First it was a volatile cocktail for Labour.

Even though Moore had jilted Laws at the altar, he had yet to fully get his head around being part of the Labour team. He was still annoyed with the behaviour and tone of many of its MPs and officials which he saw as puppets for a bigger politically correct movement in society.

Having to change your language and your thinking undermined free speech and stifled debate, which was critical if Labour was to progress as a party. He saw it as a form of intellectual bullying and was determined to fight against it.

He wrote a series of newspaper opinion pieces against political correctness and offered the public a bottle of Scotch from Bellamy's for the silliest examples.

He said he wanted to expose the shallowness of the politically correct brigade and the tactics behind their 'thought control' which he considered 'silly as well as sinister'.

He cited a kindergarten banning hot cross buns at Easter because it might offend non-Christians, how someone had wanted to change the name of Victoria University of Wellington because it was sexist and imperialist, and how he and Yvonne were criticised by a senior Labour official in the 1993 campaign for looking too heterosexual.

If you can control the vocabulary, you can control the debate and if you control that, you control the outcome, Moore said.

In March 1996 Moore launched a damning criticism of the party, saying too many of its MPs had no idea what motivated core Labour voters.

'They are not on this planet. They are Klingons,' he told the *Evening Post*.

He hadn't quite got over the collapse of the Democratic Coalition idea and talked about a centrist party being necessary under MMP.

'I have a lot of people and a lot of resources saying, "Come on, MMP needs a firm hand and the best way to help Labour is to provide another option to it as a partner in government, even as a possible partner to National".'

But it wasn't long before political circumstances moved him on by presenting another opportunity — one that almost paralysed him with indecision again.

With the 1996 general election fast approaching, it was starting to dawn on some Labour MPs — seniors and newbies — that Clark's poor polling would put many of their seats in jeopardy.

Outspoken National Cabinet minister John Banks, who had a Sunday talkback show on Radio Pacific, would stir it up by constantly referring to Clark as 'Ms Two Per cent'.

In May 1996 Labour's pollsters UMR had the party at 22 per cent, with National on 35 per cent and New Zealand First in second place on 30 per cent.

Eyes started being cast around in caucus for a potential saviour. Deputy Leader David Caygill had been loyal to Clark since his elevation after the 1993 coup. Retread MP Annette King wasn't seen then as having the gravitas for the role.

There was a crop of young up-and-coming MPs like Lianne Dalziel from Christchurch Central and Palmerston North's Steve Maharey who had been touted by many as future leaders, but they were inexperienced and strongly loyal to Clark.

That really left only St Kilda MP Michael Cullen, Roskill MP Phil Goff and Moore. But all three likely candidates were reluctant.

Cullen was the obvious successor. As finance spokesperson he'd made a great fist of the portfolio under Moore and Clark, regularly putting pressure on the government. He was ambitious, managed to straddle the conservative and liberal wings of the party and, while he hid it well, was deeply suspicious of Clark.

Cullen's wife Anne Collins, a former MP in the fourth Labour Government, was often vocal in her dislike and distrust of Clark and her supporters. Some in the party likened his quiet and intellectual demeanour as similar to their iconic Labour hero Michael Joseph Savage.

For much of his career Goff was seen by many as a future leader and, on this occasion, the most likely contender because his seat was at risk from Labour's poor polling. He'd lost his seat in 1990 and didn't want it to happen again. But Goff had always been a cautious politician.

Much of his political career had been about standing back and waiting for the opportunity to be presented to him. Many, including Moore, liked Goff and his work ethic but thought he lacked boldness. So it was again.

For Moore it was déjà vu. This was 1990 all over again. His caucus colleagues saw themselves staring at the unemployment line and once again — reluctantly — turned to their old mate Mike for help. They didn't see this as an opportunity to help promote Moore — this was all about them.

This time instead of seeing it as his obligation to try to save the party or even his main chance, Moore was annoyed. He knew they were using him for their own selfish purposes. In the past he was more than happy for that to occur. Not this time.

He was coy. If the caucus wanted him to be leader, he'd do it. But he wasn't going to campaign for it or lobby anyone. In fact, he'd do nothing. It had to be presented to him — on a plate.

Moore even told Clark what was happening. He said a group had approached him about the leadership but that he wouldn't challenge her unless a majority of the caucus wanted him. Only then would he consider it.

For the plotters, however, Moore's attitude was a thumbs-up for their plans. They had Moore or Goff as their horse against Clark.

In all coups, the numbers are always fluid. Mini-alliances and debts and favours called on make it always difficult to accurately calculate. Lions behind closed doors quickly become pussy cats when asked about their voting intentions.

The plotters kept a pink-coloured parliamentary Hansard reporter's notebook of where all the voters were, and it seemed they had the numbers in the caucus of 41 against Clark. But it wasn't straightforward.

Two of the three Labour Māori MPs, Eastern Māori's Peter Tapsell and Southern Māori's Whetu Tirikatene-Sullivan, were willing to vote against Clark but only for Moore, not Goff. Moore's good friend, Western Māori's Koro Wetere, was happy either way.

Throughout his career Moore had been respectful of the Māori MPs, showing due deference to the history and mana of their seats. The Māori MPs thought they'd lose their seats if Clark remained.

The plotters then made a fatal error. Instead of moving when they had momentum around Easter 1996, they decided to wait until after the party's election-year Congress in May. With Clark's control of the party hierarchy and its affiliated unions deeply rooted, any new leader would likely face a strong backlash at the Congress in full view of the cameras.

This would prove a fillip for Jim Anderton and the Alliance which had slumped back to 10 per cent support.

It was also decided to try to persuade Clark to stand down rather than force a vote in caucus. Some thought a secret vote in caucus was the best course of action because it would give her traditional supporters the opportunity to turn their backs on her.

Jim Sutton had drafted a letter asking Clark to stand down from the leadership and signatures had been gathered. It was basically deadlocked: some 19 or 20 votes each with a few MPs unsure but also with a few on the Clark side as possible defectors and a few on the other who were wobbly.

Many of her 1993 coup supporters had switched sides: the likes of Eastern Hutt's Paul Swain, Invercargill's Mark Peck, Hastings' Rick

Barker and Hamilton West's Martin Gallagher. In fact, Peck and Barker were helping do the numbers for the coup.

A delegation — Cullen, Sutton, Wetere, King and Goff — was then sent to Clark's office to confront her first thing in the morning.

They were met by Clark supporters including Palmerston North MP Steve Maharey, Pencarrow MP Trevor Mallard and long-time friends New Lynn MP Jonathan Hunt and Auckland Central's Judith Tizard.

The two groups of MPs nervously sat together in a meeting room waiting for Clark to arrive. Wetere was so tense that his thumbnail dug away a little hole in the edge of the wooden meeting table.

The plotters told Clark about their unhappiness with her leadership but didn't give her an ultimatum. They seemed unsure who their leadership candidate was. They seemed weak and confused.

The plotters would have to blast her out of office was the message she gave back to them. The plotters became nervous and left the meeting with the matter unresolved.

Clark later asked Cullen for a private meeting where he was offered the deputy leadership role. As soon as Cullen took it, any ongoing threat to Clark dissipated.

It was the unification card that some thought should have been played at the time of the leadership ballot in November 1993. It might have calmed the caucus down after the coup and potentially have eased Moore back into the fold.

Moore watched all this from the sidelines with amusement. He knew the plotters would be unsuccessful. They didn't have the resolve, cunning or hardnosed single-mindedness of Clark.

Bizarrely, Wetere put out a media statement on 10 June after media speculation of the showdown effectively saying a coup had been in the air but it wasn't going to happen now.

'Koro Wetere, Labour MP for Western Māori, said today that no vote on the Labour leadership would be called for at tomorrow's caucus meeting by any of the five frontbench MPs who were reported as recently meeting with Labour Leader Helen Clark to discuss leadership issues,' the statement said.

'It is clear to us that a majority of our caucus colleagues do not wish to vote on the leadership. We have no desire to prolong the internal debate.'

Following the non-coup, instead of discarding the plotters to the obscurity of the back benches, Clark made sure they had prominent roles.

In turn, they responded by becoming loyal supporters of Clark and focusing on the future. They knew they probably weren't going to win in 1996, but with it being New Zealand's first MMP election anything was possible.

Certainly, 1999 was a possibility for Labour with National likely in its third term, so long as they showed supreme unity with Clark.

Moore, while not embraced by the left in the caucus, was encouraged to participate. And with the support of his former supporters Cullen and King he started to get back some of his spirit in the House.

It was the beginning of the turnaround in fortunes for Clark. Her steely-eyed toughness saw Labour steady its polling in the early twenties, eventually overtaking New Zealand First into second place, and her leadership numbers improved. The wounds in the caucus seemed to be healing.

That's not to say there weren't tense moments to come. Moore wasn't quite ready to forgive and some of the Clark supporters weren't willing to forget.

In late August 1996 Labour launched its health policy. But on the same day Moore upstaged it by holding a media conference in the Belfast home of constituent Evan Nicol who was having problems getting funding for a caregiver for his three-year-old disabled son Jonathan.

Clark accused Moore of 'riding on the back of unfortunate circumstances'. Some Clark backers in the caucus and her staff also confronted Moore about the story. He quite happily snapped back, reminding them it was a bit rich they were preaching loyalty to the leader and the party.

The constituent later publicly defended Moore, saying the MP didn't want to go to the media with the issue and that he'd forced him.

The bitterness went beyond Moore. Yvonne, who after *Romper Room* had gone on to other roles — floor manager, reporter, researcher and presenter — with TVNZ in Christchurch, took on the role of *Nine–Noon* talkback host on Christchurch's NewstalkZB.

During the election campaign she hosted Clark in the studio and wasn't shy in her questioning. Yvonne had felt slighted by Clark on a recent visit to a Christchurch school where she helped out.

Yvonne said Moore helped get Labour 35 per cent of the vote in 1993 so asked whether Clark would consider standing down from her role if the party got 25 per cent this time.

Clark said that under MMP 20 per cent might be enough to form a government. Under persistent questioning from Yvonne she said the leadership of the party was not her decision. 'As long as I kept the confidence of the caucus I would stay there. When that changes life takes on a new pattern,' Clark said.

The 1996 election for Moore took on a slow start. His electorate — now called Waimakariri — had pushed north and became more rural and, on paper, more National. He hid his frustrations by reverting to what he always did: campaigning. He knew a nationwide profile was no substitute for grass-roots old-fashioned door-knocking.

Moore was out in the electorate with his old campaign organiser Jeff McIntyre when Clark's office called and broached the idea of the pair appearing together at a campaign event. In front of the country's media it would look like an endorsement and a burying of the hatchet between the two.

Moore didn't immediately dismiss it and he and McIntyre discussed the pros and cons of the idea as they drove around Waimakariri. Moore wasn't sure so McIntyre confronted him with a basic question: 'What do you want the end game to be Mike?'

Yvonne was vehemently against any form of endorsement of Clark, but Moore thought it was time to let go and back his party and leader. He wanted Labour back in government. It might be his last chance.

Clark had offered him a frontbench role as spokesperson for foreign affairs and trade and he had decided to accept it.

Moore was particularly concerned about the new Christian Coalition party, which was made up of Graeme Lee's Christian Democrat Party and Graham Capill's Christian Heritage New Zealand.

The Christian Coalition was taking votes from Labour's conservative working-class base and Pasifika supporters, getting close to the 5 per cent MMP threshold to enter Parliament. One poll before the election had the Christian Coalition at 6.7 per cent.

So it was arranged for Moore to greet and introduce Clark at a campaign stop in the Porirua shopping mall in front of about 200 people on 3 October 1996.

He felt uncomfortable endorsing her, but he was Labour and she was his leader.

They shook hands, he put his hand on her shoulder, and they applauded each other. It all looked stage managed and awkward, but Moore knew it was the right thing to do.

'Helen and I have talked and worked together and had differences over the ages,' he said. 'I've got to say to people that I have no hard feelings about losing the Labour leadership to Helen.'

Clark said Moore would form part of Labour's post-election coalition negotiating team, along with herself, Cullen and Party President Michael Hirschfeld.

'This guy has got the skills to do it,' she said. 'This guy has negotiated with much more difficult people.'

The pair then went to the nearby Ngāti Toa Health Clinic together.

The gloss was taken off the event, however, by Lange — who was retiring at the election — telling an Australian television news programme that there was no way Labour could lead a coalition with Alliance and New Zealand First.

It had annoyed Clark — she labelled Lange 'irrelevant' — and other Labour MPs enormously, coming as it did one week out from polling day.

Now everyone knew what he had to put up with at the last election, Moore thought.

After a tumultuous term where Clark stabbed one of Labour's most popular leaders in the back, where a popular centre party almost emerged, where she had to fight off a coup with all her guile, where New Zealand First and the Alliance were on the rise, and a Christian party challenged her base, it was little surprise that the 1996 general election was the party's worst in 60 years.

At 28 per cent of the vote, it was 20 per cent down on Labour's 1993 result.

Despite Labour's abysmal showing, it still had an outside chance to form a coalition government in 1996 with New Zealand First, which finished with 13 per cent of the vote and 17 seats.

One of the first contacts made between Labour and New Zealand First was Moore calling Laws on election night.

While it was clear to some that Peters wanted to form a coalition with National all along, Labour still wanted to see if it could stitch something together.

As the formal coalition talks took place in the glare of the news media, Moore was used as a back channel to Peters and Laws.

The optimist in Moore continued to push matters with New Zealand First. Between Moore and Laws an accidental meeting would occur at what was then one of Wellington's high-end restaurants, Il Casino. No Yangtze Restaurant for Peters.

The New Zealand First Leader went out for what was supposed to be a nice evening with Laws and his wife, and Moore arranged to take Peters' brother Wayne, a National MP, out to the same restaurant.

After 'bumping into each other', joining tables, a lot of Italian food, drinking and storytelling, Peters, Laws, Moore and a New Zealand First staffer went off to a nearby nightclub — they couldn't find any bars — for more drinks.

As the music blared out and young people danced in the background, Peters laid out the deal to Moore at the bar.

He wanted to become treasurer and deputy prime minister, when Clark was out of the country he wanted to be acting prime minister, a New Zealand First MP was to be police minister and the Cabinet manual was to be rewritten to reflect the coalition agreement.

Moore thought it was a reasonable request but knew that some of the conditions would be unacceptable to Clark and Cullen. He suspected Peters was just trying to use Labour to get a better deal with National.

Moore also suspected National were using Peters' old friends Wyatt Creech, Roger McClay, Paul East and Philip Burdon to talk to him and that Labour only had an outside chance.

While he was part of the Labour negotiation team, Moore never really thought he had the trust of Clark, Cullen and Hirschfeld. He also knew if they couldn't create a coalition government with New Zealand First and the Alliance — which they eventually failed to do — then it would be another long three years in the political wilderness.

But late 1996 was the beginning of another period in Moore's life that would, once again, present him with stark choices.

11

Justice now: finish the round

'US Secretary of State Madeleine Albright came to New Zealand and Helen and some others from the caucus were going to meet her. I was Labour's foreign affairs spokesperson but somehow got left off the invitation list. I was invited eventually but didn't have a say in the meeting. Labour's foreign affairs spokesperson wasn't asked by the leader if he had any questions. I knew it was time to go.

'I've never had such unanimous support from the Labour caucus before — everyone hoped I'd get the job.

'Leaving politics wasn't hard. It was leaving Parliament. I love the House; I love the idea of the place. You test ideas and thinking through intelligence and wit and through that you decide the course of a nation. What a civilised way to run a society. It beats who has the most men and guns. The House had so many memories for me.

'I went across to Europe a number of times, secretly and unpaid for by the government. I quickly discovered something strange — WTO candidates never went around and door-knocked and asked for support. So I thought, bugger that, I'm going to set my own rules.

'There was a heck of a lot of politics between countries at play, some of which I couldn't even understand.

'I talked to everyone. At one stage the Swedish prime minister met me like a long-lost brother and said he remembered well a conference in Malta we were at. I'd never been to Malta and just kept my mouth shut.

'As always you have to be mindful of the US in these things. They never go for anyone initially, but they must always end up on the winning side no matter what happens.

'I was staying in this shitty hotel in Geneva. God it was rough. It was a druggy kind of place, but it cost a fortune. So whenever I met an ambassador I always went around to their place or hotel.

'The New Zealand media just drove me crazy during the process. The WTO guys told me later that the New Zealand media would ring up and say: "He hasn't really got a chance, has he?" Well, it's down to two they'd say. "Oh, he has got a chance then. And how much will he earn?"

'I was going around telling people who were supporting Supachai [Panitchpakdi] that if they couldn't change their vote then to say to their governments that both candidates were good and that they should be able to vote for either.

'The Americans are always crucial in these international situations. I called on all my American contacts and depending on who I talked to, I was in or out.

'US WTO Ambassador Rita Hayes went beyond her mandate. She got all the candidates in for lunch with some of the other WTO ambassadors. The Canadian candidate wasn't coming across too well with people, so she put on more functions and invited him along. She was very smart and I owe her a lot.

'The Brits tried to ankle tap me during the process. Never trust the British in negotiations — they still think they're a superpower and cleverer than everyone else.

'A lot of people within the WTO helped me. Evan Rogerson, who had worked for me on my Eden campaign in 1972, was working there and had great advice.

'It became a bit cloak and dagger near the end. The New Zealand and Australian embassies in Geneva are together and the Japanese one is across the road. So there are cameras everywhere and they could see me and supporters coming and going for meetings.

'Jenny Shipley was very good to me and she didn't need to be. She had a real scrap with some of her Cabinet about supporting me. I can't imagine many in the then Labour caucus going out on a limb for me like Shipley did.

'The WTO is impressive. It's in this beautiful old building, the old International Labour Organization headquarters. It's got these great big murals of big muscular Viking-like men doing the lawns or something . . . fascist kind of architecture. It's on Lake Geneva and very beautiful.

'I was very excited to go but sad to say goodbye to the electorate. It's a great joy in life to help people and we had wonderful people in my electorate, and we'd built up this machine. They're working-class people who don't have much, but they give and give to the party.

'We only had five weeks to pull Seattle together. I believe it failed because the Americans didn't want it to work. They just weren't pushing as hard as they should have, as you'd expect a host to.

'The whole thing was a mess. It was hard to move around so at one of the first meetings only half the delegates were there and the American hosts hadn't turned up. So I had to chair the meeting, so I bullshitted my way through it and formally welcomed everyone.

'Clinton's economic adviser Gene Sperling was coming and going and was on his phone checking things with others. Clinton arrived and he was very charming and engaging, but he was consumed with talking about local issues like health care and we couldn't get him to engage on trade.

'I was eventually sidelined by the Americans and some others. I was left there writing notes on pieces of paper and sending them across the room. They'd read them, screw them up and throw them away. I swore to myself then that we had to change things in the WTO if we were to make progress.

'I have to admit the Seattle demonstrations were impressive — people came from everywhere to protest something. At one point I went out and met with some trade union leaders. I said to them: "Trade unions against trade, that's ironic." Everyone roared with laughter. They were actually good guys.

'In my time at the WTO some said I was aggressive and biased towards some countries. But I wanted to stand up for the developing world because few others were. I'd stood up for working people and the poor in New Zealand, now I wanted to do it on the world stage.

'The WTO is great because every country has a voice and your voice is as useful as you want to make it. It does away with phoney capitalism, trade diversion and stops governments picking its cronies. The WTO has rules about central banks, transparency and governance. These are all great foundations for functioning countries.

'The elegance of the WTO shouldn't be forgotten. One of the WTO's core principles of "Most Favoured Nation status" — the best treatment you grant to one of your trading partners should be accorded to others — is the basis of all civilised behaviour. All religions and cultures contain the concept of reciprocal treatment: you treat others as you would like to be treated yourself.

'When it's functioning well the WTO does a better job than the UN. But no one judges the director general of the WTO on whether a round is got up.

But if peace breaks out in the Middle East, they'll recognise the secretary general of the UN.

'Getting China into the WTO was more important than starting another trade round. It meant a lot to me and a lot to them so I put an enormous amount of energy into it. Having China involved in a rules-based global trading system could profoundly change the global economy, bringing enormous prosperity and global security never seen before, I thought at the time.

'I would say to the many who were nervous: "If you can't accept China as part of the global trading system then it means you're scared of the world working together."

'For China to accept there is a legal system that is outside the Communist Party's control is an important thing. Just think about that.

'The country had changed a lot since I'd visited it in the 1970s. People had food, they had houses and you could see the difference in health just between the generations. They know they're better off because of trade. It's easy to quantify for them.

'A lot of people over many years were involved in getting China into the WTO and playing a small part in that is something I'll forever be proud of — it was a great moment in my life.

'Before Doha the way agendas used to run was you could have anything in and then everyone had to agree that it would stay. I changed it and said let's agree beforehand what's on the agenda. That way the agenda would be narrow and more likely to be successful.

'Quite a few people pulled out of Doha, including staff who I never forgave. It was a dangerous time just after 9/11.

'When I had three months left, I set up an office for Supachai so he could prepare for the next ministerial meeting in Mexico. I got everything ready for him, but he wasn't interested. He didn't accept my deputies either, but that's okay.

'I left Supachai with all the goodwill in the world. After three years he went off to the United Nations Commission on Trade and Development.

'If I had had another three years at the WTO, I would have double-knotted some of the agreements and systems that we'd set up, including training for Third World and smaller countries.

'I got a lot of countries to join the WTO because I thought it should be a global organisation. But there's an argument that it's resulted in more nagging about issues and that it might have been better off as a slightly smaller organisation.

'While increasing its size might make it more cumbersome, I thought it was a good thing that countries could go to the WTO and get their ambassadors to vent. They could then report back to their capitals that they'd dumped a bucket on us — so it also provided a good outlet valve.

'Like all international bodies, the WTO isn't perfect. But the system only works if you keep fighting for it.

'The idea of the WTO is brilliant — the smallest countries in the world can take on the biggest using the law, not military or economic might. A legally binding system gives certainty and protection for businesses to invest in developing nations, in particular.

'Trump has been blocking replacements to the WTO's appellate body and now it's down from seven to its quorum of just three judges. When the terms of those judges expire then there will be no appellate body and no process for people to appeal decisions about trade disputes. The whole trade disputes process will grind to a halt.

'For Trump to spew all over the WTO is beyond contempt. America and Trump will lose from having a weak global trading system with fewer rules.'

****

Most people who knew Moore thought that if there was ever to be an organisation designed to meet his interests and skill set, the World Trade Organization was it.

Formed in 1995, the WTO replaced the post-Second World War General Agreement on Tariffs and Trade and regulates trade in goods, services and intellectual property between participating countries.

Critically, it has a legally binding disputes resolution process to allow grievances between countries, regardless of their size or international standing, to be resolved, in theory, in 12 to 16 months. It, in effect, means all members take action against a nation breaking trade rules rather than leaving it up to an individual country. This is considered central to the global trading system.

The WTO is guided by five principles which Moore always believed was the genius of the organisation and fitted with his anti-privilege view of the world: non-discrimination; reciprocity; binding and enforceable commitments; transparency; and safety values, or the ability of countries to restrict trade on the basis of issues like the environment or public health.

While many focus on the work the WTO and its director general does with the current trade round, it also runs a series of bodies and committees that oversee work in areas such as textiles, intellectual property, trade in services, trade and the environment, and trade and development.

Its disputes settlement process, with compulsory jurisdiction, requires members to comply with recommendations from a three-person independent experts' panel. Members can appeal a panel's recommendations to a seven-member appellate body and the decision by that group is final.

The pre-WTO GATT was essentially transatlantic in culture, although there were powerful voices from other regions, such as India. All the directors general had been European.

The Uruguay Round, which Moore helped launch as overseas trade minister in the fourth Labour Government and was concluded in 1994, had greatly enlarged and updated the global trading system for the new organisation to include work in services, intellectual property and disputes settlement.

One of Moore's heroes, Joe Walding, had always encouraged him to look beyond the standard Labour issues of health, education and social welfare and to carve out a unique policy pillar for himself in the party. Trade had been his major interest for almost 25 years because of that.

He'd taught himself about the issues by constantly reading about trade, economics and globalisation and involved himself with like-minded international politicians and academics.

Moore had been approached informally twice before about running for the role of director general of the GATT and the WTO but had refused to contemplate it and had suggested others.

The first time was in 1992 when he was leader of the Opposition running hard to get Labour back into government at the 1993 general election. GATT Director General Arthur Dunkel was coming up to the end of his 12 years and Moore was sounded out about the position.

It was then suggested to Moore at the signing ceremony for the end of the Uruguay Round in Marrakesh in April 1994, which he attended as a guest of the Bolger Government. With the round completed, Director General Peter Sutherland was keen to move on the following year.

Moore had only just been replaced as Labour leader and wasn't in the mood to contemplate leaving Parliament while still trying to deal with whether or not he remained in the party. He was still agitated about everything.

The suggestion was moot, anyway, because there was a belief by many that since Sutherland, an Irishman, was only going to do such a short stint that Europe should get the replacement position. The US agreed and Italian Renato Ruggiero took on the role for four years from 1995.

The director general's role is almost an undefined one. Some directors general saw themselves as administrators, others like conductors of an orchestra of disparate instruments, but none as drivers of the free trade agenda. Being a consensus-driven organisation, the director general of the day always had to deal with the reality of the global mood of the time.

Moore's goal in life had always been to be prime minister of New Zealand. Even now, he would have gladly given up being director general of the WTO for a shot at being prime minister again.

Moore was Labour's foreign affairs spokesperson but still grumpy. He was trying to motivate himself to be a contributing member of Clark's team, particularly as the National Government were increasingly in disarray, having dumped Jim Bolger for Jenny Shipley in December 1997 as prime minister.

There was a good chance Labour would win the next general election in 1999 and if he played his cards well Moore could have ended up as foreign affairs or trade minister. He knew Clark would probably have been happy to have him out of the country most of the time.

Moore had often described being minister of foreign affairs for New Zealand as one of the best jobs in the world: travelling the globe, attending stimulating international gatherings with interesting and insightful people who mattered, and having an opinion on all the world's issues but never having responsibility for any of them or having to follow through on much.

The same in status as the US secretary of state, China's foreign minister or the EU commissioner for external relations but, unlike them, powerless.

But he and Yvonne wondered whether they could be bothered with New Zealand politics any more. Could he put up with the snide remarks and what he increasingly felt was his party being taken over by affinity politics at the expense of the issues that he thought mattered to ordinary Kiwis and their families?

Clark impressively controlled her caucus and the party and, Moore felt, colleagues were still afraid to be seen fraternising with him. Many in his own caucus and party had become his enemies. He thought they felt more comfortable embracing those who had left the party, run against it and campaigned against it than those who had stayed faithful and kept it alive during the difficult years.

He felt alone and there were some internationally saying they loved and admired him and thought he could once again make a significant contribution to a cause, one that he deeply cared about.

Whether it was a campaign to make him feel unwanted or a new generation now running the caucus and party, it had the same outcome: Moore was ready to move on.

Moore had first met Uruguayan Carlos Pérez del Castillo during the launch of the GATT's Uruguay Round in Punta del Este in September 1986 when he was minister for overseas trade.

It was the GATT's eighth and most ambitious round, looking to reform trade in textiles, services, intellectual property and, importantly for New Zealand, agriculture. Moore and Pérez del Castillo had shared a few beers at that gathering and quickly became friends.

Moore spent much of his energy in the first term of the fourth Labour Government focused on the Uruguay Round. He unsuccessfully tried to interest his caucus colleagues and the news media, distracted by the almost daily Lange–Douglas economic reforms, of the strategic importance of it.

During this time Pérez del Castillo was Uruguay's top negotiator on agriculture and had played a significant role alongside Moore in setting up the Cairns Group of agricultural nations lobbying to free up trade in that sector.

Thanks to the efforts of people like Pérez del Castillo and Moore, the Cairns Group became a formidable and credible counterweight to the EC, US and Japan and their protectionist agricultural policies. Not only did it have Australia and New Zealand as members but South American and some Asian nations and, initially, Hungary.

Pérez del Castillo was similar in age to Moore, had been educated in Australia and served as a diplomat there so almost instinctively understood the New Zealand overseas trade minister's outlook and his obsession with the need to open up agricultural markets.

Pérez del Castillo went on to be the permanent secretary of the Latin American Economic System for four years, before a period in the private sector as an international economic consultant and then Uruguay's vice minister, acting minister for foreign affairs and then ambassador to the WTO in the late 1990s.

Pérez del Castillo told Moore that there was a group of countries who were keen that the WTO's third director general be a strong leader, have a clear vision for the world's trading system, be able to navigate the difficulties that globalisation brought and, most importantly, be a formidable and credible communicator with developing nations and working people.

The WTO was still in its infancy and Pérez del Castillo and like-minded people were concerned that it didn't get taken over like some other international organisations by its bigger players or equally by the forces opposed to global trade.

Uruguay had seen Moore in action and thought he was perfect for the role. They had even tested their thinking with their friends and all signs were positive. Moore would have strong support from Latin America, he was told, and other agricultural developing countries because of his work in the Uruguay Round and the Cairns Group.

Unlike with much of Moore's career, the timing seemed right. He was interested and quietly approached Prime Minister Jenny Shipley who, a little to his surprise, was very supportive.

His long-time Christchurch adversary, former Bolger trade minister Philip Burdon, who briefly flirted with the idea of going for the role himself, and the then trade minister Lockwood Smith also encouraged him.

In 1999 New Zealand was about to host the leaders of 21 economies from the Asia-Pacific to an APEC gathering in Auckland. As hosts, Shipley was keen for New Zealand to stamp its international mark as strong supporters of free trade and a global trading system that the WTO stood for.

Shipley was keen to throw the government's support behind Moore's candidacy. At the very worst, if his candidacy failed, 'New Zealand Inc' would have had an opportunity to tell its free trade story to others.

It hadn't concerned her that earlier in her parliamentary career Moore had led numerous attacks on her, particularly when she was social welfare minister and had cut benefits in the Bolger Government.

She had a reputation for not taking comments personally and saw that as the robust debate of politics.

In the late 1990s Shipley pushed a broad free trade agenda including trying to launch a new WTO round, looking at the potential of a free trade agreement with China's President Jiang Zemin and actively seeking to get that country into the WTO, and out of frustration starting a regional free trade arrangement, the P2, with Singaporean Prime Minister Goh Chok Tong that then morphed into P3, P4, TPP and the eventual CPTPP.

She was also convinced Moore was the right candidate for the time. His personal story and communications skills were what the WTO needed at a time when there was a concerted push-back by some activists against globalisation.

Moore could credibly talk with leaders from the developing world and in some of the sceptical First World about how closed economies destroyed jobs and didn't uplift working people.

But this wasn't a view universally shared by some of New Zealand's senior diplomats at the time who privately scoffed at the idea of Moore running.

More concerning for Shipley, though, was that there was a high degree of scepticism from her Cabinet about Moore's candidacy. It got petty at times with even debate about whether the government should pay for his international phone calls to lobby for the role.

First, some in the Cabinet argued, Moore was a Labour MP. But Shipley put the case firmly that he was the right candidate for progressing a WTO round, which was in New Zealand's interests. Having someone capable in that job was more important than domestic politics.

But, second, and of genuine concern, was the fact that foreign minister Don McKinnon was going for the role of secretary general of the Commonwealth Secretariat based in London and the government had decided to back that too.

With Shipley ousting Bolger, McKinnon was also replaced as deputy prime minister by Wyatt Creech. While staying on as foreign affairs minister, McKinnon had decided not to contest the 1999 general election. He, too, had cast his eyes internationally.

McKinnon was thought to be deeply anxious that Moore's campaign might undermine his.

But Shipley thought the lobbying could be sufficiently separated. Moore had strong contacts in Africa and was confident of their votes but would need the government's help with countries in Asia, the US and Australia. There wouldn't be much crossover with McKinnon's lobbying of Commonwealth countries.

Unattributed stories started to emerge in the New Zealand news media that Cabinet was divided on the issue and that they wanted to back their own man McKinnon and withdraw support for Moore.

This enraged Shipley who took it as an early test of her resolve by some of Bolger's old guard. She quickly made her views known to colleagues. She wanted to go after both roles at the same time. Both campaigns were to be pursued equally by the government.

In preparation for hosting the APEC leaders meeting in Auckland in September 1999, Shipley met with more than half of the 20 visiting economies ahead of time.

In her bilateral discussions she took the opportunity to lobby for Moore, promoting his skill set and making the case that a strong WTO was in their best interests and for security, peace and prosperity globally. With Australian Prime Minister John Howard she was more direct, expressing how Moore was a better candidate for the region, and particularly its agricultural agenda.

Australia was the major stumbling block. Australian trade minister and Deputy Prime Minister Tim Fischer had a strong affinity with South East Asia, having served in the Australian Army in the Vietnam War.

Australia had not only found an alternative candidate in Thailand's former Deputy Prime Minister and Minister of Commerce Supachai Panitchpakdi but was actively lobbying against Moore and New Zealand.

One of the lines the Australians used was that the WTO needed a representative from the developing world. Moore's riposte whenever he was told this was: 'Do you want a rich man from a poor country or a poor man from a rich country running the WTO?'

For the first time in Moore's memory everyone in the Labour caucus was unified in wishing him luck.

Moore quietly slipped out of the country for Geneva to gauge international support. He kept a low profile in Geneva, which was easy enough staying in the budget Hotel Cristal in the red-light district near the railway station. He was surprised at the good reception and encouragement he received from many at the WTO.

What was going to be a few weeks out of the country turned into three months on the road: Britain, Europe, Singapore, Canberra, the US and South America. The trip was funded from Moore's own pocket and to save on hotel costs he often took overnight flights between capitals.

It was a hard slog and at times the odds seemed overwhelming. There were many moments of self-doubt and at one stage an MFAT official even told Moore that he should head home as he risked becoming an embarrassment to New Zealand.

There were logistical problems with two international bids happening at the same time with Moore and McKinnon seeing government officials from the same country on the same day unknown to each other.

With the WTO having been formed only in 1995, the selection process for the director general role was relatively new. The WTO's General Council said there would be three basic criteria for selection: volume, depth and distribution of support. It was a numbers game, but also weighted towards the nations that were big traders and what regions in the world they were from.

With the chair of the WTO's General Council rotating, Switzerland's William Rossier would start the process and Tanzania's Ali Said Mchumo would see it through its crucial period.

All members express their preference confidentially to the chairman who then informs the General Council which candidate has the least support. This process of 'confessionals' continues until it whittles down to a winner. There is no formal vote.

Former Canadian international trade minister and current High Commissioner to Britain Roy MacLaren had also put his hat in the ring, along with former Moroccan trade and agriculture minister and current ambassador to France Hassan Abouyoub, whose early withdrawal freed up France to go with Moore. MacLaren dropped out soon after that.

While the New Zealand media showed little attention to it, the Thai media positioned the contest as the developing world versus the developed world, of Asia versus the West, and of the world versus America. Stories appeared in the Thai media of Moore variously having a brain tumour to him being a trade union leader.

Moore became increasingly worried that he was being successfully positioned by his opponents as the American candidate. His concerns were confirmed when protesters marched against him not on the New Zealand Embassy in Bangkok but on the US mission and ground rocks into photos of his face.

Moore talked with his old friends in the French trade union movement and former Socialist Prime Minister Michel Rocard, who he'd got to know when he was trade minister, and they easily convinced Socialist Prime Minister Lionel Jospin to back him, as did German Chancellor Gerhard Schröder's Social Democratic Government and Italian Prime Minister Massimo D'Alema's 'Olive Tree coalition' left-wing government.

The three guarded Europe for Moore against the efforts of the British, who were against him. The Germans once caught out the British trying to pass resolutions in favour of Supachai at an EU meeting.

Moore's commitment to the developing world within the WTO ensured he had a head start in Africa and the French and Nigerians did the rounds there to make sure. While a small bloc and not resident in Geneva, the Caribbean and Pacific nations had always been ignored. Moore paid them the respect of speaking to them and got their support.

Moore's old friend Ken Douglas even introduced him to old international trade union friends in Geneva and after a heavily wine-laden lunch they promised to do all they could for his candidacy.

A small lobbying team of Pérez del Castillo, US WTO Ambassador Rita Hayes and her offsider Andrew Stoler, and New Zealand WTO Ambassador Roger Farrell, would meet daily after work in Geneva to decide where their lobbying efforts should be directed.

With the US, Sweden, and eventually most of the Europeans, Africans, South Americans, economies in transition and small island states in the Caribbean and Pacific indicating their support, Moore ended up in an unassailable position. Even some Asian nations — breaking with Thailand — said they privately supported him but for regional political reasons couldn't do so publicly.

The Australians, British, Dutch, Japanese and ASEAN nations were left to back Supachai.

While Moore's early declaration as a candidate had caught the

Australians off guard it was done to deliberately stop them publicly declaring for Supachai and to give them a possible out.

That never happened. To the contrary, as it became clearer that Moore was the front-runner, Supachai is understood to have offered to stand down and only stayed in the race on Australia's insistence.

Despite being labelled by some as the American candidate, it wasn't plain sailing with the Clinton administration either. Originally the US Treasury wanted Supachai as the candidate, but the US Trade Representative Office and then the State Department backed Moore.

Former National Security Council official Peter Watson, who had worked with Moore on restoring the New Zealand–US relationship in 1990 and had later chaired the US Trade Commission, persuaded US Trade Representative Charlene Barshefsky to go with him.

This was a diplomatic triumph for New Zealand. Officials from the time credit Moore's strategic and campaigning skills for the success. While MFAT worked tirelessly on lobbying the right officials internationally, who, when and what to say was decided by Moore.

Again, as with much of his career, there was no grand memo or strategy paper that had been circulated to and agreed with key stakeholders. It was Moore's campaign and it was in his head.

During this period, he gave a critical speech in Wellington that outlined his vision for the WTO. It was relayed to many embassies.

'In many countries an increasing number of citizens feel locked out, forgotten, angry and hurt, believing falsely that globalisation is the cause of all their problems. They sit waiting for a train that may never come, their faces pressed against the window, easy victims to old and dangerous songs that yesterday was better.

'People are appalled and dismayed when they see the few living in splendour and the many in squalor, with half the world dieting and the other half starving.'

But, he said, a fairer and stronger world trading system was not the cause of, but the answer to, this problem.

'Those countries that have liberalised have done the best and we ought to say so. The point is not that the global economy is somehow perfect or that the widening range of public concerns is without substance or validity. The point, rather, is that the challenges we face can realistically be addressed only inside this global system.'

The issues of employment, the environment, Third World development and justice would not be solved by restricting the flow of goods and services through closing borders or undermining the WTO's rules-based approach to trade and resolving disputes.

As with most international bodies, Moore understood the importance of the US vote. In his career as a trade minister he'd amassed a detailed contact book of leaders and influencers among the US political class who he'd assiduously kept in touch with over the years.

He spoke to Democrats and Republicans alike, those in power and those close to it, who he knew shared his hopes for the WTO and would carry his water.

Moore particularly singles out US WTO Ambassador Hayes, who had been nominated for the role by President Bill Clinton and whose confirmation was unanimously agreed to by the Senate.

A skilful and astute politician from South Carolina, she became one of Moore's biggest supporters, calling on friends and favours in the US Senate, Congress and White House. People don't describe Hayes as a southern belle. She was a lot like him: brash and in people's faces. He says he would not have got the job but for Hayes.

In the end Moore won convincingly on all three criteria, Mchumo told the General Council.

But to everyone's surprise the Pakistani WTO ambassador objected immediately and vocally to the decision. People couldn't remember the last time a decision that had reached a consensus being objected to.

Even though all the participants had all agreed to the process and to be bound to it, Moore's opponents demanded the chair provide proof of his preferences.

There were angry and unruly scenes and Mchumo struggled to control the meeting and eventually adjourned the General Council.

What Moore didn't count on was Supachai's backers using the WTO's consensus ethos to, in effect, stall the process. The minority were trying to veto Moore's nomination. The whole process was now paralysed despite numerous attempts to reconvene the General Council.

It surprised Moore and made him angry. Supachai had lost a fair contest, so turns around and blows up the scoreboard. Someone was trying once again to outmanoeuvre him from a role he'd worked hard to get.

The process had now become bitter for many of the participants. Moore says that a younger version of him might have thrown in the towel at this stage. But it was now personal and unlike on some occasions in his career, he wasn't going to walk away this time. Moore dug his heels in.

A week had gone by and some suggested a compromise candidate was now needed. Enrique Iglesias, a Uruguayan economist and banker who was the president of the Inter-American Development Bank, was suggested by some.

At this point the British showed their hand. Not only had they backed Supachai but they had a compromise candidate conveniently waiting in the wings in former Thatcher Home Secretary and current European Commissioner for Trade Sir Leon Brittan, whose term in the EU was coming to an end. Brittan would be the deadlock breaker.

It caught Moore and many others by surprise. To make matters more insulting, in Moore's mind, it was a British Labour Government being deceitful and promoting a former Tory minister.

The British had all along been lobbying the EU on the side to go with their convenient compromise candidate, despite Shipley strongly making a case for Moore to Prime Minister Tony Blair. The British quickly managed to convince many of the EU members of the compromise idea, except for Sweden which stood firmly with Moore.

Sweden's Minister for Industry and Trade Leif Pagrotsky, a member of the Social Democratic Party and who Moore had met decades earlier when he was president of the Swedish Social Democratic Youth League, was an old friend.

Pagrotsky counter-lobbied the British and reminded the EU members of their commitments to Moore's candidacy, his lifelong dedication to free and fair trade, and his belief that a rules-based global trading system was the best protection for developing and small nations in a rapidly globalising world. The WTO had to move away from the US–Europe view of the world. And, besides, he told those from progressive political parties, he was Labour.

A committed socialist and internationalist, Pagrotsky had locked his mate Moore into the contest and killed off the Brittan threat.

But being stuck with Moore and Supachai didn't move the process forward.

Moore feared his campaign was close to falling over and on another round of lobbying stopped in to Singapore again to get advice from his old friend Loo Chong Yong, who made the obvious observation that the two should simply share the role.

The alternative was nothing for Moore, Chong Yong pointed out to him. Supachai, in contrast, was wealthy and from a connected family so would always fall on his feet. Moore could always rely on Chong Yong to be honest and to put his interests first and begrudgingly accepted he had to go back to Geneva with the suggestion.

This was the turning point in the selection process and led to the compromise of both Moore and Supachai sharing the director general role three years each. It was far from ideal and Moore knew that very little progress could probably be made in such a short term, particularly if he went first. Nevertheless, he wasn't prepared to stand aside and be the magnanimous one this time in his career.

To this day Moore is often described as America's WTO director general. It grates him because it's equally true that he could have been described as the puppet of Lesotho, Gabon, Mongolia, Papua New Guinea, France, Sweden, Germany or Uruguay.

This 'American branding' meant he didn't get off to a good start at the WTO and, most importantly, it meant the organisation was distracted in the lead-up to the Seattle ministerial meeting in December 1999 when it was hoped another round would be started.

The prospect of leaving Parliament was more of a wrench than he thought it would be. He'd spent most of his adult life there and, after a few hiccups at the start, Christchurch had adopted him like one of its favourite sons.

Once again it took Yvonne to encourage him and reinforce with him that he was making the right choice with his career. Like moving from Auckland more than 20 years earlier, it was time for new pastures and leaving behind the petty enmities and negativity.

He told his local party members of his decision at his Kaiapoi office in an emotional meeting. The response was a mixture of pride and disappointment that someone they'd really cared for was leaving. But many knew — but never talked about — how the loss of the leadership had hurt him and how he needed a new challenge to revive his spirits.

Moore's valedictory speech to Parliament in August 1999 was a mix of the feelings he had about leaving and its ending reflective, perhaps, of his approach to some matters and some people's attitudes to that.

He graciously thanked people, including opponents inside and outside the party, paid tribute to Labour for what it had given him, was self-deprecating, poked fun at others and reminded the party of its roots.

'My own party has changed, of course, as it must. It is the success of the welfare state that has changed my party. The sons and daughters of cleaners and carpenters can now become university lecturers, professors, or whatever. That is a good thing.

'I know I have always been a bit of a dinosaur. The movement has been good to me. Without the movement I would just be another overweight, unemployed, white-trash freezing worker in the Far North.'

But he was also sad about what was becoming of the party.

'It was Nye Bevan — some of my colleagues will not even know who Nye Bevan was — who said that Labour used to be the cream of the working class, and now it is an intellectual spittoon for the middle class.'

He said he always believed New Zealand was a special place inspired by all the cultures that made up the country. The defining issue for the nation was race relations and Treaty issues and we should measure our progress against how we dealt with them. It was 'the stone in New Zealand's shoe'.

'We could get everything right here — I doubt it, but we could — inflation, employment, health policies, and debt. But if we fail on this issue, we fail at everything.

'We keep talking about the Crown and Māori at Waitangi. I do wish we would substitute the words "New Zealand Government", "New Zealand people", and "New Zealand taxpayer" for "Crown", and I would like us to stop using the word "beneficiary" when we speak of Māori claims, and instead talk of "owner" and "stakeholder".

'Let us think of that fateful morning at Waitangi. There on the lawn were assembled Māori and representatives of the British Government. Was that the deal? Not entirely. There was a third partner: the church, God, the missionaries. It was the missionaries whose mana and prestige gave confidence to the partners.

'The church had a moral mandate based on the principle that we are all created in God's likeness, therefore we are all the children of God, and therefore we must be equal. That is the moral basis of democracy. That is the force of the democratic impulse. Those are the core values that have driven civilised society.

'That is why I get uneasy when people say that partnership could mean Māori having 50 per cent of the seats in Parliament or could mean having a state within a state.

'Sometimes I do fear for our country. We are in danger of dividing ourselves. Any nation that bases its law and destiny on the colour of skin will perish, and so it should.'

But he was hopeful, saying the next generation was better than his on just about every issue and there was a lot to be proud of.

Among the stories and humour, he talked about the kind of nation New Zealand was and had the potential to be.

'People talk of New Zealand as being a young nation. I have never seen it that way. Our people reflect the many waves of migration. We were all boat people at one time. Whether people came 1000 years ago or more, in a waka, or 1000 hours ago in a Boeing, nobody arrives here without a memory.

'It is our collective memories that build up a society. This collective memory reflects the English with their history of respect for institutions and law; the agony of the Irish and their experience as the first colony of Britain; and the Welsh, the Scots, the Croatians, the Indians, the Dutch, the Chinese, and the new arrivals from the Pacific. All those memories actually bind us together.'

He said while we have been a lonely country geographically, spiritually and intellectually we have always been part of a wider world.

'New Zealanders have always been proud, but not vain or nasty, ultra-nationalists. We are also internationalists. We have had to be. We like international engagement.

'We must, because New Zealanders realise that our peace and our progress are actually based on the peace and progress of people everywhere. Therefore we have always supported international engagement in treaties, and the rule of international law and institutions, to achieve that end.'

But Moore also used the speech to try to cleverly progress a pet project of his — giving New Zealand a constitution.

As part of his valedictory speech he sought leave of the House — which needs to be a unanimous vote — to bring forward a Constitution Convention Bill to be introduced, read a first time and referred to the Justice and Law Reform Select Committee for consideration.

The draft legislation looked to establish a process to slowly move New Zealand towards deciding on a constitution which could, although he wasn't promoting it, lead to a republic.

A leadership council, made up of all the political leaders, would be set up after the election to create an eminent persons group with the powers of a royal commission. That eminent persons group would then, over a maximum of seven years, have a public consultation process to come up with options.

Those options would then be put to a constitutional convention held in Parliament of delegates appointed at large and from MPs. A plebiscite and referendum would then be held.

Unfortunately, he said, people wanted to first focus on the issue of the head of state and republicanism. That's why it was important to have a long reflective process to first consider a constitution, including its relationship to the Treaty of Waitangi.

'There are those who believe that the Treaty should be the constitution. There are those who do not believe that the Treaty should exist at all. My bill is about a process to take us through this problem.

'We ought not to make quick decisions because of some temporary fashion or fad, or because the Aussies are doing something, or because we have a grievance and do not like the government of the day.

'We ought to think desperately about what we are doing. New Zealand is no longer an Anglo-Celtic and Māori society. We do not even have a Westminster system of government any more.'

But when the Speaker asked the House if there were any objections to leave being granted, there was, and his parliamentary career ended to the waiata 'Pokarekare Ana'.

His resignation was effective from 31 August to avoid a by-election being necessary in Waimakariri. That date was also the twenty-fifth anniversary of the death of one of his heroes, Kirk.

The next concern of Moore's was what would happen with his

replacement for the Waimakariri seat. To his surprise his good friend and protégé Clayton Cosgrove hadn't eagerly put his hand up for the candidacy.

Cosgrove had carved out a career in the corporate world, working in Australia, and had recently moved to Auckland. In recent years he'd turned his focus away from politics.

In the end Moore demanded of Cosgrove: 'Do you want to kick arse or lick arse all your life, Clayton?'

The next trick now was to win the selection for the seat. Even though it was strongly Moore's seat and the locals were loyal, experience told him head office would almost certainly try to influence the selection. It would be their last crack at Moore.

Clark congratulated Moore on his WTO appointment at caucus and asked him if he had any final words before leaving. Moore made it clear that he wouldn't countenance any interference in the selection for his seat.

The Kaiapoi High School auditorium was packed for the selection meeting with many previously unseen members of the affiliated unions in attendance. Party President Bob Harvey and General Secretary Rob Allen were the head office representatives.

For Moore, this was his last task with the party; his last selection meeting after 27 years of selection battles. Though this was Cosgrove's fight, he knew that it was seen by many as his.

Cosgrove was his pick and beating him at this selection would be the final insult to Moore. He was determined not to let all his enemies beat him this last time.

Cosgrove's main opponent was Glen Cameron, a member of the party's ruling New Zealand Council and the son of well-known and respected Canterbury Meat Workers Union Secretary and Federation of Labour executive member Wes.

Moore had known Cameron's father, who he'd taken with him on a trade mission but had fallen out with over the fourth Labour Government and his departure from Labour to the Alliance.

Cosgrove needed to get the three local votes on the selection panel. Moore and the locals decided that tactically the best approach was to have long-time loyalists Roger Pike and Dennis Hills of the Labour Electorate Committee go on as the local representatives and try to nominate LEC Chair Sally Thompson from the floor as the third vote.

Thompson, a well-known local educationalist, was their strongest candidate and the best hope for beating the stacked hall. Moore quickly nominated her and much to their surprise she won easily.

After the speeches, Cameron won the indicative straw vote from the floor.

To the surprise of LEC panel members, head office didn't try to bulldoze them during the confidential deliberations. Instead they worked through a 'job description' Moore and the LEC had devised to test each of the candidates against. When logically matched against the job description, it was hard not to pick Cosgrove.

The selection panel's deliberations seemed to go on forever and most of the union members went home. But Moore paced the hall, becoming increasingly nervous. It had the air of some of his previous failed selections. Eventually, at about 1.30 am, Harvey came out to announce Cosgrove had won.

After a few celebratory drinks and tearful farewells from locals, Moore told Cosgrove to meet him at his home at 8 am with a photographer when they would go around the electorate taking election campaign photos together. Cosgrove now had the baton.

Within days Moore was on a plane to Geneva. Once again, he felt guilty about leaving Yvonne behind to sort out the logistical arrangements of packing, storage and moving while he headed for early meetings about the rapidly approaching Seattle ministerial gathering for which he felt completely underprepared.

Yvonne had the role of taking Cosgrove around Moore's old haunts in the electorate — the sports clubs, pubs, RSA and workingmen's club — and campaigning with him.

It was a stressful time for Yvonne because her mother Rosie had had a major heart attack at the beginning of the year. Yvonne had spent time with her in Auckland and was afraid to leave her and go to Geneva.

The couple were unsure what the future held and thought it might be the last time they saw their home in Dormer Street. It held most of their Christchurch memories.

Their backyard Christmas parties for local party members, businesspeople and the news media were legendary.

There was the one year when a rising TV star called Paul Holmes enjoyed the hospitality too much and stripped off and swam naked in the pool, much to the delight of some of the pensioners there. Holmes was never sure for years later whether Yvonne had film in the camera she was using that night.

Whenever he had spare time Moore would use his old bricklayer's skills to make improvements to the backyard, including building a BBQ, for which he jokingly had a plaque made in commemoration of his old trade union mate Ken Douglas.

In Geneva the bureaucracy quickly saw Moore coming. His term wouldn't officially start for a few more weeks so Moore couldn't move into his office let alone the director general's official residence. He paid for a hotel downtown and had meetings there. The Thai representative refused to meet him initially; the ill feeling over the selection process was still evident.

Moore's initial impression was the WTO was dynamic as an organisation but the culture of the 600-strong secretariat in Geneva was, at its worst, a bit like an old boys' club. However, it wasn't a particularly bureaucratic place by the standards of international organisations. He also encountered snobbery and viciousness from some of the delegates to the WTO.

Moore had to come up to speed quickly with the issues and get to know the key players. He told staff at an early meeting that because of his three-year term he would be working twice as hard and setting a tough pace.

He knew that like all the campaigns he'd been involved with throughout his career, surrounding himself with good people was important. The key appointments were his four deputies.

Moore knew he had to have strong people who had influence in key parts of the world so appointed Ablassé Ouedrago from Burkina Faso, Paul-Henri Ravier from France, Miguel Rodríguez Mendoza from Venezuela and Andrew Stoler from the US.

Old WTO hand and Kiwi Patrick Low was made his chief of staff. Moore would also get counsel from his New Zealand friend Evan Rogerson who had worked within the WTO for many years.

He was worried that all the distractions of the director general selection process meant the WTO's third ministerial meeting to launch a new trade round, to be hosted in Seattle, hadn't been framed properly in the news media and with key stakeholders.

He was right to be concerned. Little work had been done by officials on the round because the organisation had been leaderless for five months and the director general process had polarised WTO staff. It had consumed too much time.

So in his first speech, at the Transatlantic Business Dialogue in Berlin at the end of October 1999, Moore deliberately set the bar high for Seattle to try to get some momentum. It was, in effect, his future vision for free trade and the WTO's part in it.

He said the outcome would be a test of confidence in the WTO and a sign of international commitment to trade liberalisation. 'It will influence the direction and credibility of the world trading system as we enter a new and uncertain century,' he said.

It would ultimately be a test of international leadership and of the political will of the US and Europe.

He reminded his audience that the WTO was no longer a cosy club of industrialised nations, but a global system of 135 members with China, Russia and 29 others wanting to join.

'There may be 100,000 protesters outside the conference centre but there are 1.5 billion people wanting to join our organisation.'

But he acknowledged that even though the world had seen unprecedented economic growth, many people were anxious about job security, incomes, social standards and the environment.

He said there needed to be an informed and engaged public and those at the conference needed to help communicate the benefits of free trade and the WTO.

'What the trading system cannot withstand is complacency, indifference, the corrosion of purpose and direction that comes with neglect.

'We will hear a great deal in Seattle from those who oppose the WTO. We also need to hear from those who not only understand the challenges of an open world economy but grasp its immense opportunities. We need to explain better that high-skill, high-income jobs flow from trade.

'And we need to ask what rational alternative those who oppose the WTO are offering in a world of ever-deepening interdependence. The reality of trade's benefits is proven. The onus is on those who would slow down or arrest trade to explain what other options exist.'

Moore was particularly keen on the round helping developing countries get into the global trading system. The developing world wasn't threatened by globalisation, he said, the danger was them being left outside of it.

'Trade is their bridge to the twenty-first century. With it comes access not only to markets but to investment, technology and know-how. Without it the dream of development will remain out of reach.'

He hoped the ministerial meeting could see beyond strict national interests and narrow political concerns and embrace a multilateral trading system and international institutions designed to build a better world after the conflicts of the twentieth century.

'Too much of this century was marked by force and coercion. Our dream must be a world managed by persuasion, the rule of law, the settlement of differences peacefully within the law and cooperation. It's a good thing that all our living standards are now based on the ability of our neighbours to purchase our products.'

Seattle ended up being a spectacular failure. The WTO and its members didn't get to the launch pad let alone the bar Moore had set in Berlin. The streets were lined with protesters and there were running battles between them and the police.

But it wasn't the protests or any gaps in the WTO's processes that caused it, although they didn't help. Instead, it was because members were too far apart on key issues. The US, in particular, was nervous about domestic politics.

No one — among the WTO or the hosts — seemed to own the process. On-the-ground logistics were poor and compounded by the security issues created by the protesters.

Smaller delegations felt excluded as they meandered around the corridors asking what was going on. Some delegates were accosted in the streets. A sense of siege developed as the GATT and WTO process faced its first genuine opposition since its formation almost 50 years earlier.

Moore gathered a list of all the delegates who had been excluded by the chaos or who had felt threatened in Seattle and asked US officials to apologise to them. The request was ignored.

The most successful initiative negotiated at Seattle was Moore brokering a last-attempt 'green room' meeting at about 2 am of delegates to try to resolve the issues. The hard part was not getting everyone up for the meeting but that they be allowed to smoke at the gathering.

While many at the WTO were depressed with the outcome, Moore kept his sense of humour. Boarding a plane shortly after Seattle, Moore turned to his Ministry of Foreign Affairs and Trade assistant who was seconded to him, Patrick Rata, the nephew of his old mentor Mat, and laughed. One day a movie would be made about the failed Seattle ministerial meeting 'and Denzel Washington will play you and Danny DeVito me'.

As in Eden, post-Seattle Moore spent a lot of time trying to lift the spirits of his team.

Despite this, he found resistance from some of the WTO staff. Some of the older more refined diplomats didn't like Moore's down-to-earth and informal manner. They scoffed at his academic qualifications. And the more they disliked him the more he would accentuate his New Zealand-ness — his mannerisms, accent and sayings.

He wouldn't let anything stop him; he was in a hurry. So, an ambitious outreach programme was started with the smaller often forgotten members. Seattle reinforced to him the need to restore a sense of purpose and wider legitimacy for the WTO.

Some questioned the value of his reaching out to the smaller countries like those in Africa and the Caribbean, many of whom couldn't afford to have a physical presence in Geneva.

But his belief was you needed to build from the bottom up to ensure everyone felt they had a stake in the process. He empowered the smaller, poorer and weaker nations to have a voice.

Moore's skills as a retail politician who understood marginal seats campaigning were invaluable post-Seattle.

He insisted that the US and EU representatives met regularly with him and worked on sorting out their differences, particularly on agriculture.

He was also focused on tactical initiatives that some staff dismissed as 'Mike's rats and mice'.

He created 'Geneva Week' where NGOs could come into the WTO once a year to organise their own meetings, bring in speakers and present an alternative view. He had one-on-one meetings with NGOs who wanted serious engagement.

There was a non-residents week where countries — often smaller ones — who didn't have representation at the WTO could participate. A non-residents office was established, some trips were paid for them to attend conferences and meetings, and a trust was created to pay for legal assistance for disputes.

He made the WTO's processes more inclusive for smaller and poorer members, with technical assistance and training increased.

Cooperation increased with other international organisations and a bigger effort was made with civil society and the private sector — people he'd always interacted with as a politician. He also demanded greater transparency, with documents declassified much more quickly.

All of 'Mike's rats and mice' added up and this painstaking and carefully orchestrated effort changed the dark post-Seattle mood.

For Yvonne, moving to Geneva didn't bring her any closer to her husband. He was happier than he'd been in a long while, deeply immersing himself in something he was passionate about and had a significant say in. He also no longer had to deal with some of the pettiness and backstabbing of some in the party.

But Moore spent more time away from home than ever and when he was back in Geneva, he had long hours in the office.

Old Europe has a lot of pomp and ceremony and as director general of the WTO Moore and Yvonne had to do the rounds.

There's an unwritten rule in Geneva that evening functions go from 7 pm until 10 pm when everyone goes home. Whenever the Moores were hosting that would also be the case. But for those who wanted to stay on, the guitars would then come out and they'd party until the wee hours.

Yvonne quickly became good friends with Sarah Fay, wife of former New Zealand businessman Sir Michael Fay, who was also living in Geneva.

Some of their more enjoyable and memorable moments were hosting staff and visitors from New Zealand to simple barbecues by Lake Geneva or watching the All Blacks on TV early in the morning with other expat Kiwis. BYO, BBQ, barefoot and in shorts with a beer or a glass of wine in hand; it was almost like being back at Dormer Street in Papanui.

It seemed like the couple had only just settled in when Moore's three-year term was up. Two years of it had been spent recovering from the Seattle mess — reaching out to governments, NGOs and the news media to make the case for the WTO and free trade — so that a new round could be launched.

It felt, in some respects, like his time as leader of the Opposition after the 1990 general election loss getting the Labour Party back up off the canvas only to have to leave after three years.

Moore was proud of what the WTO did in his short tenure. It successfully launched a new round, the Doha Development Agenda, in November 2001 — the first new one since 1986 — and saw the accession of more than a quarter of the world's population into its membership.

Lithuania, Moldova, Oman, Jordan, Croatia, Albania, Estonia, Georgia and, most significantly for world trade and regional security, China and Chinese Taipei, were all admitted. Russia's accession was also progressed.

The Doha Round only got launched, some say, because of the persistence and political skills of Moore. Coming so soon after the Seattle disaster, it almost didn't happen. Few others could have done it.

Moore relied on his experiences as a former politician to get the Doha Round launched. He sold the round politically but didn't become involved in the technical drafting of the documents, leaving them to the officials.

There were many obstacles in the way.

Coming so soon after the 9/11 terrorist attacks, there was nervousness about hosting the ministerial in Doha. British and US navy ships would need to be in the area for security.

Some in the EU wanted the ministerial moved and when Moore wouldn't they suggested the compromise — which was their real objective — of Qatar not chairing the meeting. This was not only an insult to Qatar but also to Moore and he had to lobby the US and others to ensure another ministerial didn't collapse on his watch.

In the WTO on rare occasions when a free and frank off-the-record discussion is required to resolve an issue, a process known as a 'green room' meeting is held.

Moore called for a 'green room' meeting the night before the round was due to be launched. There was a real chance agreement couldn't be reached.

He was active and vocal and extremely critical and aggressive with countries that expressed reservations against the launch.

He stepped beyond the job description of the director general, politically endangering himself and making many WTO staff uncomfortable. But by doing so he managed to reconcile all the diverging views into one.

For Moore the round was important because of its potential impact on the developing world. More than half the world's population lived on less than $2 a day and a successful round could lift billions of people out of poverty. The impact of that wasn't lost on his old socialist soul.

The core issue was — and still is — how do you make the system work for developing countries? It was a system that had been designed after the Second World War by the industrialised nations. Moore was the first director general who tried to answer that question, to use a lens that was not transatlantic.

That's why he called it the Doha Development Round and why its launch was the high point, for a brief moment, of international consensus that brought trade and development together.

While ambitious, it had been hoped that the round would have been completed at the 2003 Cancun Ministerial meeting. Some criticise Supachai for not making more of an effort — he went off with his sketch pad to the Mayan pyramids in the days leading up to the ministerial.

If it was to have been completed, it would have been before the end of Supachai's term in 2005. His successor, Frenchman Pascal Lamy, tried in 2008 but by then people had been allowed to move too far apart on issues to rescue the round.

Bringing China into the WTO in December 2001 was another huge achievement during Moore's time. China had applied for membership of the WTO's predecessor the GATT in July 1986 and for more than 15 years diplomats and politicians had been working on the accession.

It had required China listing its trade regime, countries negotiating bilateral agreements for market access and concessions with the most liberal then applied to everyone else and, in parallel with that, multilateral negotiations with China on rules for trading.

It was an enormously complex and technical process making a communist country, which was still converting into a market economy, a member of the WTO. But it was the politics of it all where Moore's skills were deployed.

Some thought China could have been brought into the WTO as

early as the 1990s but for nervousness from the Clinton administration around domestic political issues.

So Moore sold the politics, rather than the trade, in his discussions with nervous world leaders. China's accession would go beyond creating access to the world's biggest and fastest-growing economy. It was a geopolitical statement.

With China's increasing wealth and interconnectedness, Moore said, any of its future expansionary intentions could best be contained by the rest of the world via the WTO.

If China was part of a rules-based process that was consistent and fair for everyone, everyone would know where they stood with the country and vice versa. That was the power of trade and the WTO.

Moore had upset some seasoned WTO diplomats and bureaucrats during his tenure by demanding things be done differently or not as they were used to. When they complained to him, he'd often reply: 'Get elected, son.'

Near the end of his time he upset some in the secretariat by unfavourably comparing them to some in New Zealand's civil service who he used to think lacked capability and loyalty.

In his valedictory speech to the WTO General Council at the end of July 2002 Moore apologised if it had upset people.

'I have made some mistakes. But never out of malice. Mostly, my mistakes were born of enthusiasm to get the job done, complete our agenda and serve the public. George Bernard Shaw said reasonable people do not make change, thus all human progress is based on the unreasonable person. So, I have sometimes been unreasonable.'

One diplomat said she was sorry he was leaving as she'd only just begun to understand his New Zealand accent. 'Exactly the reason I should go,' he told her. 'And don't worry, no one in New Zealand understood me either.'

Moore's experiences of government in New Zealand — what works and doesn't — helped him see the work of the WTO from a macro level.

His WTO work, with his meetings of the superpowers in grand palaces and barely functioning countries with mud for roads, confirmed for him something he'd believed most of his career: that economies work best where there are democratic systems, a professional civil service, honest and transparent political parties, open commerce, a free and fair media, free trade unions and religious tolerance.

Moore wasn't naïve, though. He accepted that the WTO and globalisation had become dirty words in some circles, blamed for everything from global poverty and human rights abuses to the destruction of indigenous cultures. It had been misunderstood — sometimes deliberately — by some as a victory for the politics of the right.

But he remained an unabashed believer in internationalism, free trade, open markets, democracy, good governance and an active participating civil society as the pillars of development and success.

He was convinced more than ever that the free flow of goods and ideas promoted by bodies such as the WTO acted as a catalyst for development and lifted living standards worldwide and strengthened human rights.

Privilege, something he'd hated since a boy in Northland, survived and prospered best when protected by the state. Freedom and equality of opportunity was the best way to counter that. He saw protectionism and economic and political isolationism as the holdovers of colonialism and imperialism and against the goals of true social democratic thinking.

Moore argued that while the world had a long way to go, on real measures of human progress — life expectancy, infant mortality, literacy, access to clean water, democracy, human rights — an enormous amount had occurred and free trade had played more than a part in that.

In his farewell remarks to staff at the WTO's Geneva office, Moore reminded them that freedom was growing around the world, and as it grew its benefits compounded and people's lives improved even more. That expansion of individual freedoms, in turn, led to the might of the privileged and powerful contracting. That's why their work in the WTO was so important.

He told the WTO General Council that he'd continue to serve the public because he could think of no greater vocation. One day he might even join a protest outside the gates of the WTO.

'You will know me immediately,' he laughed. 'My banner will say "Justice now: finish the round".'

12

Mr Raymond Poynter

'Geneva's beautiful and is in the middle of everything, but it just wasn't home. It was great getting back to New Zealand, but I then ended up away from home a lot because I was on all these international boards. I ended up travelling and writing newspaper columns.

'Poor old Yvonne became my travel agent and my typist, I'm so useless with computers, and was left behind again.

'Mike Rann got me to do some interesting things for him in South Australia around economic development. Labour here weren't interested in me.

'I started thinking a bit about Dilworth and what it had done for me. I'd never really thanked them so I spent a bit of time at the school and we set up this fund with some serious money for the boys to manage and grow to benefit others.

'Through the WTO I'd become very fond of Africa and believed if the young people there had the educational opportunities, they'd transform the place. So the Dilworth boys would help in a small way to educate themselves and Africa. I was hoping that if it took off, we could replicate the fund elsewhere.

'After the fifth Labour Government lost, I went to a caucus function in Auckland that Phil Goff invited me to. I was talking to some MPs but when Helen Clark arrived in the room everyone moved away.

'She came up to me and we kissed on the cheeks and everyone came back and talked with me. She was going for the UNDP job and I think I gave her some bloody good advice on how to run her campaign. You have to give her credit — she's a quick learner, she took it all in.

'I was enjoying life, but I was still trying to find something to really sink my teeth into. Then out of the blue Murray McCully asked if I'd help New Zealand restore its relationship with the US. He and John Key were really worried about the progress of TPP and thought I could add value to it in Washington DC. They figured with my contact book I could open some doors.

'I had itchy feet, but it still wasn't an easy decision. New Zealand was comfortable. I wasn't sure about TPP. McCully was very keen on a ship visit too, so I said I'd only do it if they didn't touch the anti-nuclear legislation.

'At the WTO everyone wants to meet with you. In Washington DC I was a baggy-arsed ambassador for not an important country. You have to make yourself out to be important so people think it's necessary to meet you.

'I love Americans. They think they're the best in the world at everything and if anybody else is beating them, they must be cheating. There used to be a time when they were the best at everything and the world owes them a lot.

'Washington DC is a stimulating place. There are people with big minds and big ideas. The think tanks have sway with serious people working in them. It's a glorious thing. It's a place for politicians to renew their thinking and upskill themselves when out of office.

'God, we met so many clever Kiwis doing all sorts of great things in America. You come across them all the time. They're in all sorts of important roles in companies and politics and they all want to help. New Zealand needs to tap into them.

'Yvonne and I visited Walter Reed Hospital many times to see the wounded soldiers. It was a humbling experience.

'I believe in the special relationship between New Zealand and the US. Our people have fought and died together, we have shared values and we've been trading since Europeans settled in New Zealand.

'[The stroke] happened about 10 pm and luckily Yvonne was still up. I still don't remember much.

'The American system of health care is great if someone else is paying for it. I was looked after really well, and I'm grateful to Murray McCully, John Key and Brook Barrington. They were really concerned for me and Yvonne.

'My end at the embassy was a bit sad. The old and battered body had finally given out. It was also a little sour with the behaviour of a few staff.

'The tragedy of all this is I thought if I worked hard, built up some savings, got a bach then Yvonne and I would have enough to spend a good retirement together.'

****

Everyone said go on to some international boards, go on the speaking circuit, maybe set up a progressive foundation or think tank and set yourself up financially for the rest of your life.

His life had supposedly peaked and now it was time to cash in on all his contacts and experiences. Former GATT and WTO Director General Peter Sutherland had done that, going on to a successful corporate career with BP and Goldman Sachs.

After finishing his term in August 2002, Moore and Yvonne stayed on in Geneva for another year.

Moore was appointed to the board of SGS, the world's leading testing and certification company, became a commissioner for the UN Commission of Legal Empowerment of the Poor, and a commissioner for the Global Commission on International Migration.

In addition, he became a member of the Trilateral Commission, a founding member of the Global Leadership Foundation and an adviser to the UN Global Compact for Business and Development and the China Institute for Reform and Development's World Trade Organization Reference Centre.

He was given honorary and visiting professorships and had honorary doctorates conferred on him from universities in China, Australia and Britain, and regularly wrote for the *Australian Financial Review* and the *South China Morning Post.*

New Zealand trade minister Jim Sutton, an old friend, also appointed him as a special trade envoy for the country to speak on New Zealand trade policy and meet with governments and NGO leaders to discuss trade liberalisation.

But much of what he was doing wasn't him. Sitting in a boardroom listening to management presentations about selling widgets didn't fire up his belly. New Zealand beckoned and after only 12 months the couple returned home and he gave up some of his international commitments.

Back in New Zealand Moore teamed up again with his old friend from Eden days Mike Rann, who was now Premier of South Australia. Rann was trying to turn his state from a sleepy hollow into an economic success story and called on Moore's experiences to assist his newly created South Australia Economic Development Board.

Moore had kept in touch with Rann over the years, posting to him policy and campaigning ideas, and articles, and had joined him at Australia's Constitutional Convention looking into republicanism in Canberra in early 1999. Whenever the two would meet they'd talk all night about politics while finishing off one of their hotel mini bars.

Having become Premier of South Australia in March 2002, Rann was concerned about the state's heavy reliance on the car industry. The Economic Development Board was chaired by mining mogul Robert Champion de Crespigny and included the likes of South Australia's Social Inclusion Commissioner Monsignor David Cappo, well-known Australian businesswoman and mountaineer Cheryl Bart and former Prime Minister Bob Hawke.

The Board had intellectually rigorous, socially concerned and brave characters on it. He loved the debates and enjoyed their company.

The Board encouraged the South Australian Government to expand its mining base, embrace renewables and to win defence contracts. Instead of giving out incentives and subsidies for industries, the Board said the government should instead invest in infrastructure and attracting foreign students to South Australia.

Moore's belief in education as an export industry — which went back to him advocating it as an overseas trade minister in the 1980s against the wishes of some of his Cabinet colleagues — continued with his chairing of the advisory board of Carnegie Mellon University, which had been encouraged to set up a boutique campus in Adelaide in IT management and public policy.

He was also appointed to the Board of Governors of the Institute for International Trade, Business and Law at the University of Adelaide.

At home Moore became a consultant for telecommunications company TelstraClear in its battles to get Telecom New Zealand to open up its network to competitors and turned his spare time to his old school Dilworth.

The school had moved in his mind from being a 'Colditz' for young men to one of the fondest memories of his otherwise difficult upbringing. It taught him his love of books, which in turn opened his mind to the world and ideas that were the driving force of his career.

Moore believed he had a debt to repay to the school and after a number of discussions with Principal Donald MacLean — who said Moore didn't owe them anything — he thought the best way to give back to Dilworth was to establish an investment fund to be overseen by the school's students, with the dividends going to educational projects in poor communities in Africa, with a preference for Lesotho, Uganda, Rwanda and Nigeria. The Anglican Church would help give some guidance to what projects the funds would go to, but Muslim schools were to be included.

Through his work in the WTO he spent a lot of time on the continent and saw its potential. He also saw the corruption of governments, civil servants and the judiciary and was convinced that the only way to get lasting change was through young Africans becoming educated and demanding better.

The successful businesspeople he'd met during his career concurred with his thinking; many, in fact, had set up foundations with similar objectives.

Moore had been a long-time admirer of the Himalayan Trust founded by Sir Edmund and Louise Hillary in the 1960s to give practical assistance to the people of Nepal.

His thinking was that 'School Aid: Global Partnerships through Schools' would teach Dilworth year 12 and 13 students about investments and markets and about the lives of their counterparts in the developing world. It would also show them that capitalism can be used for social outcomes.

The students would need to do their own research about what to invest in, make judgement calls about responsible and ethical investments, determine what dividends to reinvest and what to distribute, and make assessments on what charities to choose. The only restriction was that equities must be limited to those in New Zealand.

It would involve real money and real choices and sometimes — and Moore thought this was its most important aspect — mean real mistakes were made by the boys. He had made many mistakes in his life, but those knocks had made him a more determined and stronger person and kept him in touch with the real world.

As part of its establishment Moore brought US environmentalist and author Robert F. Kennedy junior, the son of former senator Bobby Kennedy, to New Zealand in December 2009 as a fundraiser for the initiative. The event raised more than $150,000. Moore also donated $100,000 of his own money.

At the end of the 2019 financial year School Aid had almost $470,000 in assets and had made more than $116,000 in distributions to African charities that ranged from building classrooms, providing computer equipment and educational materials, and developing drinking wells.

Moore hoped that in time School Aid would be picked up by other New Zealand schools.

Moore also tried to establish a think tank in New Zealand for progressive and social democratic research and projects, similar to those in the US, Europe and Australia, to help counter the influence of establishment and right-wing lobby groups.

But corporate interest in funding the venture was minimal and he scrapped the idea after 12 months of trying.

All of this was interesting and stimulating work that used the skills he'd honed after decades as a politician and the contacts he'd gathered from the world stage. But it wasn't the kind of public service he thrived on and to which he still thought he could contribute. He was still itching to get back into the political ring. He still thought he had more in the tank.

Changing political winds favoured him at the end of 2008 when National won power after a nine-year absence.

Foreign Minister Murray McCully approached Moore in 2009 to replace New Zealand's Ambassador to the US Roy Ferguson, who was coming to the end of his posting.

McCully, a Northland boy too and who had known Moore in Auckland political circles going back to 1972, would regularly catch up with him for lunch to pick his brain about international issues.

Prime Minister John Key was strongly supportive of McCully's idea, although a few in the National caucus were aghast that the plum job was going to a former Labour politician.

The government sensed the relationship was on the cusp of being normalised and the Trans-Pacific Partnership (TPP) regional free trade agreement would be significantly boosted with American participation.

McCully knew that to get through the important doors in Washington DC New Zealand needed a politician of standing,and a former prime minister and WTO director general was the obvious candidate.

He thought Moore had skills and contacts that were underutilised by New Zealand.

The US had just elected a Democrat in Barack Obama as president and the incoming assistant secretary of state for East Asian and Pacific Affairs — who would have responsibility for New Zealand — was likely to be an old acquaintance of Moore's, Kurt Campbell.

It wasn't an easy decision for Moore, though. He and Yvonne had settled back into Auckland and were enjoying their time there and at their beach house in Matauri Bay, which used to be a motel owned by former Labour MP and minister Dover Samuels and was renovated by his old mate Bryan Gregory.

But it was more than deciding to go off on one last assignment. Pushing the TPP agenda created a philosophical dilemma for Moore.

As the director general of the WTO he had become a committed believer in a multilateral trading environment where the whole world benefitted. The TPP was a plurilateral trading agreement limited to its signatories. He had always seen bilateral and plurilateral deals as preferential, not truly free trade, agreements.

But the more he looked at the TPP deal the more he thought it could, if completed properly, be the impetus the WTO needed with its stalling Doha Development Round. Because of its consensus nature, WTO agreements always ended up with the lowest common denominator result.

The TPP was aiming for the elimination of tariffs on goods, liberalisation of trade in services, and new rules that reflect today's business practices — a highest common denominator agreement.

Importantly, it wasn't exclusionary; so other countries could join in later and this could create a ripple effect around the world, possibly reigniting the Doha Development Round.

The more he thought about it the more he realised that his work as New Zealand's ambassador, helping drive the TPP in the US, could help the WTO complete the round he started when he was director general.

McCully told Moore he hoped he could significantly boost the relationship with the US with the aim of resuming ship visits to New Zealand without the need to change the nuclear-free legislation.

At the senior official level, contact on a number of fronts was going well between New Zealand and the US, but at the highest political echelon it was still challenging.

A lot of good work had been done on the relationship by former New Zealand diplomats, including Ferguson.

Among other things this meant that in 2005 New Zealand was granted a special presidential waiver to be involved in a joint naval exercise with US forces for the first time in 20 years.

Soon afterwards, in May 2006, US Assistant Secretary of State for East Asia and Pacific Affairs Chris Hill said that New Zealand's anti-nuclear legislation was 'a relic' in an interview with the *Australian Financial Review* and signalled that there should be a closer relationship between the countries.

Hill praised New Zealand's involvement in Afghanistan and in the reconstruction effort in Iraq. He said there was no point trying to change each other's minds on the anti-nuclear issue but to focus on what could work in the relationship.

Despite the warming relationship, the US military still saw the lack of navy access to New Zealand as an issue.

Then there was the practical issue for New Zealand of its profile around Washington DC. The US capital is a place that is flooded with politicians, diplomats, lobbyists, businesspeople, NGOs and think tanks and is described by many as somewhere that's difficult even for the most high-profile people to get attention. It's an oxygen fight.

Key and McCully understood that this was a unique time when New Zealand and US interests could potentially converge. The right appointment could significantly step up New Zealand's profile and ensure the country had a seat at the tables where important international decisions were being made.

On his arrival in Washington DC, Moore and his team at the embassy established a profile-raising and stakeholder-engagement strategy.

They mapped out the top 100 people New Zealand needed to establish a relationship with on the Hill: the Congress and Senate leadership, key trade committee members, congressmen and -women and senators from farming states and states linked to trade, and heads of Congress and Senate coalitions.

They also established at the New Zealand Embassy a TPP war room. As a former WTO director general, Moore effectively became the 'unofficial dean' of the TPP country ambassadors, even though one of its members, the Singaporean ambassador, was the actual dean of the Washington Diplomatic Corps and well known and respected around town. The Singaporean and other ambassadors bought into Moore's coordinated lobbying approach.

Moore was energised and in his element. He was doing what he knew best — campaigning.

The US system is hard to penetrate, even for the most experienced diplomats, so a country needs regular engagement to be top of mind. Most Americans are polite and, busy diaries permitting, will receive a new visitor to the city. The trick isn't getting in the door but getting subsequent meetings.

Moore opened up a whole lot of bandwidth that only a former prime minister and WTO director general could. People were intrigued to meet him because of his back story and achievements, and then most warmed to his down-to-earth authentic style after meeting him.

He became well known in Washington in a way few politicians and diplomats could with those from the left and the right of the political spectrum. Previous career diplomats had ensured the embassy was well engaged across the system, but Moore's background and personality gave a turbo boost to New Zealand's effort, putting the country in the centre of some of the most important conversations in Washington DC.

He understood and could relate to most of the politicians he met and understood the political realities they faced in their states and districts on the issue of free trade and the TPP.

He spent a lot of time with the anti-free traders on the Hill. While it would be difficult to turn most into supporters of the TPP, Moore was hoping to at least neutralise their opposition.

One of the most ardent opponents was Democratic Congressman Mike Michaud from Maine. New Zealand diplomats had previously lobbied him. While he politely heard New Zealand out, it changed little.

Michaud was a non-university-educated former mill worker from a paper factory and a lifelong member of the trade union commonly known as the United Steelworkers. A member of the 'Blue Dog Coalition' of conservative Democrats, he was a strong supporter of veterans and had stood up for environmental causes.

Waiting in Michaud's congressional meeting room, Moore admired the Maine memorabilia around the office. When Michaud walked in and shook his hand Moore pointed to a United Steelworkers metal lunchbox and said: 'Union man, are you?' before reaching into his suit pocket to get his wallet and slide out his union membership card.

The two smiled at each other, nodded and then talked freely for 45 minutes in what was to be the first of many meetings.

Moore struck up friendships with many, including the powerful Montana Senator Max Baucus, the chair of the finance committee which has jurisdiction over trade.

Baucus had previously been on trips to New Zealand and Ferguson had built up a good relationship with him. Soon after his arrival, Moore was invited by the senator on an exclusive week-long mini-van tour of Montana with the ambassadors of Chile, China, Ireland and Japan. It was invaluable personal face time.

Soon after, with Moore's encouragement, New Zealand embassy staff were involved in regular softball matches and social activities with Baucus's office.

It was a tag team approach the almost 70 staff at the New Zealand embassy weren't used to. Moore also included the non-MFAT New Zealand secondees in the embassy, including those in uniform.

Moore told the younger staff to use his residence to host functions for staffers from the Congress and the Senate. It was highly unusual for most staff on the Hill to be invited to an ambassador's residence and it carried cachet in Washington DC.

Moore would help greet the guests, then joke to everyone that he was like the fictional balding, overweight and hunched television character Uncle Fester in the *Addams Family* and go off to his room and leave them to their evening.

Moore and the team nuanced New Zealand's message. For most Republicans it was that TPP was needed if US companies were to compete longer term with China. For most Democrats it was that a rules-based agreement like TPP was needed to protect labour standards and the environment in a relationship with China.

He would subtly tell people that America's influence was waning globally by pointing to the trade relationship between New Zealand and the US. Some 20 years earlier 18 per cent of imports in New Zealand came from the US and it had declined to 11 per cent. While the value was up, the market share was down. Moore would point out that it must, therefore, be a similar situation with other countries. While the global world trade pie had grown, the US slice of it had got smaller.

There were constant breakfasts, lunches and dinners as Moore and his team lifted New Zealand's profile.

Their fear was that the last time New Zealand was mentioned in any legislation in the US Congress or Senate was in 1987 and it was to do with the anti-nuclear and ANZUS issue. The next time would be around TPP. Congressmen and -women, senators and their staff needed to know the relationship between the US and New Zealand was older, broader and deeper than ANZUS.

He was always on the lookout for a hook to demonstrate the New Zealand–US relationship to stakeholders. If he saw a photograph of New Zealanders and Americans working together somewhere in the world, he would often get copies sent to people around Washington DC.

He demonstrated the depth of the relationship, too, by helping create events around important anniversaries such as the June 1942 arrival of US Marines in Wellington. It was important to remind the American military and political establishment, he thought, that the relationship went back a long way before the 1985 rift and that New Zealand was grateful for the friendship.

He would regularly, but politely, remind Americans that New Zealand soldiers participated in the First and Second World Wars before the US did and had served in many wars and peacekeeping missions since.

Moore knew that many of the early interactions between New Zealand and the US were military. So he hosted the 'Wounded Warriors' initiative, which is an annual function for injured US servicemen and -women from Walter Reed Hospital at nearby Bethesda.

Key US military and political figures would attend, including the influential neo-conservative former Deputy Secretary of Defense Paul Wolfowitz and the highly regarded former Deputy Secretary of State Richard Armitage.

Moore's networking skills were in overdrive in Washington DC. He continued his strong relationship with Kurt Campbell, who was assistant secretary of state for East Asian and Pacific Affairs during most of his time in Washington DC.

Moore identified the 2016 seventy-fifth anniversary of the Royal New Zealand Navy as a potential opportunity for a US warship visit and worked closely and quietly with Campbell and others on it.

Campbell was also instrumental in Secretary of State Hillary Clinton visiting the Pacific Island Forum in Rarotonga in 2012.

The US relationship with the Pacific, with which Moore had an affinity going back to his Pacific Parliament idea of the 1970s, was a pet project of his.

For most Americans, the Pacific stops at the equator and from a foreign policy perspective is limited to Japan and Guam.

It was important the US looked further south and helped provide a counterweight to China's growing influence in the region.

He turned the annual 'Pacific Night' celebration at the embassy into something broader and created a policy arm to it with seminars and lectures about the region which Secretary of State John Kerry attended.

During Moore's tenure he helped pave the way for Prime Minister John Key's visit to the White House to see President Barack Obama in July 2011 and defence minister Jonathan Coleman's visit to the Pentagon to sign the Washington Declaration, which increased defence cooperation between the two countries, with Defense Secretary Leo Panetta in June 2012.

Three months later Panetta said the Royal New Zealand Navy could use Defense Department and Coast Guard facilities around the world, and the following year Coleman and new US Defense Secretary Chuck Hagel said both countries would resume bilateral military cooperation after a near total 30-year break.

And almost a year after Moore's return to New Zealand, in November 2016, the USS *Sampson* participated in the Royal New Zealand Navy's seventy-fifth anniversary International Naval Review and coincidentally assisted after the Kaikoura earthquake.

With Key satisfied that under New Zealand's anti-nuclear law the destroyer was neither nuclear armed nor powered, it was the first warship visit to New Zealand in 33 years.

Moore found Washington DC stimulating and exciting. He spent many hours with people from think tanks to the left and the right. He loved meeting with them and particularly debating their outlooks on international issues. They all had research, data and thinking on a variety of matters. He would devour their books, papers and thinking.

Influential think tanks from across the political spectrum, from the Third Way, the Center for Strategic and International Studies, the Brookings Institution, the Heritage Foundation and the Cato Institute, were only too willing to share their ideas with him and to hear from Moore.

In his spare time he would look for books around Georgetown University and the George Washington University, and immerse himself at bookstore Politics and Prose on Connecticut Avenue.

Moore enjoyed the American spirit, the optimism, the bravery and entrepreneurial enthusiasm.

The Vietnam War had damaged America's image for his generation and the Iraq War had impacted its reputation for younger New Zealanders. He hoped that in some small way in his time as ambassador New Zealanders would still come to admire the US for all the good it had achieved in many fields — science, culture, commerce and democracy — and the potential the nation had to continue advancing the world.

That's why Moore established simple initiatives such as an internship programme for New Zealand students in US congressional offices and was happy to host barbecues at the embassy for these young people. A generation of New Zealanders would end up with invaluable networks of future US decision-makers.

Throughout their time in the US, Moore and Yvonne devoted much of their non-official duties to fundraising for the Christchurch earthquake appeal. Moore had been in Christchurch in February 2011 during the earthquake helping host the New Zealand–US Forum which included more than 110 high-ranking American and New Zealand politicians and officials. All got out safely.

But the experience of what had happened to his adopted home of Christchurch so moved Moore that on returning to Washington DC he worked with the US–New Zealand Council to set up the 'American Friends of Christchurch' charity.

It was chaired by Moore's friend Dr Peter Watson, a New Zealander who used to work for the National Security Council in President George H.W. Bush's White House, and it raised US$5 million.

Moore became obsessed about the fundraising, making special

trips to New York to meet wealthy friends of New Zealand and other high rollers to solicit donations. He told staff that when Americans rang offering donations not to passively accept them but to politely ask for more. For a while he would bluntly tell staff when they thought they'd had a hard day at the office to remember there were people in Christchurch using buckets for toilets.

He was a different ambassador to any the diplomats had experienced in the past. On a trip to the Boeing factory in Seattle when Air New Zealand was accepting a new aircraft, instead of spending his whole time with officials and management, Moore went off alone to the factory lunchroom to meet and talk with the workers.

But his work went beyond the US. Moore would always say that the road to Canberra was via Washington DC and his old friendship with Australian ambassador Kim Beazley, himself a former Labor leader, was important to maintain. Through his work on CER during the fourth Labour Government, Moore understood that Australia was still New Zealand's most important relationship.

Australia has a very different world outlook to New Zealand's. It sees itself as an international player deserved of a place at the same table as the superpowers. With its northern coastline on the backdoor of Asia, Australia needs a different relationship with the US. Moore would often say that Australia wanted to be 'indispensable' to the Americans, while New Zealand just wanted to be 'useful'.

Moore would remind Australia at the annual Anzac Day ceremony in Washington DC's National Cathedral of the bonds between the nations and come floods, bush fires or earthquakes how the two 'mates' always looked out for each other.

'No two nations have sailed, marched and flown so far to make and keep peace,' he said.

'We have never been neutral, passive or indifferent to the demands of keeping and making the peace. It's the rent we pay for civilisation.

'All contributed to the character and spirit of our nations. Sacrifice does not just build character, it reveals character.'

It wasn't a particularly difficult or stressful April day for Moore in 2015. He'd been working at the embassy and been to a New Zealand Trade and Enterprise function for a few hours.

He and Yvonne had a light dinner at the nearby New Zealand

ambassador's residence at Observatory Circle in the north-west of the city in the Embassy Row neighbourhood before watching a little TV. Moore headed off to bed about 10 pm because he had an early breakfast meeting the next day with visiting trade minister Tim Groser.

Then Yvonne heard some moaning and went into the bedroom to see Moore sitting still with a strange look on his face.

When she asked if he was alright, Moore starting talking rapidly to her. The right side of his face was drooping and his mouth wasn't working properly. He seemed frozen still and couldn't see well.

Yvonne asked him again if he was alright and Moore started mumbling: 'I'm okay, I'm okay, I'm okay.' He clearly wasn't and Yvonne screamed out for the house manager, Michael Macklin, and dialled 911.

While they were waiting for the paramedics to arrive, Yvonne made Moore do a stroke test. She had coincidentally only just seen a video about it on Facebook a couple of days earlier.

She calmly asked Moore to repeat a simple sentence, then raise his arms and tell her his name. He couldn't do them.

The paramedics arrived within 10 minutes and they confirmed he'd had a stroke.

He was rushed to the George Washington University Hospital not too far from the White House well within the three-hour window they say stroke victims should be attended to.

The hospital was used to dealing with Washington DC's VIPs and its systems were quickly enacted. Moore was given a pseudonym — 'Mr Raymond Poynter' — and a code word was assigned to him so that only those expected could get in to see him.

Few of the staff attending Moore even knew who he was.

In the emergency room they discovered Moore had already taken blood thinners that night so they couldn't give him the usual course of action for fear that it might cause a major and fatal bleed in his brain. While being checked, Moore suddenly sat up on the edge of the gurney and spoke normally before lying back down. No one could explain what had just happened.

Doctors told Yvonne that Moore had had an ischaemic stroke, the most common form. It often occurred with older people and was caused by a blood clot in an artery in the brain that had narrowed over time due to a number of factors including constant smoking.

The previous year Moore had also had a heart valve replacement operation and had atrial fibrillation or an abnormal heart rhythm. Heart issues are often thought to contribute to strokes.

He was completely paralysed down his right side and was unable to swallow, speak or move.

Yvonne was worried and upset and immediately turned to the person she knew would have a clear head and would provide good counsel, Clayton Cosgrove.

He was in South Australia and despite her urging him not to, Cosgrove arrived at the hospital within 72 hours.

It was around this stage that Moore was being moved out of the intensive care unit into a rehabilitation ward. His speech had returned quickly, but he could barely use the fingers on his right hand and walking was impossible. However, the doctors were hopeful.

Moore was like a caged animal. He hated the hospital. It brought back terrible memories of when he was going through his cancer treatment in Christchurch in 1979. The sounds and smells of the hospital were all too familiar and horrible.

His moods would swing as his recovery had good days and bad. Yvonne would make him food every day and take it to the hospital to give him some familiarity and comfort.

A young African American therapist and a hospital cleaner seemed to get on best with him. The therapist knew when to push him and when to ease back on the requests for effort. He would laugh and joke with the cleaner. They had no idea who he was.

Moore was steadily making progress after about four weeks of treatment and was managing to walk slowly from the hospital gym about 20 metres away back to his room.

It was physically and mentally difficult, but he could do it. The first time Yvonne saw him do this it was overwhelming, and she couldn't help but cry.

Walking in recent years had been difficult for him anyway. In Washington DC Moore had started wearing a brace on his right leg. It was the opposite leg to the one that had caused him problems going back to his childhood.

He thought he'd rid himself of a brace in his teenage years when he'd paid for an operation to fuse some of the bones together in his foot.

But all his cancer treatment in his thirties had meant his spine was now weaker in his old age than it would normally have been, and the brace was needed again.

The plan was to keep Moore in the hospital so long as his treatment was progressing. When his improvements appeared to plateau, it would mean he should probably check out.

Moore was constantly tired but enjoyed receiving visitors: current and former congressmen and -women, former US trade representatives, former assistant secretaries of state, current US military commanders from the Pentagon and ambassadors.

Prime Minister John Key, foreign minister Murray McCully and the CEO of the Ministry of Foreign Affairs and Trade Brook Barrington called him and Yvonne offering whatever assistance they needed. Former National and Labour parliamentary colleagues also sent well-wishes.

Kim Beazley helped fill in at functions for New Zealand, including giving Moore's Anzac Day address at the National Cathedral in Washington DC. Another old friend and now ambassador, former Manitoba Premier Gary Doer from Canada's progressive New Democratic Party, also assisted where he could.

Moore didn't realise so many people cared.

While Moore was stuck in hospital, unknown to him Yvonne was putting up with what she considered some unusual and unprofessional behaviour from a few senior staff in the embassy. Moore had another year to go in his term, but it was clear to her that some were trying to push him out earlier because of his stroke. Refusals to send Moore papers while he lay in hospital and comments to Yvonne that she thought were insensitive created pent-up anger.

Tensions were becoming apparent in the embassy so MFAT sent one of its most experienced diplomats, Carl Worker, to Washington DC as chargé d'affaires in June to help manage the situation.

Moore moved out of hospital six weeks after being admitted. The 1920s four-storeyed brick masonry residence wasn't built for someone with a disability — and Moore didn't want the money spent on adapting it since he wouldn't be there longer term. So only minor ramps were put up the steps to the library, where the couple spent most of their time, and into the bedroom, and handrails in the bathroom.

By late July he was walking with a quad cane for about 45 minutes at a time.

During his recovery period Rann, who was by now Australia's Ambassador to Italy, visited and was encouraged to see him walking slowly. But there was to be a drama one morning as Yvonne administered Moore's daily vitamin B12 injection. The needle somehow snapped off the syringe and when they couldn't find it Yvonne and Rann thought it had broken into and disappeared up his vein.

In a panic an ambulance was called and Rann grabbed a magnet from Moore's desk and held it to his arm where the needle had been inserted to try to stop it progressing to his vital organs.

Having just woken, Moore was unshaven and still wearing his nightwear, a T-shirt that said 'I got Bourbon faced on Shit Street'. Having run red lights all the way to the George Washington University Hospital's Ronald Reagan Emergency Department, a young specialist came out to meet them.

Rann explained that he'd managed to keep the magnet near where the needle had probably gone in only to be told by the doctor that they don't travel around corners in the body. After multiple X-rays and scans no needle was found and they returned to the embassy to laugh about Rann's ground-breaking medical procedure.

In November his recovery seemed to be going backwards. He needed several lumbar punctures to diagnose that he was suffering from 'normal pressure hydrocephalus', which among other things results in difficulty walking and incontinence. All of this was being caused by excessive cerebrospinal fluid. So he had to go back into hospital, this time to the nearby Johns Hopkins, for a shunt to drain the excess fluid.

After the procedure Moore was fit enough to return to New Zealand in December 2015, having been the longest continuously serving ambassador to the US.

In his farewell message to staff he said that unlike most of his career he was in the right place at the right time for this role.

'I want to thank you and your families for your commitment and to apologise for walking past you in the building full of ideas and full of hope. If I forgot to say hello or thank you that was my mistake. We will go home content that we did our best. Pity the old body gave up,' he said.

They would miss Washington DC. Away from the stuffy cocktail functions they met many New Zealand artists, sportspeople, entrepreneurs and academics doing well and having a major influence in US and global affairs.

It filled Moore with pride to see open-minded, mostly young, New Zealanders unafraid of and undaunted by the world's best. It was living proof to him of his early political beliefs that New Zealand should open up to the world and not be afraid to take it on rather than to retreat and close the economy.

The stint as ambassador also confirmed for him his long-held view that all people — even in a country like the US which is steeped in the ethos of the pioneering individual — fundamentally share Labour's values of community and shared responsibilities.

Americans don't see it that way, but Moore recognised their collectivist streak in their congregations in the south, their environmentalism on the west coast, their neighbourliness in the rural Midwest, their staunch trade unions in the rust belt and their family-oriented immigrant groups on the east coast.

The only upside of Moore's convalescence was he had to give up smoking, something he'd done since his teenage years and barely stopped during his many cancer treatments. It had proved difficult, but the nicotine patches helped. The stroke had also affected his taste buds so he no longer enjoyed a glass of wine.

What was starting to upset Moore was the thought of life after Washington DC. He knew he wouldn't be able to have a full recovery from his stroke while in the US and that he'd have to return to New Zealand. He had unfinished business around helping the government with its TPP discussions with Congress and some security discussions with the Pentagon still to complete. He was also fascinated by the upcoming 2016 presidential elections.

But what really concerned him was his life with Yvonne. Just before the stroke they'd had a two-week holiday in Nashville, Tennessee and New Orleans, Louisiana, and decided that when his term finished they would spend more time travelling together and enjoying life. He would put public life on the back burner.

After more than 40 years of marriage he realised that while he'd travelled to most parts of the world, he actually hadn't seen it. They were almost always plane, airport, hotel and meeting room trips. And but for trade missions in the 1980s, Yvonne hardly ever accompanied him.

The couple now had a home in Auckland and a beach house in Northland. For the first time in their lives they would be financially able and be free of obligations to enjoy themselves.

So, his sudden change in circumstances ate away at him.

Coming back to New Zealand to convalesce — and no more public service — was not how he'd imagined his later years.

13

A work in progress

Entreat me not to leave thee, or to return from following after thee: for whither thou goest, I will go; and where thou lodgest, I will lodge: thy people shall be my people, and thy God my God: Where thou diest, will I die, and there will I be buried: the Lord do so to me, and more also, if aught but death part thee and me.

'It's always moved me. I wrote that on a card and have carried it around in my wallet for a long time now. It's from the Book of Ruth and it's a promise from Ruth to her mother-in-law Naomi to be beside her no matter what.

'In 1941 President Roosevelt sent his closest adviser Harry Hopkins to meet with Winston Churchill to assess whether America should join the war.

'Hopkins was a boy from Iowa, whose father was a storekeeper, who became a social worker and was one of the architects of Roosevelt's New Deal that saved working people during the Depression. He was a hard-drinking and smoking man, survived cancer and couldn't stand privilege.

'Churchill took him on a tour of bombed-out Britain and at a dinner in Glasgow Hopkins was asked what he'd be recommending to Roosevelt. So Hopkins gave a toast quoting this passage.

'Hopkins went back to America and persuaded Roosevelt to create the Lend-Lease programme where Britain was given equipment and supplies and helped turn the war. It was a pledge of unbreakable loyalty and fidelity.

'Ultimately, politics is about such loyalty and fidelity to a core set of principles and those around you who will, together, carry that water. It's a simple thing to say but very few people are capable of it.

'That's formed the basis of my view of working-class Labour politics.

'The challenge for Labour over the next 70 years — as it has been since I joined in the 1960s — is the same battle the world over for progressive parties.

'Do we represent the aspirations of the working class or do we represent middle-class narrower issues and perspectives — some call it identity politics — and hope that we can form some kind of coalition of common interests in the party.

'Labour was born out of the desire for change by working people via the political process and we forget that at our peril.

'The biggest fear I have for the party is that we're becoming too narrow in the people we're attracting into it. We need more diversity of life's experiences and thought. It's got to be more than gender and ethnicity.

'Labour can't be complacent with the candidates we select. We should be the place people with talent gravitate towards.

'We just have to make sure we avoid choosing candidates who look and sound like each other.

'There's no point replacing male, pale and stale with female, pale and stale. Growing up in the same suburbs, going to the same universities, belonging to the same NGOs, hanging out in the same cafés and living with the same people doesn't foster diverse and innovative thinking.

'Maybe we should have quotas for working-class people. Labour's always at its strongest when we bring different ideas to a debate and aren't afraid to challenge each other.

'True diversity in Labour is about different upbringings, life's experiences and perspectives all bound by a common purpose and set of core values.

'I hope that in the future Labour MPs will be writing books and papers, giving speeches and organising conferences that challenge the status quo.

'That's what I used to love about the party back in the 1960s when I first joined — we'd have great and forceful debates about all sorts of things, but everyone would walk away as friends. It was like a rugby match: you'd beat each other up on the field but afterwards shake hands and have a beer together.

'The traumatic 1980s have meant people are afraid to have different views for fear of creating disunity.

'Labour and Parliament needs revolutionaries like Roger Douglas, people who think differently and are prepared to question the status quo. It also needs people like Jim Bolger, arch conservatives, who people like me need as a reminder of why we have the battles that we have.

'The world is a lot more complicated than when I joined Labour. Then we were in the middle of the Cold War and the spread of communism, there was the post-war break with colonialism, there was the evil of apartheid and French nuclear testing to focus on.

'And it was pretty clear who the bosses and the workers were. In my day an electrical worker in a factory was unionised and worked for wages — they were working class and almost certainly voted Labour. Now that same electrical worker is a small business person, not in a union, driving a ute between various contracts and probably employs a couple of apprentices. I still think that's blue collar, but are they still attracted to Labour?

'The next 70 years will be a lot more complicated. Technology, climate change and changing power balances between countries are the challenges, while at home we'll have to face some big questions about what it means to be a Kiwi.

'Automation and globalisation took many blue-collar jobs in the 1980s and 1990s. The next wave of technology — artificial intelligence — will take professional and white-collar jobs.

'Generally speaking, the blue-collar workers bought our arguments that old industries naturally died as the world became smaller and different countries had advantages over others. They bought the notion of retraining and they also wanted better jobs for their kids.

'This time last century there was a similar debate about work. Do you replace a gang of labourers with picks and shovels with a bulldozer and one driver? It's an easy answer — you train the labourers to be the bulldozer drivers, have more bulldozers, and create more roads more quickly, and lift the country's productivity in the process. This has historically been the response of nations.

'The logic of the counter-argument is that you give all the labourers spoons and ask them to continue working and create more employment. That's pure nonsense.

'But what happens when the white-collar workers lose their jobs: the lawyers, the accountants, the bank workers? Will they buy the arguments, will they stay silent?

'The working-class dream of sending our kids to university to become a lawyer or doctor will be challenged in future.

'Does that mean everyone will have to be trained and educated to become computer programmers or creative thinkers? That won't work because the sheer numbers of jobs will shrink.

'So we'll have to rethink the working week and what we do with our spare time. Do we collectively commit ourselves as a society to more voluntary or community work? I don't know.

'This is confronting because it means governments will have to think through the welfare system.

'Will it mean that those with jobs will have to help pay for those who don't, or do we have to rethink how we value the contribution people make to a community?

'The answer this time has to be more about rethinking the mix of work, recreation and community time and a coordinated approach to rapidly developing the skills the economy will need. There will always be plenty of work, but people will come in and out of it depending on what's needed in the economy.

'That means we'll have to rethink the contribution workers make to wealth creation. We value the contribution capital makes to it by writing it down in a balance sheet. But where's a worker's contribution accounted for other than a wage bill or cost?

'That means employers, workers — individually or collectively through their representatives or unions — and governments planning together. It's the same model I was convinced of as a young trade unionist and party member in the 1960s through to the compact idea in 1990.

'Allowing New Zealanders to face this uncertain future with confidence is what Labour should always be about.

'How we treat the planet is also a big challenge.

'I grew up in a time when cutting down trees and digging coal out of the ground was seen as progress and in Labour a test of manhood. I remember reading *Moby Dick* thinking the whale was the bad guy.

I even once agreed with Onehunga MP Hugh Watt's idea of filling in part of the Manukau Harbour to create more industrial land. It was just mangroves and mud flats everyone thought.

'Technological advances in energy creation and storage mean the economics of substitution will soon allow people to start transitioning out of the biggest need for fossil fuels. To advance this transition, governments will need to use carrots and sticks with industries to think differently.

'One of the reasons I'm optimistic about the future is that young people are making us think differently about the environment. Like young people always, they're impatient.

'The major foreign policy theme for the rest of this century will centre around China, its place in the world, how it behaves and how others treat it.

'I've always been fascinated with China right from when Norm Kirk recognised it soon after being elected in 1972 and Joe Walding led the country's first trade mission there in 1973.

'My many visits there as a minister and during its accession to the WTO, and lecture tours to Chinese universities since, have opened my eyes to the country's remarkable achievements.

'In the space of a generation hundreds of millions have been lifted out of extreme poverty. China is a great example of the nation-building and transformative power of trade.

'I'm unsure now whether China's growing strength will be used for global good or domination. It's important to remember that China's name for itself is 'middle kingdom' — they see themselves historically as the middle of the universe.

'Their period of poverty throughout much of the twentieth century, they argue, was an aberration and created by colonial subjugation. Their view is they're just restoring themselves to their rightful place as the middle kingdom.

'I used to be confident of China's intentions in the global community. I was reassured by a United Nations speech by paramount leader Deng Xiaoping, the driving force of the country's economic transformation in the 1980s and 1990s, that China had no desire to be a superpower.

'China was too busy taking its people out of poverty and modernising the nation. Deng warned, though, that if China ended up subjecting others to "bullying, aggression and exploitation" then the world should "expose it, oppose it and work together with the Chinese people to overthrow it".

'In recent years I've become wary of China's international goals. It has always had an interest in Africa and the Pacific, but it now seems to have a harder economic and military view of those regions.

'A world where nations, particularly the US, become insular means fewer counterpoints to countries like China and Russia which are internationally forceful and creates dangerously less ballast in the global geopolitical system.

'There will be tensions in China as its middle classes grow and demand more freedom of thought to go alongside their freedom of wealth. How will the Chinese Communist Party deal with this?

'I think part of the answer we're already starting to see as China becomes more aggressive internationally in an effort to look nationalistic back home. This has less to do with the 1960s and 1970s style of spreading communism and more to do with grabbing resources and projecting itself militarily to protect its interests.

'The key challenge for the immediate future will be how the US and China get on.

'Throughout history when the first military power starts to give way to the second there's normally conflict. The only time it really didn't happen was when America took over from Britain as the world's naval power.

'China could surpass the US if it became democratic, but I just can't see it happening. China flexing its muscles is a very different thing to America flexing its muscles.

'The US is guilty of many crimes, but they're a democratic nation. That's not a small thing and that's why we should stay close to the Americans. I hope New Zealand understands that being neutral or uncommitted is a dangerous place.

'Having said that, I don't think China has a grand plan for world domination. Deng Xiaoping once said China would "cross the river by feeling the stones", meaning they'd be cautious in their move from a centrally planned economy to an open one.

'There's a great opportunity for New Zealand here to play a significant role as the superpowers sort themselves out. China and the West trust and listen to New Zealand. We've always been non-threatening, we're humble, we're not thieves, we're good people and countries respond to that. Everyone's happy to talk with us and we shouldn't underestimate that. We can have honest conversations that aren't based on self-interest other than wanting a peaceful world.

'Fundamental to the future architecture of the world will be trade between countries based on legally enforceable laws and rules.

'I'm convinced the World Trade Organization or something similar has a place in that future. But there will probably be "A" members and "B" members. "A" members will be believers in free trade and "B" members will argue about it. And countries will slip between "A" and "B" as it suits them.

'The world may well go through a period of chaos around trade, but very soon sane minds will realise like we've done in history that some kind of order is better than resolving disputes by gunboat.

'This chaotic order may initially result in a period where trade is managed between the bigger players and smaller countries like New Zealand and the developing world just have to tag along and accept the rules set by others.

'I have more faith in the WTO being a key player in this new world order, though, than I do the United Nations. The UN will continue to exist — and that's a good thing — but it won't reform. The permanent five of the Security Council won't give up their power even though power will move to different countries in future: the US, China, Russia, India, Brazil, what's left of the EU and maybe Britain.

'With information so global I think we'll also see the emergence of super political leaders — people who lead a country but can influence the people of another through the power of their ideas and rhetoric, not so much the size of their economies or military.

'Donald Trump has become one of those for the bigoted and closed world believers. Jacinda Ardern has the potential to be the counterpoint, for those who believe in tolerance and interconnectedness.

'For New Zealand, our standing in the world and our main point of leverage is our understanding of, and influence in, the Pacific. This is one of the new battlegrounds for global resources and strategic military presence. New Zealand's historic and familial links with the Pacific place the country in a perfect position.

'We've just got to be careful that we don't become like the Brits,

French, Americans and Chinese — and increasingly the Australians — bringing the modern equivalent of beads and trinkets.

'New Zealand's role should always be about technology and capability transfer — a hand up — so that the Pacific nations can become sustainable economies, they don't need to go cap in hand to others and can become truly independent.

'Over the next 70 years the EU will break apart. It's an experiment too far. People still have to have a cultural identity and some things aren't the business of governments.

'It was really a post-World War Two and Cold War entity formed to stop another war in Europe and to counter the Soviet Union and the Eastern bloc. It was meant to keep the Germans in and the Russians out.

'As a trading group it made sense and maybe free movement of labour — like CER between Australia and New Zealand. But a common currency removed an economic lever for individual nations and impinges on sovereignty.

'When you're passing regulations on what shape bananas should be you know there's something wrong.

'That's why a federal Europe doesn't work and why I favour a United Nations of Europe approach.

'Likewise, I don't think we'll have a formal economic union with Australia. We'll get closer and New Zealand should try to leverage Australia's size to our benefit and there's an argument for similar laws and regulations in some areas of the economy, but we should continue to have a separate currency, judicial system and regulators.

'There's never been a more important time since the end of the Second World War for the role of international institutions like the United Nations, World Bank and World Trade Organization and regional arrangements like CER, Asia-Pacific Economic Cooperation, the South Pacific Forum and the Association of Southeast Asian Nations.

'Those institutions and arrangements create structures and rules for civilised engagement that help limit the influence of bullies and help avoid nations talking past each other and resorting to other means of communication. They have been the counter to tribalism and old disputes.

'They're still the best way to deal with the waves of populism and nationalism sweeping the world.

'The rule of law and strong political leaders with great communications skills are needed to make the arguments against the vested interests and crony capitalists.

'Tariffs, subsidies and trade barriers are simply taxes that don't protect working people. Instead they look after the interests of the rich and powerful who would far rather try to influence a few politicians than have to compete in an open market against the best on the merits of their products and services.

'While the US is undermining the work of the WTO it's good that many nations, including New Zealand, are making progress on bilateral and regional trade agreements. It's important to continue advancing the free trade agenda with the hope that other nations can join.

'I've always been a fan of the US with its political checks and balances. That's why I'm confident that nation will eventually reset itself and become an example of and talisman for rules-based free trade.

'We might just be in a cycle and things will come back. The US has resilience about it. The nation that most embodies the age of enlightenment — reason, science, tolerance, the separation of church and state — is America and you see it in their constitution. It was an amazing experiment and democracy has spread.

'This current insularity is being driven by globalisation and technology leaving people behind. And politicians in search of votes appeal to those who have missed out by blaming others and suggesting walls rather than bridges as the answer.

'Thankfully, New Zealand has a strong parliamentary democracy.

'I hope Parliament continues to be the marketplace of ideas where competing views of how New Zealand should be run and organised are debated — no, argued over.

'I don't buy the notion that Parliament should be a place of polite debate. It's not a school debating club. It's not Sunday school. It should be raw at times because MPs should be passionate about representing New Zealanders.

'Parliament could be pretty dull at times in our day. But it would catch fire when people talked from the heart and didn't have speeches prepared for them by their research units.

'Modern MPs are far harder working and more focused than we were. Parliament doesn't sit late into the night and MPs get more of a chance to be with their families. It's great that MPs can bring their babies into the House — it reminds us we're human beings and who we're fighting for. Parliament is a less macho place and there's less of a drinking culture, which is good.

'I hope it hasn't lost its camaraderie and human touches — like when Koro Wetere used to bring his smoked trout in to share with MPs, staff and the Press Gallery or people rallying around each other when things weren't going well at home.

'The electorate goes through phases with prime ministers and it tends to match their economic mood and the security they feel for their jobs, their families and their country.

'Our prime ministers will continue to come in three basic forms — father- or mother-like figures like Charles de Gaulle or Helen Clark, tough aunts or uncles like Margaret Thatcher or Rob Muldoon, or younger brothers or sisters like John F. Kennedy or Jacinda Ardern.

'Hopefully over the next 70 years no future government has the mess we faced in 1984.

'Kiwis are generous people. If you talk openly with them about the issues the country faces and your prescription for dealing with it, as we did in '84, most of the time they'll accept it. You have to talk with conviction and confidence. Most don't have the answers themselves and look to their leaders to lead.

'It's when you demonstrate to them that you're not even confident among yourselves about the changes you want — as we did from 1988 in that last term of the fourth Labour Government — that they rightly punish you.

'MMP has been good because it's slowed down the political process. I was never in favour of MMP, but it's proved me wrong. I always believed that executive power and decision making was important.

'It's still there under MMP but coalition governments mean being more inclusive in the process and that's a good thing because it means that when decisions are finally made they're more likely to be sustainable.

'The enormous change heralded by the fourth Labour Government may still have occurred but at a slower pace and maybe some of the eventual conflicts would have had more time to be resolved rather than the open warfare we had.

'The New Zealand system is self-balancing so long as we also have a plurality of news media, an independent judiciary, corruption-free law enforcement and a strong civil service. With the supremacy of Parliament, a place that promulgates the laws we collectively live under, it's a beautifully balanced system.

'The older I've become and the more I've witnessed internationally, the more important I see these structures are for resisting populists and tyrants whose only interests are actually themselves and not their people.

'I'm like many other members of Labour — hopeful and optimistic about New Zealand and always critical of the party's response. I always want more. New Zealand deserves the best. I'm impatient for the perfect nation Labour always seeks to build.

'It should be the place where the child of an immigrant in South Auckland or widow on the West Coast can, through the collective efforts of a nation with institutions like public health and education and ACC, compete with the child of a surgeon from Fendalton and where they are judged on their intelligence, hard work and character.

'There has always been a wealth disparity in New Zealand. But I don't see the answer being a nation that punishes the well-off in some misguided desire to create equality. The communists did that. There is no equality in everyone being poor. We have to uplift the poor because, like wealth, poverty can be inherited across generations.

'Taxation is part of the answer. It is a legitimate tool for governments to use to address economic, social and environmental issues. We on the left have allowed the privileged to successfully make the case that we should have taxes as low as possible.

'Taxation should be the mark of a civilised society. It's about saying the nation collectively agrees to put its resources together to help educate everyone or provide hospitals, that access isn't dependent on the size of your wallet.

'We need to once again argue that a progressive tax system where those who can afford to pay a little more are willing to so that the public institutions that help create opportunity can work better. That's a compelling case for Labour to put because those are Kiwi values.

'Labour has always been good at wealth distribution but the backgrounds of most of our MPs means business and entrepreneurship don't come naturally to us. Not only must Labour be good stewards of the economy but we must also be about wealth creation.

'Government has a role in wealth creation by using policy levers and investment in public infrastructure that the private sector can take advantage of.

'I like to think much of my work in the free trade area helped our exporters, made us outward looking and helped grow the economy.

'Labour needs to celebrate more how it has uplifted generations of working families. Many of New Zealand's current business, academic and public sector leaders are from modest backgrounds and have got ahead in life with the help of Labour's policies.

'Convincing the country's new leaders of the equality of opportunity mission of Labour should, therefore, be easy.

'This should also be the case for Labour's special relationship with Māori.

'We should strongly push back on those who say we've done nothing for Māori. It should always be remembered that the original four Māori seats were seen as the four quarters of prophet Ratana's body.

'Ratana understood, like the founders of Labour, that political representation was the key to giving voice to, and improving the fortunes of, his people.

'After Michael Joseph Savage was elected prime minister in 1935, Ratana pledged the allegiance of his MPs and his followers to Labour. At their meeting Ratana supposedly gave Savage a potato to represent the loss of Māori land and the sustenance of his people, a broken gold watch to remind him of the promises of the Treaty of Waitangi, a piece of pounamu to represent the mana of Māori and a feather from the extinct huia bird to wear as a great leader if he could restore the first three.

'The symbolism of that famous meeting should form the basis of Labour's continued commitment to Māori. Labour's relationship with Māori helps define us. Those symbols should form the pillars of the modern relationship.

'It was my old mentor Mat Rata who brought in the Treaty of Waitangi Act and my old friend Koro Wetere who amended it to look at claims going back to 1840. Labour created the treaty settlement process. This was brave stuff in the 1970s and 1980s and Labour did this in the face of opposition from National who played the race card around the issue.

'Creating a process to deal with past grievances, the returning of property to its legal owners, has been important for nation building. We now have iwi who are significant players in the economy.

'I just hope that when all the grievances have been settled, that Pākehā New Zealanders don't wipe their hands and say 'Māori, you're now on your own' because that's not what this process was about.

'We are all New Zealanders and we should all be concerned if any section of our country — Māori or otherwise — is on the wrong end of social statistics like education, employment and imprisonment.

'I think we'll always be asking questions about the Māori and Pākehā relationship — with plenty of angst — and I think it's a healthy thing to happen.

'Our grandchildren and their children will have intermarried and we'll be a beautiful mix of mocha-coloured New Zealanders able to trace our roots to Europe, the Pacific, Asia and Māori. It's not something we'll see in many other nations with their strict divides between the races.

'I hope in 70 years Māori language and culture will be compulsory in primary schools and when kids get to secondary school they either continue with it or pick up another language. It's unique to New Zealand and we all have a duty to protect it.

'I hope the Māori seats are retained so that we never forget our special relationship and all things Māori have a guaranteed place in the most important institution in New Zealand, the Parliament.

'Labour should never be afraid to push on these kinds of issues. This thinking ahead and planning for the great challenges in society is what Labour parties do and why I always see our agenda as a work in progress.

'National wants to keep the world the same for as long as they can because it's easy, controllable and less threatening. They tend to always find workarounds that suit their needs. Whether it's getting taxpayers to pay farmers supplementary minimum prices for lamb or the ratepayers of Auckland to pay for their golf course in Remuera, they understand protecting privilege.

'Will National stay the same over the next 70 years? It has become softer in its tone in recent years. I put this down to the affable John Key, who doesn't seem to have an ideological bone in his body, and to Bill English, a man driven by his Christian beliefs. I think they've done more to change National and its values than any previous leaders. They've become Labour-lite. The Nats have become much harder to hate. Those two have done more to endanger Labour than any other Tories.

'But we can still outflank them. In the end there are certain things they will always find hard to support — like public health and public education — because they see this like any other service that you should be able to profit from.

'I don't think the Nats' mild mannered-ness will last because many in that party know the easiest path to electoral success is appealing to the worst side in people, to Kiwis' fears — immigration, race, law and order.

'It's their old playbook and history has shown they understand the nature of power better than those of us in Labour. They think it's rightfully theirs. And they don't have bottom lines. We do.

'In 70 years there won't be New Zealand First. It only exists because of Winston Peters. Another politician with charisma might emerge and history shows that there's always room for one of those kinds of parties: nationalist and populist, who play to people's fears rather than their better sides. Most populations have one in ten people who are attracted to that.

'Winston is a likeable rogue. He's an old-fashioned Tory. He understands ordinary Kiwis.

'And he's not afraid to push back against political correctness which always threatens Labour. In our efforts not to offend anyone we stifle debate. Once people start double-thinking what they say, you go down an Orwellian worm hole.

'I'm sometimes scared that these people will end up controlling the blackboard and reinventing history and dismissing facts. If someone is in any way offended, then your argument is rendered irrelevant.

'Young people need to be offended more, I reckon. They might learn something.

'The trade union movement is at a key moment in history.

'God, I'd love to be in my twenties again and running a trade union.

'Trade unions will always have a role representing the voiceless and those in unbalanced employment relationships. But they need to ditch their cloth-capped, often English-based views of employer and employee relationships and reach out to a broader group of workers.

'Most companies these days treat employees well and employment laws protect many workers. That's the success of trade unions and we should celebrate that. The job of trade unions now is not to knock off the boss but to work with them to help grow the business — that's in everyone's interests.

'They cannot be like the guilds were in the eighteenth and nineteenth centuries, closed shops that restrict employment and create their own kind of privilege. The good ones that succeed will be those that help grow businesses and industries, and share the wealth with workers. I still believe good trade unions can be beneficial to the economy.

'Modern trade unions need to see themselves like a good insurance company — giving advice and guidance to policyholders as well as being there for the big moments. They've got to be more than bargaining agents.

'With many workplaces being scattered, small unions can survive if they have centralised services that are shared with others. They don't necessarily have to merge.

'In fact, a series of small trade unions with shared overheads with high-touch localised services — kind of like a franchise model — might be what they look like in 70 years.

'These changing and different times mean Labour and its movement need to constantly adapt. I'm confident that doing some things as a society collectively or together will continue to resonate with New Zealanders over the next 70 years.

'The key is to demonstrate that it's an economically better and more socially compassionate path when compared with the selfishness and cruelty of an unfettered free market. Dog eat dog just isn't the Kiwi way.

'Labour always needs to remember that New Zealanders also believe in reward for hard work and are aspirational. While most New Zealanders would love to win Lotto, unlike Americans they don't dream of being millionaires.

'Instead, many aspire to earn enough to be comfortable, to help their children get ahead, to save for retirement, have a beer and a barbecue with their mates at the weekend and to have enough to go on a family holiday every year.

'They don't ask for much more than a fair go.

'They're happy to pay their taxes so all children can have a good education, the family is looked after if there's an accident or someone gets sick, the streets are safe and if someone loses their job they'll be taken care of until they find another. They're happy with that social contract.

'But the moment one group appears to be given favours or avoids paying their fair share, they get upset. Labour needs to remember that simple equation.

'The ethnic composition of New Zealand is changing rapidly, particularly in the bigger cities, and Labour needs to reach out to these new Kiwis and be relevant to them.

'Labour needs to remember that most come to New Zealand for the same reason as our parents, grandparents and great-grandparents, regardless of whether it was a jet airplane, a steam liner, a tall ship or a waka. They want a better life for themselves and their children.

'It takes bravery to leave your place of birth to make a new life in a strange country and immigrants should be praised for choosing New Zealand. We should thank them for choosing us.

'Labour's desire for less bureaucracy for small business, a corruption-free police force and judiciary, public education and health, open and simple government, access to export markets overseas, a clean environment and a social safety net should all appeal to immigrants.

'The success of this experiment at the bottom of the South Pacific, created by successive Labour governments, is why they've chosen this country.

'It also means being compassionate and standing up for what's morally right. Labour has a great history of taking refugees from conflicts and some of my prouder moments as an MP have been when Polish orphan refugees from the Second World War thanked me for Peter Fraser's kindness in bringing them to New Zealand in the 1940s.

'Since Fraser helped form the United Nations after the Second World War, New Zealand has sought to make its way in the world free from Mother England with independent views.

'New Zealand will eventually become a republic. And we'll probably do it after Australia becomes one. How ironic would that be — to express our independence we'll copy Australia.

'I don't think we should be a republic, though. Everyone thinks I'm a republican but I'm not.

'I think the current system with a governor general has served us well. The governor general's power is not the power he or she holds but the power they deny others inside the system. Why create power for one politician?

'A governor general has far more balance and nuance and keeps the power in Parliament.

'The current system preserves the supremacy of Parliament. You have to win the Parliament if you want to pass any laws and that's where the ultimate power of the country should rest — with representatives who are voted for by the public.

'If you have a president — whether appointed by the Cabinet, Parliament or a public vote — the role inevitably becomes political and slowly but surely it undermines the power of Parliament.

'I know how politicians think and operate and a presidency would, despite any intentions otherwise, become political.

'Our system has served us very well. The monarchy is convenient and efficient, and its mysteriousness and rituals mean everyone pays attention. It has mana.

'Besides, she's not the Queen of England. She's the Queen of New Zealand. Kirk changed that. That's a subtle but important thing.

'The monarchy is a hereditary system and it is a form of inherited privilege. But I don't see any contradiction in supporting that and with being a socialist.

'I do hope Labour will be brave enough in the coming years to start a conversation with New Zealanders about a constitution, perhaps by creating an eminent persons group to develop a discussion paper and suggest a process over a number of years that might lead to a referendum on the issues. A constitution that sets out a core set of values we hold dear as a country provides us with another anchor as a nation.

'Because we don't have a constitution, we're ruled by convention. The Treaty of Waitangi is not a constitution, it's a founding document.

'We should be brave enough to have a long and thoughtful conversation about all of this rather than saying, "Oh, there's no urgency." That's when you have these kinds of conversations, so they're rational and thoughtful.

'It would be a coming of age moment for New Zealand.

'But I should stop worrying about the future.

'I'm hopeful of Jacinda Ardern and her generation of leaders.

'I was touched that she reached out to me before the 2017 election.

'Jacinda's special. She's a prime minister with a great human touch and an ability to draw people in. She's fresh and optimistic and appeals to the better side of our natures.

'She could teach me a lot about politics. She's a natural. But make no mistake, she's a politician and she's one of the best I've seen anywhere.

'With Jacinda we've struck it lucky. She's genuinely warm and kind and despite her many years in politics seems to be devoid of the cynicism the political system can create. I'm hopeful that her new way of looking at politics, this more empathetic approach, is the antidote, the push-back, to the rising levels of hatred and insularity everywhere. That's why she needs to succeed.

'Her style complements Grant Robertson as minister of finance. He's shown real strength and is the backbone of this government. He'd make for a good prime minister after her.

'Jacinda and Grant and the young people they've attracted to the party are the new generation to take the movement forward.

'Martin Luther King once said that the arc of the moral universe was long, but it bent towards justice. What King and the originator of the phrase, nineteenth-century abolitionist Theodore Parker, were talking about was belief.

'While they couldn't see the end of the arc, they were sure it bent in the right direction. They had faith, they believed.

'But I also think you have to continually make the case otherwise progressive thought gets pushed back by the forces of privilege. That's why Labour's work is always work that's never done. History isn't linear; the debates and the battles of the past still need to continually be made and won, and not banked and forgotten about.

'Jacinda and her generation, though, are now the lifeblood of Labour and I'm confident they've got the baton.

'I believe in them.'

Epilogue

September 2019

The laptop is still open. But now it's on a tray hovering over his waist, as his head is propped up by two carefully placed pillows against the elevated end of his hospital bed.

There are tubes poking out from under the sheets.

The meeting place has moved upstairs to his bedroom.

His dimple rises and he hangs his hand out to shake. Now, no muscles engage.

'Gidday mate,' he whispers, his lips hardly moving.

Yvonne brings in the savouries, sandwiches, slices and coffee.

The routine is the same, but everything is different.

There's a gritting of teeth, a sharp intake of air and a closing of eyes. Yvonne squirts a syringe of morphine into his mouth.

'How do you think they're going?' he asks, widening his eyes.

****

I scribbled it in my notebook at the time but never ended up using the quote.

He wasn't quite yet sworn in as prime minister by the governor general on 4 September 1990 when I heard Mike let slip at his first press conference as Labour leader something that, looking back now, seemed to be overly reflective.

'If you want something badly, it seems to move from you,' Mike told journalists. I thought it a strange comment at the time, wrote it in my notebook, and with the rest of the herd got distracted by the craziness of the remainder of the day.

I reflected on it, almost 30 years later, and he said, almost in a melancholy way, that it had been the story of his life.

Maybe it was the medication or the fact he knew he was dying, but he didn't seem satisfied with his many achievements. In one of our last conversations he suggested we write a book about dying, so that at least he could be useful again to someone.

Throughout his extraordinary life Mike was ambitious — for himself, for his electorates, for the government he was a part of and then briefly led, for the World Trade Organization's agenda, for New Zealand and US relations, for his health and for his relationship with Yvonne.

He wanted the best for all of them, yet almost everything he ever really desired he didn't quite get his hands around — from having a loving father in his childhood, through to enjoying a long-overdue retirement with Yvonne at the end.

Imagine what his life would have been if he'd been able to push on with the many achievements chronicled in the book. The truth is he probably wouldn't have been the complex, driven, interesting, funny and thoughtful person that was Michael Kenneth Moore.

The eulogies from across the political spectrum, on the announcement of his death on 2 February 2020 and at his funeral 12 days later, were fulsome and generous about his global and local contributions. He shouldn't have fretted.

Prime Minister Jacinda Ardern remembered him as a 'true believer' and lifted him into the pantheon of Labour leaders like Norman Kirk. Former Australian Labor Leader Kim Beazley recognised his achievements on the world stage. Former South Australian Premier Mike Rann, and former Cabinet ministers Bill Jeffries and Clayton Cosgrove, shared anecdotes of Mike the politician.

But it was nephew Nick Moore and neighbour Scott Williams who unveiled him as an ordinary human being who was kind and fun to be around, great with young people, and who did simple acts like give away hundreds of swan plants in the neighbourhood so there would be monarch butterflies for the children to see.

Many will remember Mike as a complex person, possibly with contradictions. That's what I thought when I first interviewed him. But I came to see him in simpler terms in the final weeks of his life.

People who follow politics talk about conviction politicians. They're the ones who campaign around their core values and beliefs and centre all their policies and thinking around being pure to them. To be labelled a conviction politician is a grand compliment indeed.

Mike was a conviction New Zealander. He was convinced that everything he did in his political career was around the core values and beliefs of ordinary New Zealanders — the same as those created, promoted and defended by the New Zealand Labour Party. That's why he believed he owed his very being to the party.

In Mike's mind he was always a defender of New Zealand and Labour core values and beliefs. He was a socialist because he believed a government's role was to create foundations like public health and education, social welfare and other collective provision to ensure ordinary people got a fair shot at life.

He didn't believe in equality of outcome — it was equality of opportunity — because he also believed in aspiration and the human spirit to do better.

But throughout his political career he was polarising. Some saw the best of Labour and New Zealand in him, while others saw a party and a country they needed to change.

Most people project themselves onto the politicians they like. They see the best of themselves in their representatives and Moore was that to many voters. That's why he was popular. He represented what it was to be a Kiwi battler.

But, for some, Mike also represented the worst of New Zealand — uncouth, uneducated, unrefined and plenty of other 'uns'.

Mike was never part of the chattering classes. He didn't go to art gallery openings or host fancy dinner parties. His idea of a party involved alcohol, charred protein and hopefully someone with a guitar. He thought tomato sauce was the perfect accompaniment to most meals.

I'm not sure whether he went out of his way to thumb his nose at them, but they certainly knew he didn't like — no, rate — them.

While he easily mixed with kings, queens, presidents and captains of industry, I sensed that deep down he felt awkward and shy, and was far more comfortable in the RSA smoking Peter Stuyvesant Red and drinking jugs of Canterbury Draught with Kiwis who used their hands rather than their minds to make a living.

Mike certainly showed up and embarrassed some in Labour. It wasn't so much his down-to-earth tastes and habits but the fact that he was more Labour than them. He was one of the people the middle-class members of the party were supposedly trying to save and they hated the idea that one of those people was telling them they weren't good enough to do that.

Mike saw them as part of the privilege he'd spent his life trying to smash. He saw them as no different from the 'white coats' at the Moerewa freezing works, surrounding themselves with the spoils while pretending to care about others.

Maybe that's why some people forgot his many achievements. And maybe that's why some were quick to label him as the man who came up with the lamb burger idea, as though that was his greatest contribution.

Mike was part of the 'fish-and-chip brigade' that helped give New Zealand the remarkable David Lange whose government forever transformed the country.

He helped grow the New Zealand economy by opening up international markets for the country's talented producers and innovators.

He helped repair the relationship with the US after the ANZUS split and, in so doing, helped create anti-nuclear consensus among New Zealand's political parties.

He helped put an end to the runaway free-market approach to economic management of Roger Douglas and Ruth Richardson, without going back to centralised planning of the economy.

And his greatest achievement saw China join a rules-based global trading system where the law took precedence, for the first time, over the Chinese Communist Party and, in turn, saw millions taken out of poverty — something Beazley described at the funeral as a significant event in world history.

But his story was part of something broader than that.

Moore and those who were key players throughout his political life — the likes of Jim Anderton, Michael Bassett, David Caygill,

Helen Clark, Michael Cullen, Roger Douglas, David Lange, Geoffrey Palmer and the many more of that generation — came into politics at a key juncture in the history of the New Zealand Labour Party and international progressive politics.

In their time the New Zealand Labour Party became an awkward coalition of trade unionists, blue-collar workers, academics, middle-class liberals, interest groups and professionals. It had been fragile for some time because the commonality of interests wasn't always aligned.

Left-wing politics was at a fork in the road for that generation. And it wasn't so much the debate about open versus closed economies. It was about who would rule and impose their values on these parties, what some now describe as the culture wars.

Was it a party that would continue to represent the mostly socially conservative aspirations of working-class people or the combined variety of interests of the middle classes?

I believe Mike and his colleagues fundamentally got caught up in that battle, one that he was always going to lose given how Labour and progressive parties were moving from their bases. Education, globalisation and technology changes were shrinking the manual working class, their core support.

Interestingly, Mike wasn't bitter about this. He was glad Labour policies enabled the children of the working classes to go to university and get professional jobs, and be socially mobile. He saw that as a measure of Labour's success.

But he was equally sad that many of the remaining working class also left Labour and became the swing voters that populists and nationalists are now targeting with their bigoted and isolationist rhetoric.

In an earlier era, Mike would have been the perfect Labour politician — a red meat-eating, jug-drinking and 'packet-a-day' man. But he became caught in this transition going on in the party. Many of the new members in Labour came from National Party-voting families. He couldn't be any more different from them and so his and their starting positions couldn't be any more divergent.

That's why he variously felt 'his' party was leaving — or was being taken away from — him.

The irony was that he was probably better-read than many of those who had been to university and he had no reason to feel inferior. His huge appetite for books meant he continued to learn, which was in contrast to some of his colleagues who had come to their conclusions about life upon graduation.

There were constant disconnects between Mike and some of the new people in Labour. Lifting import restrictions on second-hand cars, for example, meant working families could for the first time afford a decent car. He instantly got that. But to these new people in the party it meant more pollution and a lack of focus on public transport.

Each just couldn't — or didn't want to — see the other's point of view.

A number of former colleagues talked about his many funny, often self-deprecating, quips: 'A lawn-mowing democracy', 'I'm going to do something completely unheard of in the Labour Party — I'm going to praise someone behind their back', and 'The public are starting to wave at us with five fingers instead of two'. There are even lists of them in circulation.

Some of his colleagues used to laugh at him rather than with him when hearing the quips. But throughout his career Mike was able to get to the nub of an issue and communicate its essence, often with humour, so that ordinary New Zealanders could understand. Surprisingly, that's a rare skill for politicians.

One of the constant themes in our conversations was Mike's impatience to get things done, to make change. His three bouts of cancer clearly informed this view. This made him confronting and, at times, come across as brash and arrogant.

But there was something else, I noticed. He loved the workload. It was never a burden or an obligation.

The more he had to do — the busier he was and the higher the stakes — the more he seemed to see and understand. It was as though the screen widened for him and he saw something more than others did. Many former colleagues talked about this insightfulness. He enjoyed this clarity, the sense of purpose behind what he was doing, and it gave him personal fulfilment and happiness.

The downside of that was that politics became addictive and any slowing created a narrowing blurriness and banality he wanted to avoid in his life. The pace and adrenalin was his drug. The smaller and insignificant matters — like polite small talk with small-minded or ignorant colleagues — bored and annoyed him.

Mike joined Labour to be part of a movement of change. Some of the others joined it, he told me, for their own personal advancement and social status. They thought they were saving the party from itself and they were doing it a favour and that's why their loyalty was fleeting. He always thought he was lucky Labour would have him.

Even in its darkest hours he was never embarrassed about being Labour and for those who deserted it for NewLabour and then the Alliance he reserved the working class's greatest insult — scab.

The constant theme that came through in our conversations was that Mike always seemed insecure and, because of that, deep down — in the place where all politicians have to visit at some stage — he actually lacked confidence. He was never sure if he was quite good enough.

That's why he was first in the office in the mornings and last to leave at night. Hard work, he figured, would overcome any of his shortcomings.

If he'd managed to conquer that insecurity, who knows what giddier heights his remarkable life might have reached?

For a man as well travelled and experienced as Mike, it became clear to me he only ever really loved two places — Parliament's debating chamber, where his background wasn't judged, only his contribution when he took a call, and where he grew up in the Far North, where his soul was always replenished by its down-to-earth residents. In these two homes of his, he was everyone's equal.

Many people at home and abroad talk affectionately about Mike. He judged people simply and, despite his tribalism, not by their political affiliation. As with many New Zealanders, it was whether the person was 'a good sort' — friendly, interesting, enjoyed a laugh and, importantly, was loyal.

Politics for Mike was often intertwined with friendships, sometimes with people from the other side of the House.

But for much of his life he was a loner and introspective, he admitted once to me. He had the ability to withdraw himself, to hunker down, and not bother with the networking and small talk at which some politicians excel. That may have cost him at key moments in his political career.

The most influential people in his life, the ones he could be honest with, were few — his boyhood friends Bryan Gregory and Terry

Bayley, his Eden campaign gang Warren Goff and Mike Rann, his mentors Matiu Rata and Joe Walding, his Socialist Youth International roommate Loo Chong Yong, the preacher who helped him close death's door Bill Subritzky, his numbers man Bill Jeffries, his Aussie mate Kim Beazley, and his protégé — some say son he never had — Clayton Cosgrove.

Then there was mother, Audrey Goodall Moore Webber. Mike just wanted to hear and see love from her.

But the most important was Yvonne Dereany, the trainee school teacher from Blockhouse Bay — the person who pushed him forward when he was shy, scared or unsure, hugged him when he lost, made the sandwiches for Labour housie evenings, held up his election hoardings as he hammered them in, absorbed all the personal abuse at candidates meetings, held his vomit bag when he had cancer, consoled him when his mother died, wanted to have his children, shook the hands and smiled politely, held his grudges and in his final years bathed, cleaned and tucked him in at night.

It was not the life she probably envisioned when they met almost 50 years ago, but it was one devoid of the exaggeration, outrage and false modesty of politics. It was authentic and real.

Mike said he never wanted anything in return for his lifetime in politics.

I could tell in our conversations that, growing up on the wrong side of the tracks, all he ever really wanted was what all working-class people ever want — respect: acknowledgement of who he was, his skills, contribution and achievements.

That would have allowed him a simple retirement sitting on his balcony, comfortably and contentedly like the kuia used to outside the old Star Hotel, and to gaze across to the Cavalli Islands from the deck of his Matauri Bay beach house in the Far North.

There he would have imparted his wisdom — and his old stories on repeat — about all things politics and life to a younger generation of would-be believers.

Acknowledgements

This book was my idea but wouldn't have been possible except for the openness and courage shown by Mike Moore.

He lowered his shield and revealed his heart in a series of sometimes tearful interviews — for the both of us — and trusted me to write a biography that others might use to judge his life with. I want to thank Mike for his bravery and for giving me the freedom to talk to whoever I wanted and to look over his private records.

I want to acknowledge the encouragement and support of Yvonne Moore, particularly in the early stages when I was so full of doubt about the task. She was more than the coffees, waters and sandwiches that sustained the many conversations Mike and I had. She would also prompt his memory and finish his sentences when he struggled.

Without Mike's mother, the late Audrey Goodall Moore Webber, much of the research for this book would have been very difficult. She had studiously kept most of the newspaper clippings from her son's early political career and I had a boxful to wade through.

I want to thank my wife Debra who put up with me tapping away on the computer all hours of the night and day: after work, during the weekends, when we were supposed to be on holiday and when I should have been doing other things with the family.

Many people I called asking for help to fill in the gaps — old friends, journalists, former MPs, diplomats, people from the WTO and many old mates, colleagues and foes of Mike — have been forthcoming. For political, diplomatic or face-saving reasons some of the information has been given to me for non-attribution, so some people aren't listed.

But for those on the record I would like to thank former Members of Parliament Michael Bassett, Rick Barker, Murray McCully, Clayton Cosgrove, Sir Michael Cullen, Sir Roger Douglas, Phil Goff, Bill Jeffries, Dame Annette King, Michael Laws, Steve Maharey, Peter Neilson, Stan Rodger, Dame Jenny Shipley, Paul Swain and Elizabeth Tennet.

Former Council of Trade Unions President Ken Douglas, Moore political adviser Graeme Colman and Labour pollster Stephen Mills were open with their records and views too.

Then there were those idealists who helped run Mike's Eden campaign in 1972: former South Australian Labor Premier Mike Rann, and Labour and trade union stalwart and Auckland local body politician Glenda Fryer.

The former CEO of the Ministry of Foreign Affairs and Trade Dr Brook Barrington, New Zealand diplomats Ben King, Matt Hawkins and Pat Rata, and former World Trade Organization ambassador Carlos Pérez del Castillo, and officials Evan Rogerson and Patrick Low were invaluable.

Moore's many friends in the United States, particularly former White House National Security Council official Dr Peter Watson and political strategist Craig James have been generous with their information.

Dilworth School Headmaster Donald MacLean and Dilworth Trust General Manager Rob Campbell have gone out of their way to assist, as have boyhood friend Bryan Gregory and his wife Karen with their many fond memories.

Singaporean doctor and businessman Loo Chong Yong was, as he has been throughout Mike's life, happy to put aside his busy schedule to assist his dear friend.

Members of the Beagle Boys — Sue Foley and Paul Jackman — were again unafraid to front. Former Prime Minister Helen Clark's Chief Press Secretary Mike Munro was his usual friendly and professional self in his assistance.

The good people of Kawakawa, particularly Noma Shepherd and Bill Cherrington from the Kawakawa Museum, reminded me of how proud they breed them in Northland as they showed and told me the history of their town and region.

Mike's hardworking and loyal troops from Christchurch Brian Gargiulo, Jeff McIntyre, Rod Lingard and Sally Thompson willingly turned out for their old boss.

It's important to acknowledge in the days of digitisation the power of newspaper photographers. A generation of them captured the political images of Mike's era and I want to thank former *New Zealand Herald* staff shooter Geoff Dale of 'fish-and-chip brigade' photo fame for his recollections.

New Zealand is fortunate to have many dedicated staff in public institutions like the Auckland Council archives, the National Library and Ngā Taonga Sound and Vision. Many of our nation's memories are there and they were only too willing to assist me access them.

New Zealand produces wonderfully talented writers and I want to thank one of them, Sue Orr, whose advice, suggestions and ideas for the book got me started.

I also want to thank former colleague Nicole Newland who spent much of her free time transcribing and organising my interview notes and recordings.

Finally, I want to pay tribute to a great friend and fellow Beagle Boy — and my old campaign manager when I naïvely and idealistically flirted with politics — Barry Ebert for his guidance with this book, and for his knowledge of all things Labour.

To everyone who has entrusted me with their memories I hope I've portrayed them accurately, fairly and with the right perspective. If they haven't been, it's my fault alone in trying to make the book interesting to non-political types as well as historically accurate.

Peter Parussini
March 2020

Rt Hon Mike Moore, ONZ, AO

Political career

Opposition Spokesman, Foreign Affairs 1993–99
Leader, New Zealand Labour Party 1990–93
Prime Minister of New Zealand 1990
Minister of External Relations and Trade 1988–90
Deputy Minister of Finance 1988–90
Minister for the America's Cup 1988–90
Minister of Overseas Trade and Marketing 1984–90
Minister of Tourism 1984–87
Minister of Sport and Recreation 1984–87
Member of Parliament, Waimakariri (formerly Papanui and Christchurch North) 1978–99
Member of Parliament, Eden 1972–75

Honours and Awards

The Order of New Zealand — New Zealand's highest honour
Order of Australia — Honorary Officer
Privy Counsellor to HM Queen Elizabeth II
Commemoration Medal 1990 — New Zealand
Honorary Doctorate of Commerce — Lincoln University, New Zealand
Honorary Doctorate in Economics — People's University of China (Beijing)
Honorary Doctorate in Commerce — Auckland University of Technology, Auckland, New Zealand
Honorary Doctorate of Commerce, University of Canterbury, Christchurch, New Zealand
Honorary Doctorate in Law, La Trobe University, Australia
Commander of the Order of the Equatorial Star — Government of Gabon
Chancellor's Medal (Medalla Rectoral) — University of Chile
National Order of Côte d'Ivoire — Republic of Côte d'Ivoire
Order of the Golden Heart of Kenya — Government of Kenya
Order of Duke Branimir with Ribbon — Republic of Croatia

National Honour of Georgia — Government of Georgia
The Medal of the Oriental Republic of Uruguay (highest national honour) — Government of Uruguay
Pope John Paul II Annual Medal — Papal See
James Dilworth Medal

Publications

Saving Globalization
A World Without Walls
On Balance
Beyond Today
A Pacific Parliament
The Added Value Economy
Hard Labour
Fighting for New Zealand
Children of the Poor
A Brief History of the Future

Appointments

New Zealand Ambassador to the United States of America 2010–15
Commissioner, UN Commission of Legal Empowerment of the Poor
Commissioner, Global Commission on International Migration
Director General of the World Trade Organization 1999–2002
Founding member, Global Leadership Foundation
Senior Counsellor, Fonterra
Member, Trilateral Commission
Member, Economic Development Board, South Australia
Special Advisor, China Institute for Reform and Development's World Trade Organization Reference Centre
New Zealand Government Trade Envoy
Special Advisor to the UN Global Compact for Business and Development
Former Board Member to the Gottlieb Duttweiler Institute
Member, Board of Governors for the Institute for International Business, Economics and Law, University of Adelaide
Adjunct Professor, La Trobe University, Melbourne Australia and University of Adelaide, South Australia
Chairperson, Advisory Board of Carnegie Mellon University, Adelaide
Honorary Professor, Beijing Normal University, Zhuhai
Honorary Professor, Chinese University for Political Science and International Law, Beijing
Honorary Professor, Shanghai Customs College
Visiting Professor, School of Public Policy, University of Birmingham, 2003
Member, Competition Council, South Australia
Honorary President, Beijing Afforestation Foundation

About the Author

Peter Parussini's involvement in politics has been as a reporter in the Parliamentary Press Gallery, a staffer for former Prime Minister Mike Moore and as an elected member of the Wellington City Council.

He is currently the chair of one of South Auckland's biggest schools, Southern Cross Campus in Mangere, and is a governor of Radio New Zealand, on the board of the Manukau Institute of Technology and on the executive team of ANZ Bank New Zealand.

He lives in Auckland with Debra, his wife of 30 years, and they have two adult children, Mario and Francesca.